Data Analytics: Techniques and Applications

Data Analytics: Techniques and Applications

Julio Bolton

STATES
ACADEMIC PRESS
www.statesacademicpress.com

Data Analytics: Techniques and Applications
Julio Bolton
ISBN: 978-1-63989-145-0 (Hardback)

Published by States Academic Press,
109 South 5th Street,
Brooklyn, NY 11249, USA

Cataloging-in-Publication Data

Data analytics : techniques and applications / Julio Bolton.
    p. cm.
Includes bibliographical references and index.
ISBN 978-1-63989-145-0
1. Quantitative research. 2. Data sets. 3. Big data. 4. Information visualization.
5. Data mining. 6. Information science. 7. Visual analytics. I. Bolton, Julio.
QA76.9.Q36 D38 2022
001.42--dc23

For more information regarding States Academic Press and its products, please visit the publisher's website www.statesacademicpress.com

Table of Contents

Preface

Data analytics involves inspecting, transforming and modeling data with the objective of discovering useful information and conclusions. Techniques of data analytics can divulge trends and metrics that would otherwise be lost in the mass of information. This information can then be utilized to optimize processes to increase the overall efficacy of a business or system. Data analysis has multiple facets and approaches, encompassing varied techniques under a diverse range of names, and is used in different business, science, and social science domains. It is a process used for obtaining raw data, and converting it into information. This information is then employed in decision-making processes by the users. Data is collected for the purpose of analysis, hypotheses testing, or to disapprove theories. Data analysis plays a pivotal role in making decisions more scientific and helping businesses operate in a more effective manner. This book elucidates the concepts and innovative models around prospective developments with respect to data analytics. Most of the topics introduced herein cover new techniques and the applications of this field. Those with an interest in data analytics will find this book helpful.

Given below is the chapter wise description of the book:

Chapter 1- The data that is too complex to be handled through traditional data handling software is termed as big data. The process or science of analyzing raw data in order to draw conclusions is called data analytics. The topics elaborated in this chapter provide a brief introduction to the varied facets of data analytics such as big data value chain, collection and analysis of big data, and data storage.

Chapter 2- Data can be collected and analyzed in order to gain meaningful insights and make informed decisions. There are various ways in which insights can be obtained from data such as through univariate, bivariate and multivariate analysis and comparing these three types of analyses. This chapter closely examines these key concepts related to gaining insights from data in order to provide an extensive understanding of the subject.

Chapter 3- The process of collecting and analyzing data to extract useful information is called data analysis. There are various ways of analyzing data such as through support vector machines and principal component analysis. Neural networks can also be used for data analysis. All these diverse topics related to data analysis have been carefully discussed in this chapter.

Chapter 4- The task of segregating groups with similar traits and assigning them into clusters is called clustering. It plays an important role in analyzing high dimensional data. The topics elaborated in this chapter will help in gaining a better perspective about clustering as well as the methods used in it.

Chapter 5- The graphical representation of data in the form of graphs, charts, tables and maps to understand the information easily is called data visualization. This chapter discusses in detail the theories and methodologies related to visualization in 2 variables, visualization in 3 or more variables, and big data visualization.

Chapter 6- There are many applications of big data which are used in companies, offices and various organizations. This chapter gives an insight on the different open source tools which are used for data analysis, such as HADOOP and SPARK. This chapter has been carefully written to provide an easy understanding of the these applications of big data.

At the end, I would like to thank all those who dedicated their time and efforts for the successful completion of this book. I also wish to convey my gratitude towards my friends and family who supported me at every step.

Julio Bolton

Introduction to Big Data and Data Analytics

The data that is too complex to be handled through traditional data handling software is termed as big data. The process or science of analyzing raw data in order to draw conclusions is called data analytics. The topics elaborated in this chapter provide a brief introduction to the varied facets of data analytics such as big data value chain, collection and analysis of big data, and data storage.

Big Data

Recently, the word "Big Data" has become a buzzword. It is being used by almost everyone including academicians and industry experts. There are various definitions available in the literature. But the concept of big data dates back to the year 2001, where the challenges of increasing data were addressed with a 3Vs model by Laney. 3Vs, also known as the dimensions of big data, represent the increasing Volume, Variety, and Velocity of data. The model was not originally used to define big data but later has been used eventually by various enterprises including Microsoft and IBM to define the same.

In 2010, Apache Hadoop defined big data as "datasets, which could not be captured, managed, and processed by general computers within an acceptable scope". Following this, in 2011, McKinsey Global Institute defined big data as "datasets whose size is beyond the ability of typical database software tools to capture, store, manage, and analyze". International Data Corporation (IDC) defines "big data technologies as a new generation of technologies and architectures, designed to economically extract value from very large volumes of a wide variety of data, by enabling high-velocity capture, discovery, and/or analysis".

Academicians define big data as huge size of unstructured data produced by high-performance heterogeneous group of applications that spans from social network to scientific computing applications. The datasets range from a few hundred gigabytes to zetabytes that it is beyond the capacity of existing data management tools to capture, store, manage and analyze.

Though big data has been defined in various forms but there is no specific definition. Few have defined what it does while very few have focused on what it is. The definition of the big data on the basis of 3Vs is relative. What is defined, as big data may not be the same tomorrow? For instance, in future, with the advancements in the storage technologies, the data that is deemed as big data today might be captured. In addition to defining big data, there is a need to understand how to make the best use of this data to obtain valuable information for decision making.

Dimensions of Big Data

Initially, big data was characterized by the following dimensions, which were, often, referred as 3V model:

- Volume: Volume refers to the magnitude of the data that is being generated and collected. It is increasing at a faster rate from terabytes to petabytes (1024 terabytes). With increase in storage capacities, what cannot be captured and stored now will be possible in future. The classification of big data on the basis of volume is relative with respect to the type of data generated and time. In addition, the type of data, which is often referred as Variety, defines "big" data. Two types of data, for instance, text and video of same volume may require different data management technologies.

- Velocity: Velocity refers to the rate of generation of data. Traditional data analytics is based on periodic updates- daily, weekly or monthly. With the increasing rate of data generation, big data should be processed and analyzed in real- or near real-time to make informed decisions. The role of time is very critical here. Few domains including Retail, Telecommunications and Finance generate high-frequency data. The data generated through Mobile apps, for instance, demographics, geographical location, and transaction history, can be used in real-time to offer personalized services to the customers. This would help to retain the customers as well as increase the service level.

- Variety: Variety refers to different types of data that are being generated and captured. They extend beyond structured data and fall under the categories of semi-structured and unstructured data. The data that can be organized using a pre-defined data model are known as structured data. The tabular data in relational databases and Excel are examples of structured data and they constitute only 5% of all existing data. Unstructured data cannot be organized using these pre-defined model and examples include video, text, and audio. Semi-structured data that fall between the categories of structured and unstructured data. Extensible Markup Language (XML) falls under this category.

Later, few more dimensions have been added, which are enumerated below:

- Veracity: Coined by IBM, veracity refers to the unreliability associated with the data sources. For instance, sentiment analysis using social media data (Twitter, Facebook, etc.) is subject to uncertainty. There is a need to differentiate the reliable data from uncertain and imprecise data and manage the uncertainty associated with the data.

- Variability: Variability and Complexity were added as additional dimensions by SAS. Often, inconsistency in the big data velocity leads to variation in flow rate of data, which is referred to as variability. Data are generated from various sources and there is an increasing complexity in managing data ranging from transactional data to big data. Data generated from different geographical locations have different semantics.

- Low-Value density: Data in its original form is unusable. Data is analyzed to discover very high value. For example, logs from the website cannot be used in its initial form to obtain business value. It must be analyzed to predict the customer behavior.

Sources of Big Data

Having understood what big data are and their dimensions, here various sources of big data are briefed. Digitization of content by industries is the new source of data. Advancements in technology also lead to high rate of data generation. For example, one of the biggest surveys in Astronomy, Sloan Digital Sky Survey (SDSS) has recorded a total of 25TB data during their first and second surveys combined. With the advancements in the resolution of the telescope, the amount of data collected at the end of their third survey is 100 TB. Use of "smart" instrumentation is another source of big data. Smart meters in the energy sector record the electricity utilization measurement every 15 minutes as compared to monthly readings before.

In addition to social media, Internet of Things (IoT) has, now, become the new source of data. The data can be captured from agriculture, industry, medical care, etc. of the smart cities developed based on IoT. Table below summarizes the various types of data produced in different sectors.

Table: Different Sources of Data.

Sector	Data Produced	Use
Astronomy	Movement of stars, satellites, etc.	To monitor the activities of asteroid bodies and satellites.
Financial	News content via video, audio, twitter and news report.	To make trading decisions.
Healthcare	Electronic medical records and images.	To aid in short-term public health monitoring and long-term epidemiological research programs.
Internet of Things (IoT)	Sensor data	To monitor various activities in smart cities.
Life Sciences	Gene sequences	To analyze genetic variations and potential treatment effectiveness.
Media/Entertainment	Content and user viewing Behavior	To capture more viewers.
Social Media	Blog posts, tweets, social networking sites, log details.	To analyze the customer behavior pattern.
Telecommunications	Call Detail Records (CDR)	Customer churn management.
Transportation, Logistics, Retail, Utilities	Sensor data generated from fleet transceivers, RFID tag readers and smart meters.	To optimize operations.
Video Surveillance	Recordings from CCTV to IPTV cameras and recording system.	To analyze behavioral patterns for service enhancement and security.

Big Data Value Chain

Value Chain, the concept introduced by Porter, refers to a set of activities performed by a firm to add value at each step of delivering a product/service to its customers. In a similar way, data value chain refers to the framework that deals with a set of activities to create value from available data. It can be divided into seven phases: data generation, data collection, data transmission, data pre-processing, data storage, data analysis and decision making.

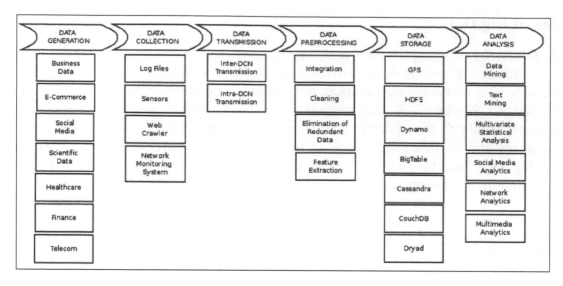

- Data Generation: The first and foremost step the big data value chain is the generation of data. Data is generated from various sources that include data from Call Detail Records (CDR), blogs, Tweets and Facebook Page.

- Data Collection: In this phase, the data is obtained from all possible data sources. For instance, in order to predict the customer churn in Telecom, data can be obtained from CDRs and opinions/complaints of the customers on Social Networking Sites such as Twitter (in the form of tweets) and Facebook (opinions shared on the company's Facebook page). The most commonly used methods are log files, sensors, web crawlers and network monitoring software.

- Data Transmission: Once the data is collected, it is transferred to data storage and processing infrastructure for further processing and analysis. It can be carried out in two phases: Inter-Dynamic Circuit Network (DCN) transmission and Intra-DCN transmissions. Inter-DCN transmission deals with the transfer of data from the data source to the data center while the latter helps in the transfer within the data center. Apart from storage of data, data center helps in collecting, organizing and managing data.

- Data Pre-processing: The data collected from various data sources may be redundant, noisy and inconsistent, hence, in this phase; the data is pre-processed to improve the data quality required for analysis. This also helps to improve the accuracy of the analysis and reduce the storage expenses. The data can be pre-processed with the help of following steps:

  ◦ Integration: The data from various sources are combined to provide a unified and uniform view of the available data. Data federation and data warehousing are the two commonly used traditional methods. Data warehousing executes the Extract, Transform, and Load (ETL) process. During extract process, the data is selected, collected, processed and analyzed. The process of converting the extracted data to a standard format is called Transformation process. In Loading, the extracted and transformed data is imported into a storage infrastructure. In order to make data integration dynamic, data can be aggregated from various data sources using a virtual database. It does not contain any data but the details regarding the information related to original data or metadata can be obtained.

- ○ Cleaning: The data is checked for accuracy, completeness and consistency. During this process, the data may be deleted and modified to improve the data quality. The general process followed includes following five processes: error types are defined and determined, errors are identified from the data, errors are corrected, error types and corresponding examples are documented, and data entry procedure may be modified to avoid future errors.

- ○ Elimination of Redundant Data: Many datasets have surplus data or data repetitions and are known as data redundancy. This increases the storage cost, leads to data inconsistency and affects the quality of data. In order to overcome this, various data reduction methods such as data filtering and compression, are used. The limitation of these data reduction techniques is that they increase the computational cost. Hence, a cost-benefit analysis should be carried before using data reduction techniques.

- Data Storage: The big data storage systems should provide reliable storage space and powerful access to the data. The distributed storage systems for big data should consider factors like consistency (C), availability (A) and partition tolerance (P). According to the CAP theory proposed by Brewer, the distributed storage systems could meet two requirements simultaneously, that is, either consistency and availability or availability and partition tolerance or consistency and partition tolerance but not all requirements simultaneously. Considerable research is still going on in the area of big data storage mechanism. Little advancement in this respect is Google File System (GFS), Dynamo, BigTable, Cassandra, CouchDB, and Dryad.

- Data Analysis: Once the data is collected, transformed and stored, the next process is data exploitation or data analysis, which is enumerated using the following steps:

  - ○ Define Metrics: Based on the collected and transformed data, a set of metrics is defined for a particular problem. For instance, to identify a potential customer who is going to churn out, a number of times he/she contacted (be it through a voice call, tweets or complaints on Facebook page) can be considered.

  - ○ Select architecture based on analysis type: Based on the timeliness of analysis to be carried out, suitable architecture is selected. Real-time analysis is used in the domain where the data keeps on changing constantly and there is a need for rapid analysis to take actions. Memory-based computations and parallel processing systems are the existing architectures. Fraud detection in retail sectors and telecom fraud are the examples of real-time analysis. The applications that do not require high response time is carried out using offline analysis. The data can be extracted, stored and analyzed relatively later in time.

  - ○ Selection of appropriate algorithms and tools: One of the most important steps of data analysis is selection of appropriate techniques for data analysis. Few traditional data analysis techniques like cluster analysis, regression analysis and data mining algorithms, still hold good for big data analytics. Cluster analysis is an unsupervised technique that group"s objects based on some features. Data mining techniques help to extract unknown, hidden and useful information from a huge data set. Various tools are available for data analysis including open source software and commercial software. Few examples of open source softwares are R for data mining and visualization, Weka/ Pentaho for machine learning and RapidMiner for machine learning and predictive analysis.

○ Data Visualization: The need for inspecting details at multiple scales and minute details gave rise to data visualization. Visual interfaces along with statistical analyzes and related context help to identify patterns in large data over time. Visual Analytics (VA) is defined as "the science of analytical reasoning facilitated by visual interactive interfaces". Few visualization tools are Tableau, QlikView, Spotfire, JMP, Jaspersoft, Visual Analytics, Centrifuge, Visual Mining and Board.

○ Decision Making: Based on the analysis and the visualized results, the decision makers can decide whether and how to reward a positive behavior and change a negative one. The details of a particular problem can be analyzed to understand the causes of the problems take informed decisions and plan for necessary actions.

An industry regardless of sector should consider three criteria before implementing big data analytics: can useful information be obtained in addition to those obtained from the existing systems, will there be any improvement in the accuracy of information obtained using big data analytics and finally, will implementation of big data analytics help in improving the timeliness of response.

Collection and Analysis of Big Data

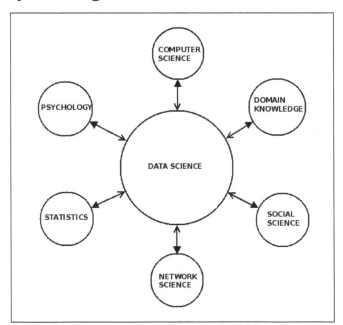

Figure: Evolution of Data Science.

Advancement in computing architecture is required to handle both the data storage requirements and the heavy server processing required to analyze large volumes and variety of data economically. With the availability of high computational capacity at a relatively inexpensive cost allows researchers to explore the underlying opportunities of big data with the field of data science. Increasingly, data are not solely being captured for record keeping, but to explore them with intelligent systems to derive new insights, which may not have been envisioned at the time of collecting the data. By initiating interesting questions and refining them without experts" intervention, it becomes capable of discovering new information on its own. For instance, if an information can be derived that a specific group of people are prone to cancer and also gives other information such as their diets, daily habits and nature of drugs causing this effect. It would be amazing to develop these kinds of models, which may look like a fiction story at this point of time.

Advancements in these technologies help managers in scenario building analysis. Big data analytics has huge application in various fields including astronomy, healthcare, and telecommunication. Despite advantages, big data analytics has its own limitations and challenges. Security and Privacy issues are main concern for researchers. These advancements as well as limitations resulted in a new interdisciplinary domain called data science, which utilizes the knowledge subjects including psychology, statistics, economics, social science, network science and computer science.

Tools that are being used to collect data encompass various digital devices (for example, mobile devices, camera, wearable devices, and smart watches) and applications that generate enormous data in the form of logs, text, voice, images, and video. In order to process these data, several researchers are coming up with new techniques that help better representation of the unstructured data, which makes sense in big data context to gain useful insights that may not have been envisioned earlier.

Not only Structured Query Languages (NoSQL)

Relational Database Management System (RDBMS) is the traditional method of managing structured data. RDBMS uses a relational database and schema for storage and retrieval of data. A Data warehouse is used to store and retrieve large datasets. Structured Query Language (SQL) is most commonly used database query language. The data is stored in a data warehouse using dimensional approach and normalized approach. In dimensional approach, data are divided into fact table and dimension table which supports the fact table. In normalized approach, data is divided into entities creating several tables in a relational database.

Due to Atomicity, Consistency, Isolation and Durability (ACID) constraint, scaling of a large volume of data is not possible. RDBMS is incapable of handling semi-structured and unstructured data. These limitations of RDBMS led to the concept of NoSQL.

NoSQL stores and manages unstructured data. These databases are also known as "schema-free" databases since they enable quick upgradation of structure of data without table rewrites. NoSQL supports document store, key value stores, and BigTable and graph database. It uses looser consistency model than the traditional databases. Data management and data storage functions are separate in NoSQL database. It allows the scalability of data. Few examples of NoSQL databases are HBase, MangoDB, and Dynamo.

Hadoop

In 2005, an open source Apache Hadoop project was conceived and implemented on the basis of Google File System and Map Reduce programming paradigm.

Hadoop Distributed File System (HDFS)

HDFS is the fault-tolerant, scalable, highly configurable distributed storage system for a Hadoop cluster. Data in the Hadoop cluster is broken down into pieces by HDFS and are distributed across different servers in the Hadoop cluster. A small chunk of the whole data set is stored on the server.

Hadoop MapReduce

MapReduce is a software framework for distributed processing of vast amounts of data in a reliable, fault-tolerant manner. The two distinct phases of MapReduce are:

- Map Phase: In Map phase, the workload is divided into smaller sub-workloads. The tasks are assigned to Mapper, which processes each unit block of data to produce a sorted list of (key, value) pairs. This list, which is the output of mapper, is passed to the next phase. This process is known as shuffling.

- Reduce: In Reduce phase, the input is analyzed and merged to produce the final output which is written to the HDFS in the cluster.

Table: Big Data Capabilities and their Primary Technologies.

Big Data Capability	Primary Technology	Features
Storage and management capability	Hadoop Distributed File System (HDFS)	Open source distributed file system, Runs on highperformance commodity hardware, Highly scalable storage and automatic data replication.
Database capability	Oracle NoSQL	Dynamic and flexible schema design, Highly scalable multi-node, multiple data center, fault tolerant, ACID operations, High-performance key-value pair database.
	Apache HBase	Automatic failover support between Region servers, Automatic and configurable sharding of tables.
	Apache Cassandra	Fault tolerance capability for every node, Column indexes with the performance of log-structured updates and built-in caching.
	Apache Hive	Query execution via MapReduce, Uses SQL-like language HiveQL, Easy ETL process either from HDFS or Apache HBase.
Processing capability	MapReduce	Distribution of data workloads across thousands of nodes, Breaks problem into smaller sub-problems.
	Apache Hadoop	Highly customizable infrastructure, Highly scalable parallel batch processing, Fault tolerant.

Data integration capability	Oracle big data connectors, Oracle data integrator	Exports MapReduce results to RDBMS, Hadoop, and other targets, Includes a Graphical User Interface.
Statistical analysis capability	R and Oracle R Enterprise	Programming language for statistical analysis.

Limitations of Hadoop

In spite of Hadoop's advantages over RDBMS, it suffers from the following limitations:

- Multiple Copies of Data: Inefficiency of HDFS leads to creation of multiple copies of the data (minimum 3 copies).

- Limited SQL Support: Hadoop offers a limited SQL support and they lack basic functions such as sub-queries, "Group by" analytics etc.

- Inefficient Execution: Lack of query optimizer leads to inefficient cost-based plan for execution thus resulting in larger cluster compared to similar database.

- Challenging Framework: Complex transformational logic cannot be leveraged using the MapReduce framework.

- Lack of Skills: Knowledge of algorithms and skills for distributed MapReduce development are required for proper implementation.

One of the biggest challenges is to have a computing infrastructure that can analyze high-volume and varied (structured and unstructured) data from multiple sources and to enables real-time analysis of unpredictable content with no apparent schema or structure.

Software Tools for Handling Big Data

There are many tools that help in achieving these goals and help data scientists to process data for analyzing them. Many new languages, frameworks and data storage technologies have emerged that supports handling of big data.

R is an open-source statistical computing language that provides a wide variety of statistical and graphical techniques to derive insights from the data. It has an effective data handling and storage facility and supports vector operations with a suite of operators for faster processing. It has all the features of a standard programming language and supports conditional arguments, loops, and user-defined functions. R is supported by a huge number of packages through Comprehensive R Archive Network (CRAN). It is available on Windows, Linux, and Mac platforms. It has a strong documentation for each package. It has a strong support for data munging, data mining and machine learning algorithms along with a good support for reading and writing in distributed environment, which makes it appropriate for handling big data. However, the memory management, speed, and efficiency are probably the biggest challenge faced by R. R Studio is an Integrated Development Environment that is developed for programming in R language. It is distributed for standalone Desktop machines as well as it supports client-server architecture, which can be accessed from any browser.

Python is yet another popular programming language, which is open source and is supported by Windows, Linux and Mac platforms. It hosts thousands of packages from third-party or community contributed modules. NumPy, Scikit, and Pandas support some of the popular packages for machine learning and data mining for data preprocessing, computing and modeling. NumPy is the base package for scientific computing. It adds support for large, multi-dimensional arrays and matrices with Python. Scikit supports classification, regression, clustering, dimensionality reduction, feature selection, and preprocessing and model selection algorithms. Pandas help in data munging and preparation for data analysis and modeling. It has strong support for graph analysis with its NetworkX library and nltk for text analytics and Natural language processing. Python is very user-friendly and great for quick and dirty analysis on a problem. It also integrates well with spark through the pyspark library.

Scala is an object-oriented language and has an acronym for "Scalable Language". The object and every operation in Scala is a method-call, just like any object-oriented language. It requires java virtual machine environment. Spark, an in-memory cluster computing framework is written in Scala. Scala is becoming popular programming tool for handling big data problems.

Apache Spark is an in-memory cluster computing technology designed for fast computation, which is implemented in Scala. It uses Hadoop for storage purpose as it has its own cluster management capability. It provides built-in APIs for Java, Scala, and Python. Recently, it has also started supporting R. It comes with 80 high-level operators for interactive querying. The inmemory computation is supported with its Resilient Distributed Data (RDD) framework, which distributes the data frame into smaller chunks on different machines for faster computation. It also supports Map and Reduce for data processing. It supports SQL, data streaming, graph processing algorithms and machine learning algorithms. Though Spark can be accessed with Python, Java, and R, it has a strong support for Scala and is more stable at this point of time. It supports deep learning with sparkling water in H_2O.

Apache Hive is an open source platform that provides facilities for querying and managing large datasets residing in distributed storage (For example, HDFS). It is similar to SQL and it is called as HiveQL. It uses Map Reduce for processing the queries and also supports developers to plug in their custom mapper and reducer codes when HiveQL lacks in expressing the desired logic.

Apache Pig is a platform that allows analysts to analyzing large data sets. It is a high-level programming language, called as Pig Latin for creating MapReduce programs that requires Hadoop for data storage. The Pig Latin code is extended with the help of User-Defined Functions that can be written in Java, Python and few other languages. It is amenable to substantial parallelization, which in turns enables them to handle very large data sets.

Amazon Elastic Compute Cloud (EC2) is a web service that provides compute capacity over the cloud. It gives full control of the computing resources and allows developers to run their computation in the desired computing environment. It is one of the most successful cloud computing platforms. It works on the principle of the pay-as-you-go model. Few other frameworks that support big data are MongoDB, BlinkDB, Tachyon, Cassandra, CouchDB, Clojure, Tableau, Splunk and others.

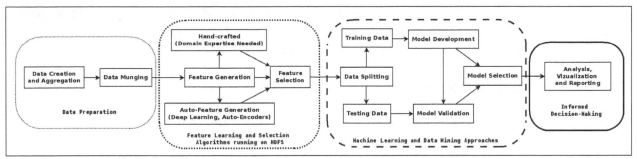

Big data processes illustration

Data Storage

Punch cards were the first effort at Data Storage in a machine language. Punch cards were used to communicate information to equipment "before" computers were developed. The punched holes originally represented a "sequence of instructions" for pieces of equipment, such as textile looms and player pianos. The holes acted as on/off switches. Basile Bouchon developed the punch card as a control for looms in 1725.

In 1837, a little over 100 years later, Charles Babbage proposed the Analytical Engine, a primitive calculator with moving parts that used punch cards for instructions and responses. Herman Hollerith developed this idea, and made the Analytical Engine a reality by having the holes represent, not just a sequence of instructions, but stored data the machine could read.

He developed a punch card data processing system for the 1890 U.S. Census, and then started the *Tabulating Machine Company* in 1896. By 1950, punch cards had become an integral part of the American industry and government. The warning, "Do not fold, spindle, or mutilate," originated from punch cards. Punch cards were still being used quite regularly until the mid-1980s. (Punch cards continue to be used in recording the results of standardized tests and voting ballots.)

In the 1960s, "magnetic storage" gradually replaced punch cards as the primary means for data storage. Magnetic tape was first patented in 1928, by Fritz Pfleumer. (Cassette tapes were often used for homemade "personal computers," in the 1970s and 80s.) In 1965, Mohawk Data Sciences offered a magnetic tape encoder, described as a punch card replacement. By 1990, the combination of affordable personal computers and "magnetic disk storage" had made punch cards nearly obsolete.

In the past, the terms "Data Storage" and "memory" were often used interchangeably. However, at present, Data Storage is an umbrella phrase that includes memory. Data Storage is often considered long term, while memory is frequently described as short term.

Vacuum Tubes for Random Access Memory

In 1948, Professor Fredrick Williams, and colleagues, developed "the first" Random Access Memory (RAM) for storing frequently used programming instructions, in turn, increasing the overall speed of the computer. Williams used an array of cathode-ray tubes (a form of vacuum tube) to act as on/off switches, and digitally store 1024 bits of information.

Data in RAM (sometimes called volatile memory) is temporary and when a computer loses power, the data is lost, and often frustratingly irretrievable. ROM (Read Only Memory), on the other hand, is permanently written and remains available after a computer has lost power.

Magnetic Core, Twistor and Bubble Memory

In the late 1940s, magnetic core memory was developed, and patented, and over ten years, became the primary way early computers wrote, read, and stored data. The system used a grid of current carrying wires (address and sense wires), with doughnut-shaped magnets (called Ferrite Cores) circling where the wires intersected. Address lines polarized a Ferrite Core's magnetic field one way or the other, creating a switch that represents a zero or one (on/off). The arrangement of address and sense wires feeding through the ferrite cores allows each core to store one bit o' data (on/off). Each bit is then grouped into units, called words, to form a single memory address when accessed together.

In 1953, MIT purchased the patent, and developed the first computer to use this technology, called the Whirlwind. Magnetic core memories, being faster and more efficient than punch cards, became popular very quickly. However, manufacturing them was difficult and time consuming. It involved delicate work, using women with steady hands and microscopes to tediously thread thin wires through very small holes.

The Twistor Magnetic Memory was invented in 1957 by Andrew Bobeck. It creates computer memories using very fine magnetic wires interwoven with current-carrying wire. It is similar to core memory, but the wrapped magnetic wires replace the circular magnets, and each intersection on the network represents one bit o' data. The magnetic wires were specifically designed to only allow magnetization along specific sections of the length, so only designated areas of the Twistor would be magnetized, and capable of changing polarization (on/off).

Semiconductor Memory

In 1966, the newly formed *Intel Corporation* began selling a semiconductor chip with 2,000 bits of memory. A semiconductor memory chip stores data in a small circuit referred to as a memory cell. Memory cells are made up of miniaturized transistors and/or miniaturized capacitors, which act as on/off switches.

A semiconductor can conduct electricity under specific conditions, making it an excellent medium for controlling electricity. Its conductivity varies depending on the current or voltage applied to a control electrode. A semiconductor device offers a superior alternative to vacuum tubes, delivering hundreds of times more processing power. A single microprocessor chip can replace thousands of vacuum tubes, and requires significantly less electricity.

Magnetic Disk Storage

Magnetic drums were the first incarnation of magnetic disk storage. Gustav Taushek, an Austrian inventor, developed the magnetic drum in 1932. The drums read/write heads were designed for each drum track, using a staggered system over the circumference. Without head movement to control, access time is quite short, being based on one revolution of the drum. If multiple heads are used, data can be transferred quickly, helping to compensate for the lack of RAM in these systems.

IBM is primarily responsible for driving the early evolution of magnetic disk storage. They invented both the floppy disk drive and the hard disk drive and their staff are credited with many of the improvements supporting the products. IBM developed and manufactured disk storage devices between 1956 to 2003, and then sold its "hard disk" business to Hitachi in 2003.

IBM switched its focus to 8-inch floppy disks from 1969 until the mid-1980s. A floppy disk is an easily removed (and easily installed) portable storage device. It is made of magnetic film encased in a flexible plastic, and is inexpensive to manufacture. IBM developed the 8-inch floppy specifically for the System/370 mainframe. On the downside, a floppy disk is very easy to damage.

In 1976, Allan Shugart improved on IBM's floppy disk, by developing a smaller version of it. This is because IBM's 8-inch floppy disk was too big for a standard desktop computer. The new 5.25-inch floppy disk was cheaper to manufacture and could store 110 kilobytes of data. These disks became extremely popular and were used on most personal computers.

The 3.5-inch floppy disc (introduced in 1982) gradually became more popular than the 5.25-inch floppy disk. The 3.5 version came with a significant advantage. It had a rigid cover protecting the magnetic film inside. However, both formats remained quite popular until the mid-1990s. (Over time, several size variations were introduced, but with very little marketing success.)

Optical Discs

In the 1960s, an inventor named James T. Russel thought about, and worked on, the idea of using light as a mechanism to record, and then replay "music." And no one took his invention of the optical disc seriously, until 1975. This was when Sony paid Russel millions of dollars to finish his project. This investment led to his completing the project in 1980, in turn leading to CDs (Compact Discs) and DVDs (Digital Video Recordings) and Blu-Ray. (The word "disk" is used for magnetic recordings, while "disc" is used for optical recordings. IBM, who had no optical formats, preferred the "k" spelling, but in 1979, Sony, and a Dutch company named Philips, preferred to use the "c" spelling in developing and trademarking the compact disc.

Magneto-Optical Discs

The Magneto-Optical disc, as a hybrid storage medium, was presented in 1990. This disc format uses both magnetic and optical technologies for storing and retrieving digital data. The discs normally come in 3.5 and 5.25 inch sizes. The system reads sections of the disc with different magnetic alignments. Laser light reflected from the different polarizations varies, per the Kerr effect, and provides an on/off, bit of data storage system.

When the disc is prepped for writing, each section of the disc is heated, using a strong laser, and is then cooled while under the influence of a magnetic field. This has the effect of magnetizing the storage areas in one direction, "off." The writing process reverses the polarization of specific areas, turning them on, for the storage of data.

Flash Drives

Flash drives appeared on the market, late in the year 2000. A flash drive plugs into computers with a built-in USB plug, making it a small, easily removable, very portable storage device. Unlike a traditional hard drive, or an optical drive, it has no moving parts, but instead combines chips and transistors for maximum functionality. Generally, a flash drives storage capacity ranges from 8 to 64 GB. (Other sizes are available, but can be difficult to find.)

A flash drive can be rewritten nearly a limitless number of times and is unaffected by electromagnetic interference (making them ideal for moving through airport security). Because of this, flash drives have entirely replaced floppy disks for portable storage. With their large storage capacity and low cost, flash drives are now on the verge of replacing CDs and DVDs.

Flash drives are sometimes called pen drives, USB drives, thumb drives, or jump drives. Solid State Drives (SSD) are sometimes referred to as flash drives, but they are larger and clumsy to transport.

Solid State Drives (SSD)

Variations of Solid State Drives have been used since the 1950s. An SSD is a nonvolatile storage device that basically does everything a hard drive will do. It stores data on interlinked flash memory chips. The memory chips can either be part of the system's motherboard or a separate box that is designed and wired to plug into a laptop, or a desktop hard drive. The flash memory chips are different than those used for USB thumb drives, making them faster and more reliable. As a result, an SSD is more expensive than a USB thumb drive of the same capacity. SSDs "can" be portable, but will not fit in your pocket.

Data Silos

Data Silos are a data storage system, of sorts. Data Silos store data for a business, or a department of the business, that is incompatible with their system, but is deemed important enough to save for later translation. For many businesses, this was a huge amount of information. Data Silos eventually became useful as a source of information for Big Data and came to be used deliberately for that purpose. Then came Data Lakes.

Data Lakes

Data Lakes were formed specifically to store and process Big Data, with multiple organizations pooling huge amounts of information into a single Data Lake. A Data Lake stores data in its original format and is typically processed by a NoSQL database (a Data Warehouse uses a hierarchical database). NoSQL processes the data in all its various forms, and allows for the processing of raw data. Most of this information could be accessed by its users via the internet.

Cloud Data Storage

The Internet made the Cloud available as a service. Improvements within the Internet, such as continuously lowering the cost of storage capacity and improved bandwidth, have made it more economical for individuals and businesses to use the Cloud for data storage. The Cloud offers essentially an infinite amount of data storage to its user. Cloud services provide near-infinite scalability, and accessibility to data from anywhere, at any time. Is often used to backup information initially stored on site, making it available should the company's own system suffer a failure. Cloud security is a significant concern among users, and service providers have built security systems, such as encryption and authentication, into the services they provide.

Data Analytics

Data Analytics (DA) is the science of examining raw data with the purpose of drawing conclusions about that information. The data that is captured by any data collection agent or tool or software is in its raw form, i.e., unformatted or unstructured or unclean with noises/errors or redundant or inconsistent. Hence, analytics covers a spectrum of activities starting from data collection till visualization. The science of data analytics is generally divided into three broad categories:

- Exploratory Data Analysis (EDA).

- Confirmatory Data Analysis (CDA).

- Qualitative Data Analysis (QDA).

Exploratory Data Analysis (EDA)

EDA is an approach/philosophy for data analysis that employs a variety of techniques enticing the data to reveal its structural secrets, and being always ready to gain some new, often unsuspected, insight into the data. Most EDA techniques are graphical in nature.

Advantages	Disadvantages
a) Flexible ways to generate hypotheses.	a) Usually does not provide definitive answers.
b) More realistic statements of accuracy.	b) Difficult to avoid optimistic bias produced by over fitting.
c) Does not require more than data can support.	c) Requires judgment and artistry - can't be cook booked.
d) Promotes deeper understanding of processes by Statistical learning.	

Confirmatory Data Analysis (CDA)

This approach for data analysis is aimed towards proving or disproving existing hypotheses. CDA, a deductive approach is inferential in nature. It relies heavily on probability models and hypotheses are determined at outset. CDA provides precise information in the right circumstances and backed with well-established theory and methods.

Advantages	Disadvantages
a) Provide precise information in the right circumstances	a) Misleading impression of precision in less than ideal circumstances.
b) Well-established theory and methods	b) Analysis driven by preconceived ideas.
	c) Difficult to notice unexpected results

Qualitative Data Analysis (QDA)

QDA is all about drawing conclusions from non-numerical data for analysis, which might be further used for decision making.

Advantages	Disadvantages
a) Allow for a broader study, involving a greater number of subjects, and enhancing the generalization of the results.	a) Collect a much narrower and sometimes superficial dataset.
b) Can allow for greater objectivity and accuracy of results. Generally, quantitative methods are designed to provide summaries of data that support generalizations about the phenomenon under study. In order to accomplish this, quantitative research usually involves few variables and many cases, and employs prescribed procedures to ensure validity and reliability.	b) Results are limited as they provide numerical descriptions rather than detailed narrative and generally provide less elaborate accounts of human perception.
c) Using standards means that the research can be replicated, and then analyzed and compared with similar studies. Kruger confirms that 'quantitative methods allow us to summarize vast sources of information and facilitate comparisons across categories and over time'.	c) The research is often carried out in an unnatural, artificial environment so that a level of control can be applied to the exercise. This level of control might not normally be in place in the real world yielding laboratory results as opposed to real world results.
d) personal bias can be avoided by researchers keeping a 'distance' from participating subjects and employing subjects unknown to them.	d) In addition preset answers will not necessarily reflect how people really feel about a subject and in some cases might just be the closest match.
	e) The development of standard questions by researchers can lead to 'structural' bias and false representation, where the data actually reflects the view of them instead of the participating subject.

Data Analytics vs. Data Mining

Data analytics is distinguished from data mining by the scope, purpose and focus of the analysis. Data miners sort through huge data sets using sophisticated software to identify undiscovered patterns and establish hidden relationships. Data analytics focuses on inference, the process of deriving a conclusion based solely on what is already known by the researcher.

Big Data Analytics

Big data analytics refers to the process of collecting, organizing and analyzing very large sets of data ("big data") to discover patterns and other useful information. With big data analytics, data scientists and others can analyze huge volumes of data that conventional analytics and business intelligence solutions can't touch. Consider that your organization could accumulate billions of rows of data with hundreds of millions of data combinations in multiple data stores and abundant formats. High-performance analytics is necessary to process that much data in order to figure out what's important and what isn't. Analyzing big data allows analysts, researchers, and business users to make better and faster decisions using data that was previously inaccessible or unusable. Using advanced analytics techniques such as text analytics, machine learning, predictive analytics, data mining, statistics, and natural language processing, businesses can analyze previously untapped data sources independent or together with their existing enterprise data to gain new insights resulting in significantly better and faster decisions.

Types of Data Analytics

Social Network Analysis (SNA)

The qualitative and quantitative analysis process of the social network such as (Facebook, Twitter, Research Gate, LinkedIn etc.) is carried in SNA. Such kind of method is done to measure the activities of the customers. This process of analyzing is done by monitoring their interaction through chat, post, comments etc. This type of social network analysis can be carried in groups, community and organization by measuring the flow of data among the customers. It helps to provide the information in both analysis methods like mathematical or visual so that they can understand the needs of the customer and it also helps to improve their business strategies.

Business Analytics (BA)

This type of analysis is used by the organization to measure the performance of their company. It also carried for evaluating their position in the market and to find where they should improve their strategies. This type of analytics uses statistical methods that can be applied for specific product or process by the company. The main goal of company to run the business analytics is to monitor their flow of business and to identify the disadvantages of the existing processes and highlight meaningful data. This helps the company to know the area of improving in their business for future growth and to handle the challenges. The business analytics plays a vital role to make decisions, improves the business strategies to keep a business competitive.

Social Media Analytics (SMA)

The term Social media analytics is used to collect and analyze the data from different social Medias and blogs etc. The monitoring of data is done after the data is collected and this strategy is used for improving the process of the company and makes them to produce a better and quality product. This analytics helps to understand the concept carried in the business functions such as marketing, customer service etc. It also helps to improve the customer experience. The Social Media Analytics is the best way to understand real-time choices and behaviour of the customers. The tactics followed by the organization or company behind social media analytics is they can get detailed information about customer base on a more emotional level. The main task during the social media analytics is to find out the which business objective can gain profit to the company, the company maximize their earnings by reducing the extra expenditure of the customer service, the suggestions can be collected from different customers on the services and products, it also able to enhance the business strategy by collecting the public opinions about their product which helps to improve the growth of the company.

Business Impact Analysis (BIA)

The analytics carried by the business impact helps to identify impact of critical and non-critical systems. The company can gain knowledge by processing the business analytics and they can take some precautionary steps at the time of disaster. This type analysis includes information about the estimated recovery times and recovery requirement, it also used for measuring the risks of failure against the costs of upgrading a particular system, find out the major risks and their fallout like losing all the data on the company main servers. These strategies should be carried out by every organization so that it helps to improve their methodologies and their strategies to understand the impact of their decisions at present and into the future.

Big Data Analytics (BDA)

The very important type of analytic in the present world, is known as big data analytics, which has the ability to analyze massive volume of data. It refers to the strategy of analyzing massive volumes of data, which is known big data. The origin of big data can be collected anywhere, such as social networking sites, the sensors used to collect climate data, videos and digital images, sale transaction records and cell phone GPS signals. It helps to explore concealed patterns, unidentified connections and provide accurate and valuable information about the data. The main task of big data analytics is to assist organizations in making better business decisions. It also helps data scientists and other users to evaluate or process massive volumes of transaction data and other data sources, which might be not, exploited by traditional Business Intelligence (BI) systems. This is because traditional systems often fail to analyze large data sources, which include Web server logs, social networking activity reports, Internet click-stream data and sensor captured data. The regular data warehouse cannot be suited to process big data. So they use some new technologies such as Hadoop, MapReduce and NoSQL databases. This technology is used for managing large volume of data in an efficient way for analytics purpose. The big data analytics helps to extract significant value from big data from the overall analytics, and they have fast analyses of data. The new type of visualizations and analytic techniques helps to capitalize on the unique characteristics of big data.

Statistical Methods for Exploratory Data Analysis

Data can be collected and analyzed in order to gain meaningful insights and make informed decisions. There are various ways in which insights can be obtained from data such as through univariate, bivariate and multivariate analysis and comparing these three types of analyses. This chapter closely examines these key concepts related to gaining insights from data in order to provide an extensive understanding of the subject.

Univariate Analysis

Types of Data

Data can be classified as categorical or numerical:

- Categorical data are observations or records that are arranged according to category. For example: the favorite color of a class of students; the mode of transport that each student uses to get to school; the rating of a TV program, either "a great program", "average program" or "poor program". Postal codes such as "3011", "3015" etc.

- Numerical data are observations based on counting or measurement. Calculations can be performed on numerical data. There are two main types of numerical data:

  - Discrete data, which takes only fixed values, usually whole numbers. Discrete data often arises as the result of counting items. For example: the number of siblings each student has, the number of pets a set of randomly chosen people have or the number of passengers in cars that pass an intersection.

  - Continuous data can take any value in a given range. It is usually a measurement. For example: the weights of students in a class. The weight of each student could be measured to the nearest tenth of a kg. Weights of 84.8kg and 67.5kg would be recorded. Other examples of continuous data include the time taken to complete a task or the heights of a group of people.

Representing Data

Data is often represented in frequency charts, column charts, histograms and dot plots. Remember: the frequency of an observation is the number of times that observation occurs.

Dot plots:

- A dot plot is an alternative to a frequency distribution table.

- A dot plot is recorded for every piece of data in the correct position above horizontal line.

- Dot plot can be used with both categorical and numerical data.

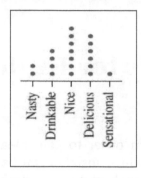

Example: The following frequency distribution table gives the number of days of each weather type for the month of January. Represent the information using a column chart.

Weather type	Hot	Warm	Mild	Cold
Frequency	8	15	5	3

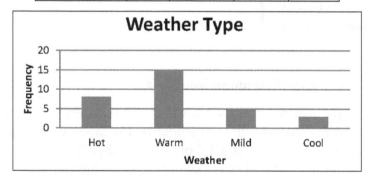

Example: The following table shows the number of cinema visits during a month by each of 20 students. It is an example of ungrouped data because each score is a separate group in itself.

Number of visits	0	1	2	3	4
Frequency	6	7	4	2	1

Represent the data in: (a) histogram and (b) frequency polygon.

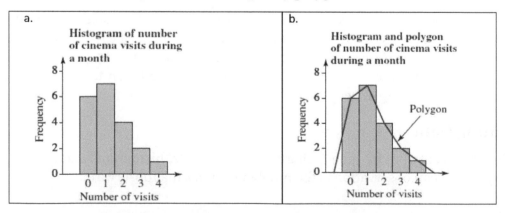

Notice that for a histogram there is no gap between the bars and the number of visits are positioned at the center of each bar.

Types of Average

There are three types of average which can represent a set of data. An average is a measure of central tendency.

The Mean

The most common average is the mean.

$\bar{x}$ is used to denote the mean.

$$\bar{x} = \frac{\text{sum of all scores}}{\text{number of all scores}}$$

Example: The following data gives the number of pets kept in each of 10 different households.

   3, 5, 4, 4, 2, 3, 0, 1, 4, 5

The mean number of pets is given by:

$$\frac{3+5+4+4+2+3+0+1+4+5}{10} = 3.1$$

The mean is sometimes not the best average to use as it is affected by extreme scores or outliers.

The Median

The median of a set of scores is the middle score when the data are arranged in order of size.

The median's position is given by $\frac{n+1}{2}$ th score, where n is the number of scores.

In previous example the median's position is given by the $\frac{10+1}{2}$ th score. This is the 5.5th score or halfway between the 5th and 6th score, after the scores have been arranged in order of size.

Arranging the data in order of size:

   0, 1, 2, 3, 3, 4, 4, 4, 5, 5

Median number of pets is: 3+4/2 = 3.5 (as there are two middle scores we take their mean. The median is not affected by extreme values or outliers.

The Mode

The mode of a group of scores is the score that occurs most often. That is the score with the highest frequency. In previous example the modal number of pets is 4. More than one mode is possible.

Frequency Tables

Example: The table shows the number of cinema visits made by each of 20 students.

Find:

- The mean of the data.

- The median of the data.

- The mode of the data.

Number of visits	0	1	2	3	4
frequency	6	7	4	2	1

The table indicates that 6 students made 0 cinema visits, 7 students made 1 cinema visit, 4 students made 2 cinema visits etc.

The mean number of visits can be found by adding an extra column to the table and multiplying the number of visits by the frequency.

Number of visits (x)	Frequency (f)	$f \times x$
0	6	0
1	7	7
2	4	8
3	2	6
4	1	4
total	20	25

a. Mean number of visits $= \dfrac{\text{total of } f \times x}{\text{total of } f} = \dfrac{25}{20} = 1.25$

b. The median number of visits can be found by finding the position of the median as the number of visits are in order of size in the table.

The median's position is the $\dfrac{n+1}{2}$ th score $= \dfrac{20+1}{2}$ th $= 10.5$th position. Halfway between the 10th and 11th scores. The median's position falls within the second row and is therefore 1.

c. The mode is the score with the highest frequency. The mode is 1.

Alternatively, the mean and median can be found using Lists and Spreadsheet in the calculator.

1: Enter the data into Lists and Spreadsheet view	2: Hit Menu, Statistics, Stat Calculations, One Variable Statistics.

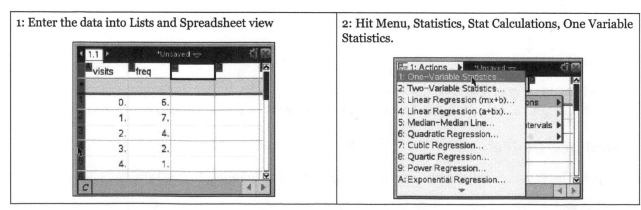

3. Click OK when number of lists appears.
4. In the pop up, click in the X1 List box and select visits from the drop down list. Hit the Tab
key to move to the next box and select frequency from the drop down list in the Frequency List box

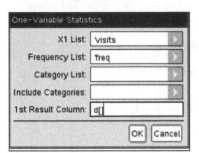

There is no need to enter data into the other boxes.
5. Click OK.

6. The statistical data appears.
The mean is given by $\bar{x}=1.25$
The median is 1.
n is useful as it gives the frequency total.

A visits	B freq	C	D	E
			=OneVa	
1	0.	6.	Title	One-V...
2	1.	7.	$\bar{x}$	1.25
3	2.	4.	Σx	25.
4	3.	2.	Σx^2	57.
5	4.	1.	sx := sn...	1.164...
6			$\sigma x := \sigma$...	1.134...
7			n	20.
8			MinX	0.
9			Q_1X	0.
10			Median...	1.

Grouped Data

When data is presented in a frequency table within class intervals, and we do not know the actual values within each class interval, we assume that all values are equal to the midpoint of the class interval in order to find the mean.

Example: The ages of a group of 30 people attending a superannuation seminar are recorded in the frequency table below, calculate the mean age.

Age (Class Intervals)	Frequency
20-29	1
30-39	6
40-49	13
50-59	6
60-69	3
70-79	1
total	30

To find the mean age, assume all people in the class interval 20 - 29 are 24.5 years of age (This value is obtained by finding the midpoint of 20 - 29); all people in the class interval 30 - 39 are 34.5 years of age and so on. The mean age can be found from the table below:

Age (Class Intervals)	Frequency f	Midpoint of Class Interval m	f×m
20-29	1	24.5	24.5
30-39	6	34.5	207
40-49	13	44.5	578.5
50-59	6	54.5	327
60-69	3	64.5	193.5
70-79	1	74.5	74.5
Total	30		1405

The mean age $\bar{x} = \dfrac{\text{total of } f \times m}{\text{total of } f} = \dfrac{1405}{30} = 46.8$ years (correct to 1 decimal place)

The above can be more easily done using Lists and Spreadsheet on the calculator.

1. In Lists and Spreadsheets view enter the data for the midpoints and the frequency into the first two columns. Label the columns as shown.

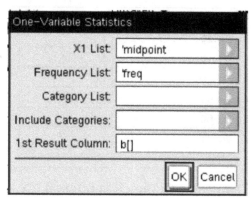

2. Press Menu, Statistics, Stat Calculations, One Variable Statistics.

3. Leave the Number of Lists as 1 and select OK.

4. In the pop up box, click in the X1 List box and select midpoint from the drop down list. Press the Tab key to move to the Frequency List box and select freq from the drop down list.

One-Variable Statistics	
X1 List:	'midpoint
Frequency List:	'freq
Category List:	
Include Categories:	
1st Result Column:	b[]
	OK Cancel

5. Press the TAB key to move to the OK button.

- The mean $\bar{x} = 46.833$

- The mean age = 46.8 years

Measures of Variability or Spread

It is useful to be able to measure the spread or variability of the data. How dispersed is the data?

The Range

The simplest measure of spread is the range. The range is the difference between the smallest score and the largest.

Example: The set of data 3, 5, 4, 4, 2, 3, 0, 1, 4, 5 (which gave the number of pets in each of 10 households) has a range of:

$5 - 0 = 5$

The Interquartile Range (IQR)

The lower quartile, Q_1 is $\dfrac{1}{4}$ of the way through the set of data.

The upper quartile, Q_3 is $\dfrac{3}{4}$ of the way through the set of data.

The IQR=Q_3-Q_1

The upper and lower quartile and the interquartile range can be found by using the following steps:

Step 1. Arrange the data in order of size.

Step 2. Divide the data into halves by finding median. If there is an odd number of scores then the median will be one of the original scores. If there is an even number of scores the median will lie halfway between two scores and will divide the data nearly into two equal sets.

Step 3. Find the lower quartile by locating the median of the lower half of the data.

Step 4. Find the upper quartile by locating the median of the upper half of the data.

Step 5. Find the interquartile range by calculating the difference between the upper and lower quartiles.

Example: Determine the interquartile range of the following data:

      12, 9, 4, 6, 5, 8, 9, 4, 10, 2.

1. First arrange the data in order of size.

      2, 4, 4, 5, 6, 8, 9, 9, 10, 12

2. Find the position of the median. The median is the $\dfrac{n+1}{2}$th score.

2, 4, 4, 5, 6, 8, 9, 9, 10, 12

↑
median

3. The median is the $\frac{10+1}{2}$ th score- that is, the 5.5^{th} score. That is, halfway between the 5th and 6th scores.

4. The data have been divided into halves, each containing 5 values. The lower quartile is the median of the lower half. The upper quartile is the median of the upper half.

5. The position of the upper half median is the $\frac{5+1}{2}$ th score- that is, the 3rd score.

2, 4, 4, 5, 6, | 8, 9, 9, 10, 12

$Q_1 = 4$

$Q_3 = 9$

6. The interquartile range is the difference between the upper and lower quartiles.

$IQR = Q_3 - Q_1$

$= 9 - 4 = 5$

The Standard Deviation

The standard deviation gives a measure of the spread of the data about the mean. The formula to find the standard deviation is complex and we usually find it directly from the calculator. On the calculator it is denoted by the symbol. The bigger the standard deviation, the greater the spread of data.

Example: Find the standard deviation of the set of data: 12, 9, 4, 6, 5, 8, 9, 4, 10, 2. This is the same data as in previous example.

1. In Lists and Spreadsheet view, enter the data.	3. Leave the Number of Lists as 1 and select OK.
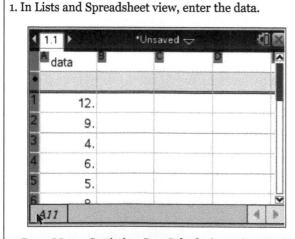	4. Enter the data into the pop up box as shown. 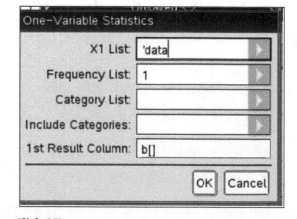
2. Press Menu, Statistics, Stat Calculations, One Variable Statistics.	5. Click OK.

The statistical data appears.

data	B	C	D
		=OneVar	
1	12. Title	One-Va...	
2	9. x̄	6.9	
3	4. Σx	69.	
4	6. Σx²	567.	
5	5. sx := Sn...	3.17805	
6	8. σx := σ...	3.01496	
7	9. n	10.	
8	4. MinX	2.	
9	10. Q₁X	4.	
10	2. Median...	7.	
11	Q₃X	9.	
12	MaxX	12.	

The standard deviation is given by

$sx = 3.17805$

Notice that the lower quartile is given by

$Q_1 X = 4$ and the upper quartile is given by

$Q_3 X = 9$

This agrees with the solutions to previous examples.

The $IQR = 9 - 4 = 5$

The standard deviation is a measure of the spread of data from the mean. Consider the two sets of data shown below:

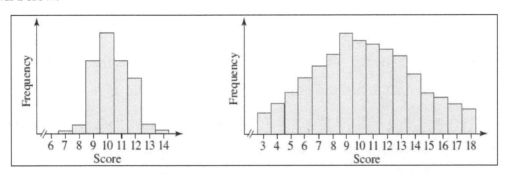

Each set of data has a mean of 10. The set of data above left has a standard deviation of 1 and the set of data above right has a standard deviation of 3. As we can see, the standard deviation, the more spread are the data from the mean.

Stem and Leaf Plots

Example: The data below shows the weights in kg of 20 possums arranged in order of size:

0.7	0.9	1.1	1.5	1.5	1.6
1.7	1.7	1.8	1.9	1.9	2.0
2.1	2.1	2.2	2.3	2.3	2.5
3.0	3.2				

We can represent this data in a stem and leaf plot as shown below:

Key: 0|7 = 0.7kg

Stem	Leaf
0	7 9
1	1 4 5 6 7 7 8 8 9
2	0 1 1 2 3 3 5
3	0 2

In a stem and leaf plot the numbers are arranged in order of size. The key is given as 0|7 kg means stem 0 and leaf 7 which represents 0.7 kg. You should always include a key in the stem and leaf plot.

When preparing a stem and leaf plot keep the number s in neat vertical columns because a neat plot will show the distribution of the scores. It is like a sideways bar chart or histogram. The inter-quartile range can be found from the stem and leaf plot.

1. Find the median weight. The median weight Q_2 is the $\frac{(20+1)}{2}$ th score. i.e. the 10.5th score.

The median lies between the 10th and 11th scores. Count through the data to find the position of the median. It can be seen from the plot that the median lays between 1.8 and 1.9. The median weight is $\frac{(1.8+1.9)}{2}$ th = 1.85 kg.

2. The lower quartile Q_1 will be the $\frac{(10+1)}{2}$ th score in the lower half. i.e. the 5.5th score in the lower half. Count through the data to find the position of the lower quartile. $Q_1 = \frac{(1.5+1.6)}{2}$ th = 1.55 kg.

3. The upper quartile Q_3 will be the 5.5th score in the upper half of the plot. Count through the data to find the position of the upper quartile. $Q_3 = \frac{(2.2+2.3)}{2}$ th = 2.25 kg

4. The interquartile range = $Q_3 - Q_1$ = 2.25 − 1.55 = 0.7 kg

5. See diagram below:

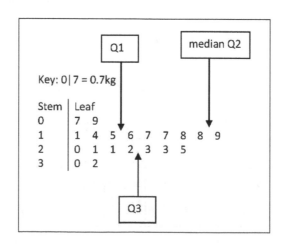

Example: Find the interquartile range of the data presented in the following stem and leaf plot.

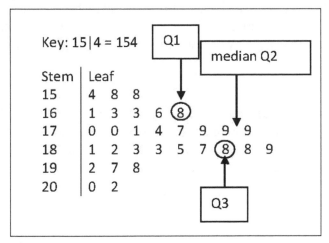

The median is the $\dfrac{(30+1)}{2}$ th score. i.e. the 15.5th score which lies between 179 and 179. So the median is 179.

The lower quartile Q_1 will be the $\dfrac{(15+1)}{2}$ th score in the lower half. i.e. the 8th score in the lower half. $Q_1 = 168$.

The upper quartile Q_2 will be the 8th score in the upper half of the data. ie 188.

The interquartile range = $Q_3 - Q_1 = 188 - 168 = 20$.

Using CAS, You could check your answers by entering the data into your CAS calculator to determine the median, lower and upper quartiles.

Boxplots

Five-Number Summary

A five number summary is a list consisting of the lowest score (Xmin), lower quartile (Q_1), median (Q_2), upper quartile (Q_3) and the greatest score (Xmax) of a set of data. A five number summary gives information about the spread or variability of a set of data.

Box Plots

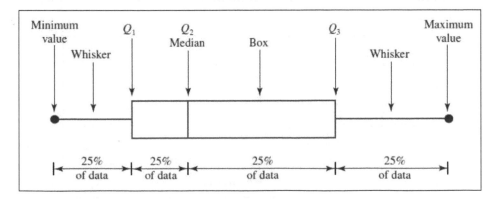

A box plot is a graph of the 5-number summary. It is a powerful way of showing the spread of data. A box plot consists of a central divided box with attached "whiskers". The box spans the interquartile range. The median is marked by a vertical line inside the box. The whiskers indicate the range of scores. Box plots are always drawn to scale and a scale is often attached.

Interpreting a Boxplot

A boxplot divides the data into four sections. 25% of the scores lie between the lowest score and the lower quartile, 25% between the lower quartile and the median, 25% between the median and the upper quartile and 25% between the upper quartile and the greatest score.

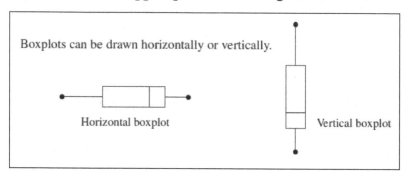

Extreme Values or Outliers

Extreme values often make the whiskers appear longer than they should and hence give the appearance that the data is spread over a much greater range than they really are. If an extreme value occurs in a set of data it can be denoted by a small cross on the boxplot. The whisker is then shortened to the next largest or smallest score. The boxplot below shows that the lowest score was 5. This was an extreme value as the rest of the scores were located within the range 15 to 42.

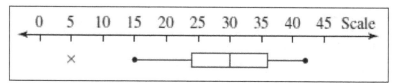

When one observation lies well away from other observations in a set, we call it an outlier. For example the histogram shows the weights of a group of 5-year old boys. Clearly the weight of 33kg is an outlier.

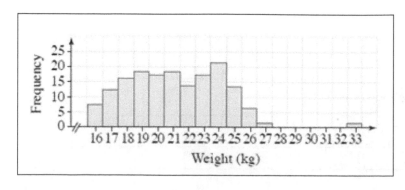

Determining whether an Observation is an Outlier

To identify possible outliers we can use the following rule:

An outlier is a score, x, which is either less than $Q_1 - 1.5 \times IQR$ or greater than $Q_3 + 1.5 \times IQR$.

Where Q_1 is the lower quartile and Q_3 is the upper quartile and IQR is the interquartile range.

In summary, an outlier is a score, X, which lies outside the interval.

$$Q_1 - 1.5 \times IQR \leq x \leq Q_3 + 1.5 \times IQR$$

Example: The times (in seconds) achieved by the 12 fastest runners in the 100m sprint at a school athletics meeting are listed below:

11.2	12.3	11.5	11.0	11.6	11.4
11.9	11.2	12.7	11.3	11.2	11.3

Draw a boxplot to represent the data, describe the shape of the distribution and comment on the existence of any outliners.

1. Determine the five number summary statistics by first ordering the data and obtain the interquartile range.

11.0	11.2	11.2	11.2	11.3	11.3	11.4	11.5	11.6	11.9	12.3	12.7

Lowest score= 11.0

Highest score= 12.7

Median= Q_2= 11.35

$\qquad Q_1$=11.2

$\qquad$ IQR=11.75-11.2 =0.55

2. Identify any outliers by applying the outliers rule.

$\qquad Q_1$-1.5 × IQR= 11.2-1.5 × 0.55 =10.375

The lowest score lies above 10.375, so there are no outliers below.

$\qquad Q_3$+1.5×IQR= 11.75 × 1.5×0.55 =12.575

The score lies above 12.575, so it is an outlier and 12.3 becomes the end of the upper whisker.

3. Draw the boxplot with the outlier.

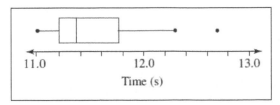

4. Describe the shape of the distribution. Data peak to the left and trail off to the right with one outlier.

The data are positively skewed with 12.7 seconds being an outlier. This may be due to incorrect timing or recording but more likely the top eleven runners were significantly faster than the other competitors in the event.

Distribution of Data

In the figures below, a symmetric distribution is represented in the histogram and in the boxplot. The characteristics of this boxplot are that the whiskers are about the same length and the median is located about halfway along the box.

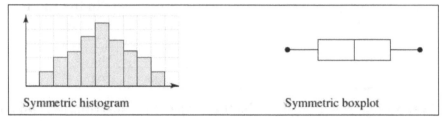

Symmetric histogram   Symmetric boxplot

The figures below show a negative skewed distribution. In such a distribution, the data peak to the right on the histogram and trail off the left.

In corresponding fashion on the boxplot, the bunching of the data to the right means that the left hand whisker is longer and the right hand whisker is shorter, that is, the lower 25% of data are sparse and spread out whereas the top 25% of data are bunched up. The median occurs further towards the right end of the box.

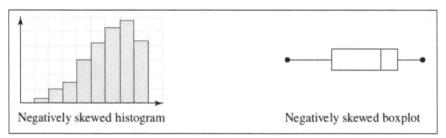

Negatively skewed histogram   Negatively skewed boxplot

In the figures shown below, we have a positively skewed distribution. In such a distribution, the data peak to the left on the histogram and trail off to the right.

In corresponding fashion on the boxplot, the bunching of the data to the left means that the left hand whisker is shorter and the right hand whisker is longer, that is, the lower 25% of data are sparse and spread out whereas the top 25% of data are bunched up. The median occurs further towards the left end of the box.

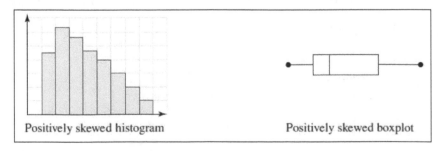

Positively skewed histogram   Positively skewed boxplot

Comparing Two Sets of Data

Back to Back Stem and Leaf Plots

Two sets of data can be compared using back to back stem and leaf plots. The data below shows the life time of a sample of 40 batteries in hours of each of two brands when fitted into a child's toy. Some of the toys are fitted with an ordinary battery and some with Brand X. Which battery is best?

Key: 6|9 = 69 hours

Ordinary Brand Leaf	Stem	Brand X Leaf
8 6 2 0 0	6	9
9 9 9 8 8 6 4 0	7	3 5
8 8 7 5 3 1 1 1 0	8	2 4 8
9 6 6 4 2 2 2 0 0	9	0 1 4 5 5 9
8 7 5 3 1 1 1	10	0 0 2 5 8 8 9 9
4 2	11	0 0 1 1 3 3 6 7 9
	12	1 4 6 6 6 7 8 8
	13	3 5
	14	6

The spread of each set of data can be seen graphically from the stem and leaf plot. It can be seen that although brand X showed a little more variability than the ordinary brand the batteries generally lasted longer.

Parallel Box Plots

The above data can also be compared by using parallel boxplots. The boxplots share a common scale. Quantitative comparisons can be made between the sets of data.

The 5-Number Summaries of both types of batteries are given below. You can work them out from the stem plots or by using your calculator.

Brand X:

Xmin	Lower Quartile Q1	Median Q2	Upper Quartile Q3	Xmax
69	95	109.5	122.5	146

Ordinary Brand:

Xmin	Lower Quartile Q1	Median Q2	Upper Quartile Q3	Xmax
60	78.5	87.5	97.5	114

The following parallel boxplots can be drawn to compare the data.

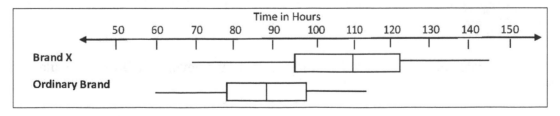

From the box plots it can be seen that:

- Brand X showed more variability in its performance than the ordinary brand. Brand X range = 77, ordinary brand range = 54. Brand X interquartile range = 27.5 and ordinary brand interquartile range =19.0.

- The longest lifetime recorded was that of a Brand X battery of 146 hours.

- The shortest lifetime recorded was that of an ordinary battery of 60 hours.

- Brand X battery median lifetime (109.5 hours) was better than that of an ordinary battery (87.5 hours).

- Over one quarter of Brand X batteries were better performers than the best ordinary brand battery (that is, had longer lifetimes than the longest of the ordinary brand batteries' lifetimes).

The Mean, Standard Deviation and Normal Distribution

The Mean

The mean of a set of data, $\bar{x}$, is given by:

$$\bar{x} = \frac{\sum x}{n}$$

Where $\sum x$ represents the sum of all the observations in the data set and n represents the number of observations in the data set.

For example the mean of 4, 7, 9, 12 and 18 is given by:

$$\bar{x} = \frac{4 + 7 + 9 + 12 + 18}{5} = 10$$

The mean is often used as the everyday average and gives a measure of the center of a distribution. The mean is sometimes affected by outliers (extreme values) and the median is often a better average to use as it is not affected by extreme values.

The Standard Deviation

The standard deviation gives a measure of how the data is spread around the mean. The formula for the standard deviation is given below:

$$s = \sqrt{\frac{\sum (x - \bar{x})^2}{n - 1}}$$

Fortunately, the calculator can be used to find the standard deviation. On the calculator it is denoted by sx.

The standard deviation is a measure of the spread of data from the mean. Consider the sets of data shown below:

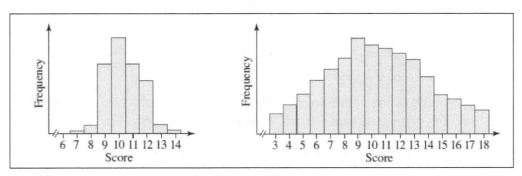

Each set of data has a mean of 10. The set of data above left has a standard deviation of 1 and the set of data above right has a standard deviation of 3. As we can see, the larger the standard deviation, the more spread are the data from the mean.

The 68%-95%-99.7% Rule Applied to the Normal Distribution

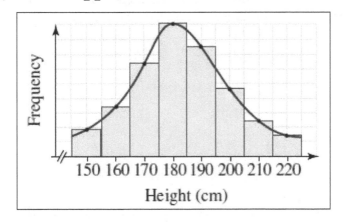

Many sets of data are approximately symmetric forming a "bell-shaped" curve. We refer to this type of data as a normal distribution. Examples include birth weights, people's heights etc. Data that is normally distributed have their symmetrical bell-shaped distribution centered on the mean value, $\bar{x}$.

The above data of the heights of people form a bell-shape and approximates a normal distribution. An astounding feature of this type of distribution is that we can predict what percentage of the data lie 1, 2 or 3 standard deviations either side of the mean using what is termed as the 68-95-99.7 rule.

The 68-95-99.7 rule for a bell shaped curve states that approximately:

- 68% of data lie within 1 standard deviation either side of the mean.

- 95% of data lie within 2 standard deviation either side of the mean.

- 99.7% of data lie within 3 standard deviations either side of the mean.

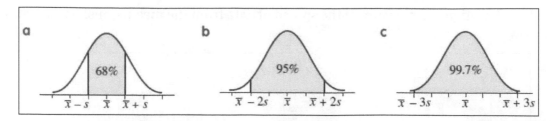

In the figure a above, 68% of the data shown lie between the value which is 1 standard deviation below the mean, that is $\bar{x}$ -s, and the value which is 1 standard deviation above the mean, that is $\bar{x}$ +s.

In figure b above, 95% of the data shown lie between the value which is 2 standard deviations below the mean, that is, $\bar{x}$ -2s, and the value which is 2 standard deviations above the mean, that is $\bar{x}$ +2s.

In figure c above, 99% of the data shown lie between the value which is 3 standard deviations below the mean, that is, $\bar{x}$ -3s, and the value which is 3 standard deviations above the mean, that is $\bar{x}$ +3s.

Using the 68-95-99% rule, we can work out the various percentages of the distribution which lie between the mean and 1 standard deviation from the mean and between the mean and 2 standard deviations from the mean and so on. The diagram below summarizes this:

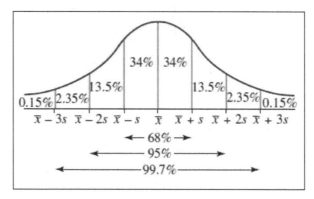

Using the symmetry of the bell-shaped curve and the above rules various percentages can be calculated.

Z-Scores

To compare scores in different distributions we can make use of z-scores. The z-score, also known as the standardized score, indicates the position of a score in relation to the mean. It gives the number of standard deviations that the score is from the mean. A z score can be both positive and negative. A z-score of 0 indicates that the score is equal to the mean; a negative z-score indicates that the score is below the mean and a positive z-score indicates that the score is above the mean. A score that is exactly 1 standard deviation above the mean has a z-score of 1. A score that is exactly 2 standard deviations below the mean has a score that is exactly 2 standard below the mean has z-score of -2. To calculate a z-score we use the formula:

$$z = \frac{x - \bar{x}}{s}$$

Where,

x= the score.

$\overline{X}$ = the mean.

S= the standard deviation.

Not all z-scores will be whole numbers; in fact most will not be. A whole number indicates only that the score is an exact number of standard deviations above or below the mean.

For example, if the mean value of the IQ's of a group of students is 100 and the standard deviation is 15, an IQ of 88 would be represented by a z score of −0.8, as shown below:

$$z = \frac{x - \overline{x}}{s} = \frac{88 - 100}{15} = -0.8$$

The negative value indicates that the IQ of 88 is below the mean but by less than one standard deviation.

Using Z-Scores to Compare Data

An important use of z-scores is to z-scores from different data sets. Suppose that in your maths exam your result was 74 and in English your result was 63. In which subject did you achieve the better result?

At first glance, it may appear that the maths result is better, but this does not take into account the difficulty of the test. A mark of 63 on a difficult English test many in fact be a better result than 74 if it was an easy maths test.

The only way that we can fairly compare the results is by comparing each result ith its mean and standard deviation. This is done by converting each result to a z-score.

If, for maths, $\overline{X}$ =60 and s= 12, then,

$$z = \frac{x - \overline{x}}{s}$$

$$= \frac{74 - 60}{12}$$

$$= 1.17$$

And if, For English, $\overline{X}$ =50 and s=8, then

$$z = \frac{x - \overline{x}}{s}$$

$$= \frac{63 - 50}{8}$$

$$= 1.625$$

The English result is better because the higher z-score shows that the 63 is higher in comparison to the mean of each subject. In each example, the circumstances must be read carefully to see whether a higher or lower z-score is better. For example, if we are comparing times for runners for different distances, the lower z-score would be better one.

Bivariate and Multivariate Analysis

Bivariate analysis is one of the simplest forms of quantitative (statistical) analysis. It involves the analysis of two variables (often denoted as X, Y), for the purpose of determining/understanding the association or dependence (empirical relationship) between them, if any. We thus restrict our attention to the two numeric attributes of interest; say X_1 and X_2, with the data D represented as an n×2 matrix:

$$D = \begin{pmatrix} X_1 & X_2 \\ X_{11} & X_{12} \\ X_{21} & X_{22} \\ \cdot & \cdot \\ \cdot & \cdot \\ x_{n1} & x_{n2} \end{pmatrix}$$

Geometrically, we can think of D in two ways. It can be viewed as n points or vectors in 2-dimensional space over the attributes X_1 and X_2.

With bivariate analysis, we are testing hypotheses of "association" and causality. In its simplest form, association simply refers to the extent to which it becomes easier to predict a value for the Dependent variable if we know a case's value on the independent variable.

A measure of association helps us to understand this relationship. These measures of association relate to how much better this prediction becomes with knowledge of the independent variable or how well an independent variable relates to the dependent variable. We have already discussed this in more abstract terms of "correlation". A measure of association often ranges between –1 and 1. Where the sign of the integer represents the "direction" of correlation (negative or positive relationships) and the distance away from 0 represents the degree or extent of correlation – the farther the number away from 0, the higher or "more perfect" the relationship is between the IV and DV.

Statistical significance relates to the generalizability of the relationship AND, more importantly, the likelihood the observed relationship occurred by chance. In political science, we typically consider a relationship significant if it has a significance level of.05 – In only 5/100 times will the pattern of observations for these two variables that we have measured occur by chance. Often significance levels, when n (total number of cases in a sample) is large, can approach.001 (only 1/1000 times will the observed association occur). Measures of association and statistical significance that are used vary by the level of measurement of the variables analyzed.

Measures of Location and Dispersion

Common examples of measures of statistical dispersion are the variance, standard deviation and inter-quartile range. Dispersion is contrasted with location or central tendency, and together they are the most used properties of distributions.

- Mean: The bivariate mean is defined as the expected value of the vector random variable X:

$$\mu = E[X] = E\left[\begin{pmatrix} X_1 \\ X_2 \end{pmatrix}\right] = \begin{pmatrix} E[X_1] \\ E[X_2] \end{pmatrix} = \begin{pmatrix} \mu_1 \\ \mu_2 \end{pmatrix}$$

- Variance: We can compute the variance along each attribute, namely $\sigma 1^2$ for X_1 and $\sigma 2^2$ for X_2 using: $\sigma^2 = var(X) = E\left[(X-\mu)^2\right]$

$$= \begin{cases} \sum(X-\mu)2f(x) \\ \int_{-a}^{a}(x-\mu)2f(x)\,d(x) \end{cases}$$

The total variance is given as: $Var(D) = \sigma 1^2 + \sigma 2^2$

Measures of Association

Variance is a measure of the variability or spread in a set of data. Mathematically, it is the average squared deviation from the mean score. We use the following formula to compute variance:

$$Var(X) = \Sigma\left(X_i - X\right)^2 / N = \Sigma\, x_i^2 / N$$

Where,

N is the number of scores in a set of scores.

X is the mean of the N scores.

X_i is the ith raw score in the set of scores.

x_i is the ith deviation score in the set of scores.

Var(X) is the variance of all the scores in the set.

Covariance is a measure of the extent to which corresponding elements from two sets of ordered data move in the same direction. We use the following formula to compute covariance:

$$Cov(X, Y) = \Sigma(X_i - X)(Y_i - Y)/N = \Sigma\, x_i y_i / N.$$

Where,

N is the number of scores in each set of data.

X is the mean of the N scores in the first data set.

X_i is the ithe raw score in the first set of scores.

x_i is the ith deviation score in the first set of scores.

Y is the mean of the N scores in the second data set.

Y_i is the ith raw score in the second set of scores.

y_i is the ith deviation score in the second set of scores.

Cov(X, Y) is the covariance of corresponding scores in the two sets of data.

Variance-Covariance Matrix: Variance and covariance are often displayed together in a variance covariance matrix, (aka, a covariance matrix). The variances appear along the diagonal and covariances appear in the off diagonal elements, as shown below:

$$V = \begin{bmatrix} \sum x_1^2/N & \sum x_1 x_2/N & \cdots & \sum x_1 x_c/N \\ \sum x_2 x_1/N & \sum x_2^2/N & \cdots & \sum x_2 x_c/N \\ \cdots & \cdots & \cdots & \cdots \\ \sum x_c x_1/N & \sum x_c x_2/N & \cdots & \sum x_c^2/N \end{bmatrix}$$

Where,

V is a c x c variance-covariance matrix.

N is the number of scores in each of the c data sets.

x_i is a deviation score from the ith data set.

$\Sigma x_i 2/N$ are the variance of elements from the ith data set.

$\Sigma x_i x_j/N$ are the covariance for elements from the ith and j^{th} data sets.

Example: Steps for Creating Variance-covariance Matrix

The table below displays scores on math, English, and art tests for 5 students. Note that data from the table is represented in matrix A, where each column in the matrix shows scores on a test and each row shows scores for a student.

Student	Maths	English	Art
1	90	60	90
2	90	90	30
3	60	60	60
4	60	60	90
5	30	30	30

$$\Rightarrow A = \begin{bmatrix} 90 & 60 & 90 \\ 90 & 90 & 30 \\ 60 & 60 & 60 \\ 60 & 60 & 90 \\ 30 & 30 & 30 \end{bmatrix}$$

Given the data represented in matrix A, compute the variance of each test and the covariance between the tests.

The solution involves a three-step process.

Step 1: Transform the raw scores in matrix A to deviation scores in matrix a, using the transformation formula.

$$a = A - 11'A \, (1 \, / \, n)$$

Where, 1 is a 5 × 1 column vector of one

a is an 5 × 3 matrix of deviation scores: a_{11}, a_{12},..., a_{53}

A is a 5 × 3 matrix of raw scores: A_{11}, A_{12}. A_{53} n is the number of rows in matrix A.

$$a = \begin{bmatrix} 90 & 60 & 90 \\ 90 & 90 & 30 \\ 60 & 60 & 60 \\ 60 & 60 & 90 \\ 30 & 30 & 30 \end{bmatrix} - \begin{bmatrix} 1 & 1 & 1 & 1 & 1 \\ 1 & 1 & 1 & 1 & 1 \\ 1 & 1 & 1 & 1 & 1 \\ 1 & 1 & 1 & 1 & 1 \\ 1 & 1 & 1 & 1 & 1 \end{bmatrix} \begin{bmatrix} 90 & 60 & 90 \\ 90 & 90 & 30 \\ 60 & 60 & 60 \\ 60 & 60 & 90 \\ 30 & 30 & 30 \end{bmatrix} (1/5)$$

$$a = \begin{bmatrix} 90 & 60 & 90 \\ 90 & 90 & 30 \\ 60 & 60 & 60 \\ 60 & 60 & 90 \\ 30 & 30 & 30 \end{bmatrix} - \begin{bmatrix} 66 & 60 & 60 \\ 66 & 60 & 60 \\ 66 & 60 & 60 \\ 60 & 60 & 90 \\ 66 & 60 & 60 \end{bmatrix} = \begin{bmatrix} 24 & 0 & 30 \\ 24 & 30 & -30 \\ -6 & 0 & 0 \\ -6 & 0 & 30 \\ -36 & -30 & -30 \end{bmatrix}$$

Step 2: Compute a'a - the deviation score sums of squares matrix, as shown below:

$$a'a = \begin{bmatrix} 24 & 24 & -6 & -6 & -36 \\ 0 & 30 & 0 & 0 & -30 \\ 30 & -30 & 0 & 30 & -30 \end{bmatrix} \begin{bmatrix} 24 & 0 & 60 \\ 24 & 30 & 60 \\ -6 & 0 & 60 \\ -6 & 0 & 90 \\ -36 & -30 & 60 \end{bmatrix} = \begin{bmatrix} 2520 & 1800 & 900 \\ 1800 & 1800 & 0 \\ 900 & 0 & 3600 \end{bmatrix}$$

Step 3: And finally, to create the variance-covariance matrix, we divide each element in the deviation sum of squares matrix by n, as shown below:

$$V = a'a \, / \, n = \begin{bmatrix} 2520/5 & 1800/5 & 900/5 \\ 1800/5 & 1800/5 & 0/5 \\ 900/5 & 0/5 & 3600/5 \end{bmatrix} = \begin{bmatrix} 504 & 360 & 180 \\ 360 & 360 & 0 \\ 180 & 0 & 720 \end{bmatrix}$$

We can interpret the variance and covariance statistics in matrix V to understand how the various test scores vary and covary:

- Shown along the diagonal, we see the variance of scores for each test. The art test has the biggest variance; and the English test, the smallest (360). So we can say that art test scores are more variable than English test scores.

- The covariance is displayed in the off-diagonal elements of matrix V.

   ○ The covariance between math and English is positive (360), and the covariance between math and art is positive (180). This means the scores tend to covary in a positive way. As scores on math go up, scores on art and English also tend to go up; and vice versa.

   ○ The covariance between English and art, however, is zero. This means there tends to be no predictable relationship between the movement of English and art scores.

If the covariance between any tests had been negative, it would have meant that the test scores on those tests tend to move in opposite directions. That is, students with relatively high scores on the first test would tend to have relatively low scores on the second test.

Correlation

The strength of the linear association between two variables is quantified by the correlation coefficient.

Given a set of observations $(x_1, y_1), (x_2, y_2)... (x_n, y_n)$, the formula for computing the correlation coefficient is given by:

$$r = \frac{1}{n-1}\sum\left(\frac{x-\bar{x}}{s_x}\right)\left(\frac{y-\bar{y}}{s_y}\right)$$

The correlation coefficient always takes a value between -1 and 1, with 1 or -1 indicating perfect correlation (all points would lie along a straight line in this case). A positive correlation indicates a positive association between the variables (increasing values in one variable correspond to increasing values in the other variable), while a negative correlation indicates a negative association between the variables (increasing values is one variable correspond to decreasing values in the other variable). A correlation value close to 0 indicates no association between the variables.

Since the formula for calculating the correlation coefficient standardizes the variables, changes in scale or units of measurement will not affect its value. For this reason, the correlation coefficient is often more useful than a graphical depiction in determining the strength of the association between two variables.

The following is a sample calculation of the above discussed measures for the IRIS data set:

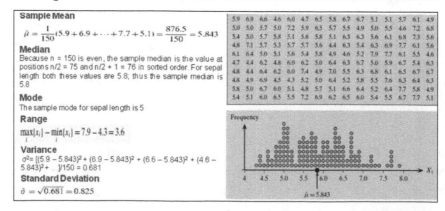

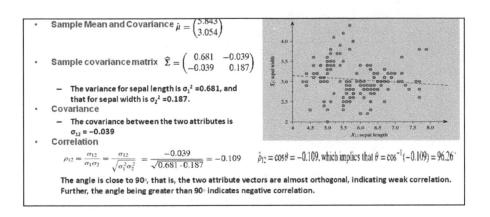

Multivariate Analysis

Multivariate analysis is essentially the statistical process of simultaneously analyzing multiple independent (or predictor) variables with multiple dependent (outcome or criterion) variables. Using matrix algebra (most multivariate analyses are correlational).

Simpson's Paradox

When you compare a population with labeled subpopulations with another population (or "the same" at a different time), it's extremely likely that the two populations will have different proportions of their subpopulations. This is the heart of Simpson's paradox.

Simpson's paradox occurs when your sample is composed of separate classes with different mean values of a statistical value. In this case, if the class distribution within sample changes between two measures, the trend observed on average might be opposed to the trend observed in each of the two classes.

Example: One of the best-known examples of Simpson's paradox is a study of gender bias among graduate school admissions to University of California, Berkeley. The admission figures for the fall of 1973 showed that men applying were more likely than women to be admitted, and the difference was so large that it was unlikely to be due to chance.

	Applicants	Admitted
Men	8442	44%
Women	4321	35%

But when examining the individual departments, it appeared that six out of 85 departments were significantly biased against men, whereas only four were significantly biased against women. In fact, the pooled and corrected data showed a "small but statistically significant bias in favor of women." The data from the six largest departments is listed below:

Department	Men		Women	
	Applicants	Admitted	Applicants	Admitted
A	825	62%	108	82%

B	560	63%	25	68%
C	325	37%	593	34%
D	417	33%	375	35%
E	191	28%	393	24%
F	373	6%	341	7%

The research concluded that women tended to apply to competitive departments with low rates of admission even among qualified applicants (such as in the English Department), whereas men tended to apply to less-competitive departments with high rates of admission among the qualified applicants (such as in engineering and chemistry). The conditions under which the admissions' frequency data from specific departments constitute a proper defense against charges of discrimination are formulated in the book Causality by Pearl.

Example: Let's say that a teacher has a class with 100 students, 10 among them come from a disadvantaged background and their average in year 1 is 80/100. All the other students are normal and have an average of 90/100. Thus the average of her class was at 89/100. Since disadvantaged student were feeling themselves well with that particular teacher they advised other disadvantaged students to sign in into the course and in the year 2 the same teacher had 50 students from a disadvantageous background and 50 normal students. Normal student average became 91 and disadvantaged ones - 81. However, the average of the class dropped to 86 and she gets a call from the dean asking her why did she become so bad at teaching.

Always look for a meaningful split of your data into classes that might have different behavior. If not, you might obtain a correlation opposed to the real one. If your data don't look like a Gaussian, don't try to pretend it is a Gaussian and proceed anyway: instead try to split it into classes that look Gaussian.

The examples discussed above in general indicate that, in real world data collection, it is common to have many relevant variables (e.g. in market research surveys; typical surveys have ~200 variables). Typically researchers pore over many crosstabs, however, it can be difficult to make sense of these, and the crosstabs may be misleading. Multivariate analysis (MVA) can help summarize the data and also can reduce the chance of obtaining spurious results.

Multivariate Analysis Methods

There are two general types of Multivariate analysis as given below:

- Analysis of dependence: If the variables are dependent on others, they are called analysis of dependence. i.e., a category of multivariate statistical techniques; dependence methods explain or predict a dependent variable(s) on the basis of two or more independent variables E.g. Multiple and Partial Least Square(PLS) regression, Multiple Discriminant Analysis(MDA).

- Analysis of interdependence: If the variables are not dependent on others, they are called analysis of interdependence.ie, a category of multivariate statistical techniques; interdependence methods give meaning to a set of variables or seek to group things together E.g. Cluster analysis, factor analysis.

Data Normalization

When analyzing two or more attributes it is often necessary to normalize the values of the attributes, especially in those cases where the values are vastly different in scale.

Range Normalization

Let X be an attribute and let $x_1, x_2, ..., x_n$ be a random sample drawn from X. In range normalization each value is scaled by the sample range of X.

$$x_i' = \frac{x_i - min_i(x_i)}{\hat{r}} = \frac{x_i - min_i\{x_i\}}{max_i\{x_i\} - min_i\{x_i\}}$$

The mean vector is often referred to as the centroid and the variance-covariance matrix as the dispersion or dispersion matrix. Also, the terms variance-covariance matrix and covariance matrix are used interchangeably. After transformation the new attribute takes on values in the range [0,1].

Standard Score Normalization

There are various techniques available for transforming indicators in pure, dimensionless numbers, a process called normalization. Standardization or z-scores is the most commonly used method. It converts (using equation given below) all indicators to a common scale with an average of zero and standard deviation of one:

$$x_i' = \frac{x_i - \hat{\mu}}{\hat{\sigma}}$$

Where, μ is the sample mean and σ^2 is the sample variance of X. After transformation, the new attribute has mean $\mu' = 0$, and standard deviation $\sigma' = 1$.

A Z-Score is a statistical measurement of a score's relationship to the mean in a group of scores. A Z-score of 0 means the score is the same as the mean. A Z- score can also be positive or negative, indicating whether it is above or below the mean and by how many standard deviations.

Difference between Univariate, Bivariate and Multivariate Analysis

Three categories of data analysis include Univariate analysis, bivariate analysis, and multivariate analysis.

Univariate Analysis

Univariate analysis is the simplest form of data analysis where the data being analyzed contains only one variable. Since it's a single variable it doesn't deal with causes or relationships. The main purpose of Univariate analysis is to describe the data and find patterns that exist within it. You can think of the variable as a category that your data falls into. One example of a variable in Univariate analysis might be "age". Another might be "height". Univariate analysis would not look at these two variables at the same time, nor would it look at the relationship between them.

Some ways you can describe patterns found in Univariate data include looking at mean, mode, median, range, variance, maximum, minimum, quartiles, and standard deviation. Additionally, some ways you may display Univariate data include frequency distribution tables, bar charts, histograms, frequency polygons, and pie charts.

Bivariate Analysis

Bivariate analysis is used to find out if there is a relationship between two different variables. Something as simple as creating a scatterplot by plotting one variable against another on a Cartesian plane (think X and Y axis) can sometimes give you a picture of what the data is trying to tell you. If the data seems to fit a line or curve then there is a relationship or correlation between the two variables. For example, one might choose to plot caloric intake versus weight.

Multivariate Analysis

Multivariate analysis is the analysis of three or more variables. There are many ways to perform multivariate analysis depending on your goals. Some of these methods include:

- Additive Tree.

- Canonical Correlation Analysis.

- Cluster Analysis.

- Correspondence Analysis / Multiple Correspondence Analysis.

- Factor Analysis.

- Generalized Procrustean Analysis.

- MANOVA.

- Multidimensional Scaling.

- Multiple Regression Analysis.

- Partial Least Square Regression.

- Principal Component Analysis / Regression / PARAFAC.

- Redundancy Analysis.

Regression Analysis

In statistics, regression analysis includes many techniques for modeling and analyzing several variables, when the focus is on the relationship between a dependent variable and one or more independent variables. More specifically, regression analysis helps one understand how the typical value of the dependent variable changes when any one of the independent variables is varied, while the other independent variables are held fixed. Most commonly, regression analysis estimates the conditional expectation of the dependent variable given the independent variables — that is, the average value of the dependent variable when the independent variables are fixed. Less commonly, the focus is on a quartile, or other location parameter of the conditional distribution of the dependent variable given the independent variables. In all cases, the estimation target is a function of the independent variables called the regression function. In regression analysis, it is also of interest to characterize the variation of the dependent variable around the regression function, which can be described by a probability distribution.

Regression analysis is widely used for prediction and forecasting, where its use has substantial overlap with the field of machine learning. Regression analysis is also used to understand which among the independent variables are related to the dependent variable, and to explore the forms of these relationships. In restricted circumstances, regression analysis can be used to infer causal relationships between the independent and dependent variables. However this can lead to illusions or false relationships, so caution is advisable. See correlation does not imply causation.

A large body of techniques for carrying out regression analysis has been developed. Familiar methods such as linear regression and ordinary least squares regression are parametric, in that the regression function is defined in terms of a finite number of unknown parameters that are estimated from the data. Nonparametric regression refers to techniques that allow the regression function to lie in a specified set of functions, which may be infinite-dimensional. The performance of regression analysis methods in practice depends on the form of the data generating process, and how it relates to the regression approach being used. Since the true form of the data-generating process is generally not known, regression analysis often depends to some extent on making assumptions about this process. These assumptions are sometimes testable if a large amount of data is available. Regression models for prediction are often useful even when the assumptions are moderately violated, although they may not perform optimally. However, in many applications, especially with small effects or questions of causality based on observational data, regression methods give misleading results.

The earliest form of regression was the method of least squares, which was published by Legendre in 1805, and by Gauss in 1809. Legendre and Gauss both applied the method to the problem of determining, from astronomical observations, the orbits of bodies about the Sun. Gauss published a further development of the theory of least squares in 1821, including a version of the Gauss–Markov theorem.

The term "regression" was coined by Francis Galton in the nineteenth century to describe a biological phenomenon. The phenomenon was that the heights of descendants of tall ancestors tend to regress down towards a normal average (a phenomenon also known as regression toward the mean). For Galton, regression had only this biological meaning, but his work was later extended by Udny Yule and Karl Pearson to a more general statistical context. In the work of Yule and Pearson, the joint distribution of the response and explanatory variables is assumed to be Gaussian. This assumption was weakened by R.A. Fisher in his works of 1922 and 1925. Fisher assumed that the conditional distribution of the response variable is Gaussian, but the joint distribution need not be. In this respect, Fisher's assumption is closer to Gauss's formulation of 1821.

In the 1950s and 1960s, economists used electromechanical desk calculators to calculate regressions. Before 1970, it sometimes took up to 24 hours to receive the result from one regression. Regression methods continue to be an area of active research. In recent decades, new methods have been developed for robust regression, regression involving correlated responses such as time series and growth curves, regression in which the predictor or response variables are curves, images, graphs, or other complex data objects, regression methods accommodating various types of missing data, nonparametric regression, Bayesian methods for regression, regression in which the predictor variables are measured with error, regression with more predictor variables than observations, and causal inference with regression.

Underlying Assumption

Classical assumptions for regression analysis include:

- The sample is representative of the population for the inference prediction.

- The error is a random variable with a mean of zero conditional on the explanatory variables.

- The independent variables are measured with no error. (If this is not so, modeling may be done instead using errors-in-variables model techniques).

- The predictors are linearly independent, i.e. it is not possible to express any predictor as a linear combination of the others.

- The errors are uncorrelated, that is, the variance–covariance matrix of the errors is diagonal and each non-zero element is the variance of the error.

- The variance of the error is constant across observations (homoscedasticity). (If not, weighted least squares or other methods might instead be used).

These are sufficient conditions for the least-squares estimator to possess desirable properties, in particular, these assumptions imply that the parameter estimates will be unbiased, consistent, and efficient in the class of linear unbiased estimators. It is important to note that actual data rarely satisfies the assumptions. That is, the method is used even though the assumptions are not true. Variation from the assumptions can sometimes be used as a measure of how far the model is from being useful. Many of these assumptions may be relaxed in more advanced treatments. Reports of statistical analyses usually include analyses of tests on the sample data and methodology for the fit and usefulness of the model.

Assumptions include the geometrical support of the variables. Independent and dependent variables often refer to values measured at point locations. There may be spatial trends and spatial autocorrelation in the variables that violates statistical assumptions of regression. Geographic weighted regression is one technique to deal with such data. Also, variables may include values aggregated by areas. With aggregated data the Modifiable Areal Unit Problem can cause extreme variation in regression parameters. When analyzing data aggregated by political boundaries, postal codes or census areas results may be very different with a different choice of units.

Linear Regression Models

We consider the modeling between the dependent and one independent variable. When there is only one independent variable in the linear regression model, the model is generally termed as a simple linear regression model. When there are more than one independent variables in the model, then the linear model is termed as the multiple linear regression models.

The Linear Model

Consider a simple linear regression model:

$$y = \beta_0 + \beta_1 X + \varepsilon$$

Where y is termed as the dependent or study variable and X is termed as the independent or explanatory variable. The terms β_0 and β_1 are the parameters of the model. The parameter β_0 is termed as an intercept term, and the parameter β_1 is termed as the slope parameter. These parameters are usually called as regression coefficients. The unobservable error component ε accounts for the failure of data to lie on the straight line and represents the difference between the true and observed realization of y. There can be several reasons for such difference, e.g., the effect of all deleted variables in the model, variables may be qualitative, inherent randomness in the observations etc. We assume that ε is observed as independent and identically distributed random variable with mean zero and constant variance σ^2. Later, we will additionally assume that ε is normally distributed.

The independent variables are viewed as controlled by the experimenter, so it is considered as non-stochastic whereas y is viewed as a random variable with,

$$E(y) = \beta_0 + \beta_1 X$$

and

$$Var(y) = \sigma^2.$$

Sometimes X can also be a random variable. In such a case, instead of the sample mean and sample variance of y, we consider the conditional mean of y given X = x as:

$$E(y|x) = \beta_0 + \beta_1 X$$

and the conditional variance of y given X = x as:

$$Var(y|x) = \sigma^2.$$

When the values of β_0, β_1 and σ^2 are known, the model is completely described. The parameters, β_0, β_1 and σ^2, are generally unknown in practice and ε is unobserved. The determination of the statistical model $y = \beta_0 + \beta_1 X + \varepsilon$ depends on the determination (i.e., estimation) of β_0, β_1 and σ^2. In order to know the values of these parameters, n pairs of observations $(x, y)(i = 1, \ldots, n)$ on (X, y) are observed/collected and are used to determine these unknown parameters. Various methods of estimation can be used to determine the estimates of the parameters. Among them, the methods of least squares and maximum likelihood are the popular methods of estimation.

Least Squares Estimation

Suppose a sample of n sets of paired observations (x, y) $(i = 1, 2, \ldots, n)$ is available. These observations are assumed to satisfy the simple linear regression model, and so we can write,

$$y_i = \beta_0 + \beta_1 x_i + \varepsilon_i \, (i = 1, 2 \ldots n)$$

The principle of least squares estimates the parameters β_0 and β_1 by minimizing the sum of squares of the difference between the observations and the line in the scatter diagram. Such an idea is viewed from different perspectives. When the vertical difference between the observations and the line in the scatter diagram is considered, and its sum of squares is minimized to obtain the estimates of β_0 and β_1, the method is known as direct regression.

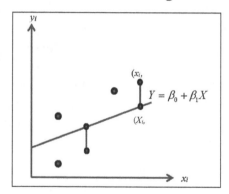

Alternatively, the sum of squares of the difference between the observations and the line in the horizontal direction in the scatter diagram can be minimized to obtain the estimates of β_0 and β_1. This is known as a reverse (or inverse) regression method.

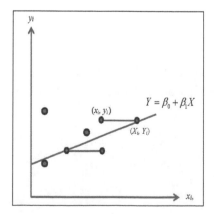

Instead of horizontal or vertical errors, if the sum of squares of perpendicular distances between the observations and the line in the scatter diagram is minimized to obtain the estimates of β_0 and β_1, the method is known as orthogonal regression or major axis regression method.

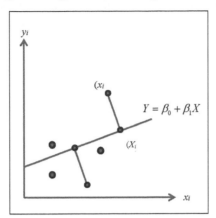

Instead of minimizing the distance, the area can also be minimized. The reduced major axis regression method minimizes the sum of the areas of rectangles defined between the observed data points and the nearest point on the line in the scatter diagram to obtain the estimates of regression coefficients. This is shown in the following figure:

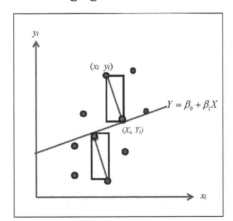

The method of least absolute deviation regression considers the sum of the absolute deviation of the observations from the line in the vertical direction in the scatter diagram as in the case of direct regression to obtain the estimates of β_0 and β_1.

No assumption is required about the form of the probability distribution of ε_i in deriving the least squares estimates. For the purpose of deriving the statistical inferences only, we assume that ε_i s is random variable with $E(\varepsilon_i)=0$, $Var(\varepsilon_i)=\sigma^2$ and $Cov(\varepsilon_i,\varepsilon_j)=0$ for all $i \neq j (i,j=1,2,...,n)$. This assumption is needed to find the mean, variance and other properties of the least-squares estimates. The assumption that ε_i s are normally distributed is utilized while constructing the tests of hypotheses and confidence intervals of the parameters.

Based on these approaches, different estimates of β_0 and β_1 are obtained which have different statistical properties. Among them, the direct regression approach is more popular. Generally, the direct regression estimates are referred to as the least-squares estimates or ordinary least squares estimates.

Direct Regression Method

This method is also known as the ordinary least squares estimation. Assuming that a set of n paired observations on $(x, y), i = 1, 2, \ldots, n$ are available which satisfy the linear regression model $y = \beta_0 + \beta_1 X + \varepsilon$. So we can write the model for each observation as $y_i = \beta_0 + \beta_1 x_i + \varepsilon_i, (i = 1, 2, \ldots, n)$.

The direct regression approach minimizes the sum of squares,

$$S(\beta_0, \beta_1) = \sum_{i=1}^{n} \varepsilon_i^2 = \sum_{i=1}^{n} (y_i - \beta_0 - \beta_1 x_i)^2$$

With respect to β_0 and β_1.

The partial derivatives of $S(\beta_0, \beta_1)$ with respect to β_0 is,

$$\frac{\partial S(\beta_0, \beta_1)}{\partial \beta_1} = -2 \sum_{i=1}^{n} (y_i - \beta_0 - \beta_1 x_i)$$

and the partial derivative of $S(\beta_0, \beta_1)$ with respect to β_1 is,

$$\frac{\partial S(\beta_0, \beta_1)}{\partial \beta_1} = -2 \sum_{i=1}^{n} (y_i - \beta_0 - \beta_1 x_i) x_i$$

The solutions of β_0 and β_1 are obtained by setting,

$$\frac{\partial S(\beta_0, \beta_1)}{\partial \beta_0} = 0$$

$$\frac{\partial S(\beta_0, \beta_1)}{\partial \beta_1} = 0$$

The solutions of these two equations are called the direct regression estimators, or usually called as the ordinary least squares (OLS) estimators of β_0 and β_1.

This gives the ordinary least squares estimates b_0 of β_0 and of b_1 of β_1 as,

$$b_0 = \bar{y} - b_1 \bar{x}$$

$$b_1 = \frac{S_{xy}}{S_{xx}}$$

where,

$$S_{xy} = \sum_{i=1}^{n} (x_i - \bar{x})(y_i - \bar{y}), S_{xx} = \sum_{i=1}^{n} (x_i - \bar{x})^2, \bar{x} = \frac{1}{n} \sum_{i=1}^{n} x_i, \bar{y} = \frac{1}{n} \sum_{i=1}^{n} y_i.$$

Further, we have:

$$\frac{\partial^2 S(\beta_0, \beta_1)}{\partial \beta_0^2} = 2 \sum_{i=1}^{n} (-1) = 2n,$$

$$\frac{\partial^2 S(\beta_0, \beta_1)}{\partial \beta_1^2} = 2 \sum_{i=1}^{n} x_i^2$$

$$\frac{\partial^2 S(\beta_0, \beta_1)}{\partial \beta_0 \partial \beta_1} = 2 \sum_{i=1}^{n} x_i = 2n\bar{x} .$$

The Hessian matrix which is the matrix of second-order partial derivatives, in this case, is given as:

$$H^* = \begin{pmatrix} \dfrac{\partial^2 S(\beta_0, \beta_1)}{\partial \beta_0^2} & \dfrac{\partial^2 S(\beta_0, \beta_1)}{\partial \beta_0 \partial \beta_1} \\ \dfrac{\partial^2 S(\beta_0, \beta_1)}{\partial \beta_0 \partial \beta_1} & \dfrac{\partial^2 S(\beta_0, \beta_1)}{\partial \beta_1^2} \end{pmatrix}$$

$$= 2 \begin{pmatrix} n & n\bar{x} \\ n\bar{x} & \sum_{i=1}^{n} x_i^2 \end{pmatrix}$$

$$= 2 \begin{pmatrix} 1' \\ x' \end{pmatrix} (1, x)$$

where, $l = (1, 1 \ldots 1)'$ is a n -vector of elements unity and $x = (x_1 \ldots x_n)'$ is a n -vector of observations on X.

The matrix H* is positive definite if its determinant and the element in the first row and column of H* are positive. The determinant of H* is given by:

$$|H^*| = \left(4n \sum_{i=1}^{n} x_i^2 - n^2 \bar{x}^2 \right)$$

$$= 4n \sum_{i=1}^{n} (x_i - \bar{x})^2$$

$$\geq 0 .$$

The case when $\sum_{i=1}^{n} (x_i - \bar{x})^2 = 0$ is not interesting because all the observations, in this case, are identical, i.e. $x_i = c$ (some constant). In such a case, there is no relationship between x and y in the context of regression analysis. $\sum_{i=1}^{n} (x_i - \bar{x})^2 > 0$, Therefore $|H| > 0$. So H is positive definite for any (β_0, β_1), therefore, o 1 S (β_0, β_1) has a global minimum at (b_0 b_1).

The fitted line or the fitted linear regression model is,

$$y = b_0 + b_1 x.$$

The predicted values are:

$$\hat{y}_i = b_0 + b_1 x_i \left(i = 1, 2, \ldots, n \right).$$

The difference between the observed value y_i and the fitted (or predicted) value $\hat{y}_i$ is called a residual. The ith residual is defined as:

$$e_i = y_i \sim \hat{y}_i \left(i = 1, 2, \ldots, n\right)$$
$$= y_i \sim \hat{y}_i$$
$$= y_i - \left(b_0 + b_1 x_i\right)$$

Properties of the Direct Regression Estimators

Unbiased Property

Note that $b_1 = \dfrac{S_{xy}}{S_{xx}}$ and $b_0 = \overline{y} - b_1 \overline{x}$ are the linear combinations of $y_i \left(i = 1, \ldots, n\right)$

Therefore,

$$b_1 = \sum_{i=1}^{n} k_i y_i$$

Where, $k_i = \left(x_i - \overline{x}\right) / S_{xx}$. Note that $\sum_{i=1}^{n} k_i = 0$ and $\sum_{i=1}^{n} k_i x_i = 1$ so,

$$E\left(b_1\right) = \sum_{i=1}^{n} k_i E\left(y_i\right)$$
$$= \sum_{i=1}^{n} k_i \left(\beta_0 + \beta_1 x_i\right)$$
$$= \beta_1$$

This b_1 is an unbiased estimator of β_1. Next,

$$E\left(b_0\right) = E\left[\overline{y} - b_1 \overline{x}\right]$$
$$= E\left[\beta_0 + \beta_1 \overline{x} + \overline{\varepsilon} - b_1 \overline{x}\right]$$
$$= \beta_0 + \beta_1 \overline{x} - \beta_1 \overline{x}$$
$$= \beta_0$$

Thus b_0 is an unbiased estimator of β_0.

Variances

Using the assumption that y_i' s are independently distributed, the variance of b_1 is,

$$= \sigma^2 \dfrac{\sum_i \left(x_i - \overline{x}^2\right)}{S_{xx}^2} \quad Cov\left(y_i, y_j\right) = 0 \text{ as } y_1, \ldots, y_n \text{ are independent}$$
$$= \dfrac{\sigma^2 S_{xx}}{S_{xx}^2}$$
$$= \dfrac{\sigma^2}{S_{xx}}$$

The variance of b_0 is,

$$\text{Var}(b_0) = \text{Var}(\bar{y}) + \bar{x}^2 \, \text{Var}(b_1) - 2\bar{x}\text{Cov}(\bar{y}, b_1).$$

First, we find that,

$$\text{Cov}(\bar{y}, b_1) = E\Big[\{\bar{y} - E(\bar{y})\}\{b_1 - E(b_1)\}\Big]$$

$$= E\Big[\bar{\varepsilon}\Big(\sum_i c_i y_i - \beta_i\Big)\Big]$$

$$= \frac{1}{n} = E\Big[\Big(\sum_i \varepsilon_i\Big)\Big(\beta_0 \sum_i c_i + \beta_1 \sum_i c_i x_i + \sum_i c_i \varepsilon_i - \beta_1 \sum_i \varepsilon_i\Big)\Big]$$

$$= \frac{1}{n}[0 + 0 + 0 + 0]$$

$$= 0$$

So,

$$\text{Var}(b_0) = \sigma^2\left(\frac{1}{n} + \frac{\bar{x}^2}{S_{xx}}\right).$$

Covariance

The covariance between b_0 and b_1 is

$$\text{Cov}(b_0, b_1) = \text{Cov}(\bar{y}, b_1) - \bar{x}\,\text{Var}(b_1)$$

$$= -\frac{x}{S_{xx}}\sigma^2$$

.

It can further be shown that the ordinary least squares estimators b_0 and b_1 possess the minimum variance in the class of linear and unbiased estimators. So they are termed as the Best Linear Unbiased Estimators (BLUE). Such a property is known as the Gauss-Markov theorem.

Residual Sum of Squares

The residual sum of squares is given as:

$$\text{SS}_{res} = \sum_{i=1}^{n} e_i^2 = \sum_{i=1}^{n}(y_i - \hat{y}_i)^2$$

$$= \sum_{i=1}^{n}(y_i - b_0 - b_1 x_i)^2$$

$$= \sum_{i=1}^{n}[y_i - \bar{y} + b_1\bar{x} - b_1 x_i]^2$$

$$= \sum_{i=1}^{n}\Big[(y_i - \bar{y}) - b_1(x_i - \bar{x})\Big]^2$$

$$= \sum_{i=1}^{n} \left[(y_i - \bar{y}) + b_1^2 \sum_{i=1}^{n} (x_i - \bar{x})^2 - 2b_1 \sum_{i=1}^{n} (x_i - \bar{x})(y_i - \bar{y}) \right]$$

$$= S_{yy} + b_1^2 S_{xx} - 2b_1^2 S_{xx}$$

$$= S_{yy} - b_1^2 S_{xx}$$

$$= S_{yy} - \left(\frac{S_{xy}}{S_{xx}} \right)^2 S_{xx}$$

$$= S_{yy} - \frac{S_{xy}^2}{S_{xx}}$$

$$= S_{yy} - b_1 S_{xy}$$

Where $S_{yy} = \sum_{i=1}^{n}(y_i - \bar{y})^2$, $\bar{y} = \frac{1}{n}\sum_{i=1}^{n} y_i$.

Estimation of σ^2

The estimator of σ^2 is obtained from the residual sum of squares as follows. Assuming that y_i is normally distributed, it follows that SS_{res} has a χ^2 distribution with $(n-2)$ degrees of freedom, so,

$$\frac{SS_{res}}{\sigma^2} \sim \chi^2(n-2).$$

Thus using the result about the expectation of a chi-square random variable, we have:

$$E(SS_{res}) = (n-2)\sigma^2.$$

Thus an unbiased estimator of σ^2 is,

$$s^2 = \frac{SS_{res}}{n-2}$$

Note that SS_{res} has only $(n-2)$ degrees of freedom. The two degrees of freedom are lost due to estimation of b_0 and b_1. Since S^2 depends on the estimates b_0 and b_1, so it is a model-dependent estimate of σ^2.

Estimate of Variances of b_0 and b_1

The estimators of variances of b_0 and b_1 are obtained by replacing σ^2 by its estimate $\hat{\sigma}^2 = s^2$ as follows:

$$\widehat{Var}(b_0) = s^2 \left(\frac{1}{n} + \frac{\bar{x}^2}{S_{xx}} \right)$$

and

$$\widehat{Var}(b_1) = \frac{s^2}{S_{xx}}$$

It is observed that since $\sum_{i=1}^{n}(y_i - \hat{y}_i) = 0$, so $\sum_{i=1}^{n} e_i = 0$. In the light of this property, e_i can be regarded as an estimate of unknown ε_i $(i = 1,...,n)$. This helps in verifying the different model assumptions on the basis of the given sample $(x_i, y_i), i = 1, 2,..., n$.

Further, note that:

- $\sum_{i=1}^{n} x_i e_i = 0$.

- $\sum_{i=1}^{n} \hat{y}_i e_i = 0$.

- $\sum_{i}^{n} y_i = \sum_{i=1}^{n} \hat{y}_i$.

- The fitted line always passes through $(\overline{x}, \overline{y})$.

Centered Model

Sometimes it is useful to measure the independent variable around its mean. In such a case, the model $y_i = \beta_0 + \beta_1 X_i + \varepsilon_i$ has a centered version as follows:

$$y_i = \beta_0 + \beta_1(x_i - \overline{x}) + \beta_1\overline{x} + \varepsilon \quad (i = 1, 2,..., n)$$
$$= \beta_0^* + \beta_1(x_i - \overline{x}) + \varepsilon_i$$

where, $\beta_0^* = \beta_0 + \beta_1\overline{x}$. The sum of squares due to error is given by:

$$S(\beta_0^*, \beta_1) = \sum_{i=1}^{n} \varepsilon_i^2 = \sum_{i=1}^{n}\left[y_i - \beta_0^* - \beta1(x_i - \overline{x})\right]^2 .$$

Now solving,

$$\frac{\partial S(\beta_0^*, \beta_1)}{\partial \beta_0^*} = 0$$

$$\frac{\partial S(\beta_0^*, \beta_1)}{\partial \beta_1^*} = 0$$

We get the direct regression least squares estimates of β_0^* and β_1 as,

$$b_0^* = \overline{y}$$

and

$$b_1 = \frac{S_{xy}}{S_{xx}},$$

respectively.

Thus the form of the estimate of slope parameter β_1 remains the same in the usual and centered model whereas the form of the estimate of intercept term changes in the usual and centered models.

Further, the Hessian matrix of the second order partial derivatives of $S(\beta_0^*, \beta_1)$ with respect to β_0^* and β_1 is positive definite at $\beta_0^* = \beta_0$ and $\beta_1 = b_1$ which ensures that $S(\beta_0^*, \beta_1)$ is minimized at $\beta_0^* = \beta_0$ and $\beta_1 = b_1$.

Under the assumption that $E = (\varepsilon_i) = 0, \mathrm{Var}(\varepsilon_i) = \sigma^2$ and $\mathrm{Cov}(\varepsilon_i \varepsilon_j)$ for all $i \neq j = 1, 2, \ldots, n$, it follows that:

$$E(b_0^*) = \beta_0^*, E(b_1) = \beta_1$$

$$\mathrm{Var}(b_0^*) = \frac{\sigma^2}{n}, \mathrm{Var}(b_1) = \frac{\sigma^2}{S_{xx}}.$$

In this case, the fitted model of $y_i = \beta_0^* + \beta_1(x_i - \bar{x}) + \varepsilon_i$ is,

$$y = \bar{y} + b_1(x - \bar{x}),$$

and the predicted values are,

$$\hat{y}_i = \bar{y} + b_1(x_i - \bar{x}), \quad (i=1,\ldots,n)$$

Note that in the centered model:

$$\mathrm{Cov}(b_0^*, b_1) = 0.$$

No Intercept Term Model

Sometimes in practice, a model without an intercept term is used in those situations when $x_i = 0 \Rightarrow y_i = 0$ for all $(i = 1, 2, \ldots, n)$. A no-intercept model is:

$$y_i = \beta_1 x_i + \varepsilon_i \quad (i = 1, 2, \ldots, n).$$

For example, in analyzing the relationship between the velocity (y) of a car and its acceleration (X), the velocity is zero when acceleration is zero.

Using the data (x_i, y_i), $i = 1, 2, \ldots, n$, the direct regression least-squares estimate of β_1 is obtained by

minimizing $S(\beta_1) = \sum_{i=1}^{n} \varepsilon_i^2 = \sum_{i=1}^{n} (y_i - \beta_1 x_i)^2$ and solving,

$$\frac{\partial S(\beta_1)}{\partial \beta_1} = 0$$

Gives the estimator of β_1 as:

$$b_1^* = \frac{\sum_{i=1}^{n} y_i x_i}{\sum_{i=1}^{n} x_i^2}.$$

The second-order partial derivative of $S(\beta_1)$ with respect to β_1 at $\beta_1 = b_1$ is positive which insures that b_1 minimizes $S(\beta_1)$.

Using the assumption that $E(\varepsilon_i) = 0, \operatorname{Var}(\varepsilon_i) = \sigma^2$ and $\operatorname{Cov}(\varepsilon_i \varepsilon_j) = 0$ for all $i \neq j = 1,2,\ldots,n$, the properties of b_1^* can be derived as follows:

$$E(b_1^*) = \frac{\sum\limits_{i=1}^{n} x_i E(y_i)}{\sum\limits_{i=1}^{n} x_i^2}$$

$$= \frac{\sum\limits_{i=1}^{n} x_i^2 \beta_1}{\sum\limits_{i=1}^{n} x_i^2}$$

$$= \beta_1$$

This b_1^* is an unbiased estimator of β_1. The variance of b_1^* is obtained as follows:

$$\operatorname{Var}(b_1^*) = \frac{\sum\limits_{i=1}^{n} x_i^2 \operatorname{Var}(y_i)}{\left(\sum\limits_{i=1}^{n} x_i^2\right)^2}$$

$$= \sigma^2 \frac{\sum\limits_{i=1}^{n} x_i^2}{\left(\sum\limits_{i=1}^{n} x_i^2\right)^2}$$

$$= \frac{\sigma^2}{\sum\limits_{i=1}^{n} x_i^2}$$

and an unbiased estimator of σ^2 is obtained as:

$$\frac{\sum\limits_{i=1}^{n} y_i^2 - b_1 \sum\limits_{i=1}^{n} y_i x_i}{n-1}.$$

Maximum Likelihood Estimation

We assume that $\varepsilon_i'(s)(i = 1,2,\ldots,n)$, are independent and identically distributed following a normal distribution $N(0,\sigma^2)$. Now we use the method of maximum likelihood to estimate the parameters of the linear regression model,

$$y_i = \beta_0 + \beta_1 x_i + \varepsilon_i \quad (i = 1,2,\ldots,n),$$

The observations $y_i(i = 1, 2, ..., n)$ are independently distributed with $N(\beta_0 + \beta_1 x_i, \sigma^2)$ for all $i = 1, 2, ..., n$.

The likelihood function of the given observations (x_i, y_i) and unknown parameters β_0, β_1 and σ^2 is,

$$L(x_i, y_i; \beta_0, \beta_1, \sigma^2) = \prod_{i=1}^{n} \left(\frac{1}{2\pi\sigma^2}\right)^{1/2} \exp\left[-\frac{1}{2\sigma^2}(y_i - \beta_0 - \beta_1 x_i)^2\right].$$

The maximum likelihood estimates of β_0, β_1 and σ^2 can be obtained by maximizing $L(x_i, y_i; \beta_0, \beta_1, \sigma^2)$ or equivalently in $\ln L(x_i, y_i; \beta_0, \beta_1, \sigma^2)$ where,

$$\ln L(x_i, y_i; \beta_0, \beta_1, \sigma^2) = -\left(\frac{n}{2}\right)\ln 2\pi - \left(\frac{n}{2}\right)\ln \sigma^2 - \left(\frac{1}{2\sigma^2}\right)\sum_{i=1}^{n}(y_i - \beta_0 - \beta_1 x_i)^2.$$

The normal equations are obtained by partial differentiation of log-likelihood with respect to β_0, β_1 σ^2 and equating them to zero as follows:

$$\frac{\partial \ln L(x_i, y_i; \beta_0, \beta 1, \sigma^2)}{\partial \beta_0} = -\frac{1}{\sigma^2}\sum_{i=1}^{n}(y_i - \beta_0 - \beta_1 x_i) = 0$$

$$\frac{\partial \ln L(x_i, y_i; \beta_0, \beta 1, \sigma^2)}{\partial \beta_1} = -\frac{1}{\sigma^2}\sum_{i=1}^{n}(y_i - \beta_0 - \beta_1 x_i)x_i = 0$$

and,

$$\frac{\partial \ln L(x_i, y_i; \beta_0, \beta_1, \sigma^2)}{\partial \sigma^2} = -\frac{n}{2\sigma^2} + \frac{1}{2\sigma^4}\sum_{i=1}^{n}(y_i - \beta_0 - \beta_1 x_i)^2 = 0$$

The solution of these normal equations gives the maximum likelihood estimates of β_0, β_1 and σ^2 as:

$$\tilde{b}_0 = \bar{y} - \tilde{b}_1 \bar{x}$$

$$\tilde{b}_1 = \frac{\sum_{i=1}^{n}(x_i - \bar{x})(y_i - \bar{y})}{\sum_{i=1}^{n}(x_i - \bar{x})^2} = \frac{S_{xy}}{S_{xx}}$$

and

$$\tilde{S}^2 = \frac{\sum_{i=1}^{n}(y_i - \tilde{b}_0 - \tilde{b}_1 x_i)^2}{n}$$

respectively.

It can be verified that the Hessian matrix of second-order partial derivation of $\ln L$ with respect to β_0, β_1, and σ^2 is negative definite at $\beta_0 = \tilde{b}_0, \beta_1 = \sigma^2 = \tilde{S}^2$ which ensures that the likelihood function is maximized at these values.

Note that the least-squares and maximum likelihood estimates of β_0 and β_1 are identical. The least-squares and maximum likelihood estimates of σ^2 are different. In fact, the least-squares estimate of σ^2 is:

$$S^2 = \frac{1}{n-2}\sum_{i=1}^{n}(y_i = y)^2$$

so that it is related to the maximum likelihood estimate as:

$$\tilde{S}^2 = \frac{n-2}{n}s^2$$

Thus $\tilde{b}_0$ and $\tilde{b}_1$ are unbiased estimators of β_0 and β_1 whereas 2 s% is a biased estimate of σ^2, but it is asymptotically unbiased. The variances of $\tilde{b}_0$ and $\tilde{b}_1$ are same as of b_0 and b_1 respectively but $\text{Var}\left(\tilde{S}^2\right) < \text{Var}\left(s^2\right)$.

Testing of Hypotheses and Confidence Interval Estimation for Slope Parameter

Now we consider the tests of hypothesis and confidence interval estimation for the slope parameter of the model under two cases, viz., when σ^2 is known and when σ^2 is unknown.

Case: When σ^2 is known

Consider the simple linear regression model $y_i = \beta_0 + \beta_1 x_i + \varepsilon_i$ $(i = 1, 2, \ldots, n)$. It is assumed that ε_i's are independent and identically distributed and follow $N(0, \sigma^2)$.

First, we develop a test for the null hypothesis related to the slope parameter,

$$H_0 : \beta_1 = \beta_{10}$$

Where β_{10} is some given constant.

Assuming σ^2 to be known, we know that $E(b_1) = \beta_1$, $\text{Var}(b_1) = \frac{\sigma^2}{s_{xx}}$ and b_1 is a linear combination of normally distributed y_i' s. So,

$$b_1 \sim N\left(\beta_1, \frac{\sigma^2}{s_{xx}}\right)$$

and so the following statistic can be constructed:

$$Z_1 = \frac{b_1 - \beta_{10}}{\sqrt{\dfrac{\sigma^2}{s_{xx}}}}$$

Which is distributed as N (0, 1) when H_0 is true.

A decision rule to test $H_1 : \beta_1 \neq \beta_{10}$ can be framed as follows:

Reject H_0 if $|Z_1| > Z_{\alpha/2}$

Where $Z_{\alpha/2}$ is the $\alpha/2$ percent points on the normal distribution.

Similarly, the decision rule for one-sided alternative hypothesis can also be framed.

The 100 $(1-\alpha)$% confidence interval for β_1 can be obtained using the Z_1 statistic as follows:

$$P\left[-Z_{\alpha/2} \leq z_1 \leq Z_{\alpha/2}\right] = 1-\alpha$$

$$P\left[-Z_{\alpha/2} \leq \frac{b_1 - \beta_1}{\sqrt{\dfrac{\sigma^2}{S_{xx}}}} \leq Z_{\alpha/2}\right] = 1-\alpha$$

$$P\left[b_1 - Z_{\alpha/2}\sqrt{\frac{\sigma^2}{S_{xx}}} \leq \beta_1 + Z_{\alpha/2}\sqrt{\frac{\sigma^2}{S_{xx}}}\right] = 1-\alpha$$

So 100 $(1-\alpha)$% confidence interval for β_1 is,

$$\left[b_1 - z_{\alpha/2}\sqrt{\frac{\sigma^2}{S_{xx}}}, b_1 + z_{\alpha/2}\sqrt{\frac{\sigma^2}{S_{xx}}}\right]$$

Where $z_{\alpha/2}$ is the $\alpha/2$ percentage point of the $N(0, 1)$ distribution.

Case: When σ^2 is unknown

When σ^2 are unknown then we proceed as follows. We know that,

$$\frac{SS_{res}}{\sigma^2} \sim \chi^2(n-2)$$

and

$$E\left(\frac{SS_{res}}{n-2}\right) = \sigma^2$$

Further, SS_{res}/σ^2 and b_1 are independently distributed. This result will be proved formally later in the next module on multiple linear regression. This result also follows from the result that under normal distribution, the maximum likelihood estimates, viz., the sample mean (estimator of population mean) and the sample variance (estimator of population variance) are independently distributed, so b_1 and s^2 are also independently distributed.

Thus the following statistic can be constructed:

$$t_0 = \frac{b_1 - \beta_1}{\sqrt{\dfrac{\hat{\sigma}^2}{S_{xx}}}}$$

$$= \frac{b_1 - \beta_1}{\sqrt{\dfrac{SS_{res}}{(n-2)SS_{xx}}}}$$

Which follows a t -distribution with (n-2) degrees of freedom, denoted as t_{n-2}, when H_0 is true.

A decision rule to test 1 1 10 H: $\beta \neq \beta$ is to reject H_0 if $|t_0| \, t_{n-2,\alpha/2}$,

Where $t_{n-2,\alpha/2}$ is the $\alpha/2$ percent point of the t -distribution with (n −2) degrees of freedom. Similarly, the decision rule for the one-sided alternative hypothesis can also be framed.

The 100 (1−α) % confidence interval of β_1 can be obtained using the 0t statistic as follows:

Consider,

$$P\left[-t_{\alpha/2} \leq t_{\alpha/2}\right] = 1 - \alpha$$

$$P\left[-t_{\alpha/2} \, \frac{b_1 - \beta_1}{\sqrt{\dfrac{\hat{\sigma}^2}{S_{xx}}}} \leq t_{\alpha/2}\right] = 1 - \alpha$$

$$P\left[b_1 - t_{\alpha/2}\sqrt{\dfrac{\hat{\sigma}^2}{S_{xx}}} \leq \beta_1 \leq b_1 + t\alpha/2\sqrt{\dfrac{\hat{\sigma}^2}{S_{xx}}}\right] = 1 - \alpha.$$

So the 100 (1 −α)% confidence interval $\beta 1$ is

$$\left[b_1 - t_{n-2,\alpha/2}\sqrt{\dfrac{SS_{res}}{(n-2)S_{xx}}} \, b_1 + t_{n-2,\alpha/2}\sqrt{\dfrac{SS_{res}}{(n-2)S_{xx}}}\right].$$

Testing of Hypotheses and Confidence Interval Estimation for Intercept Term

Now, we consider the tests of hypothesis and confidence interval estimation for intercept term under two cases, viz., when σ^2 is known and when σ^2 is unknown.

Case: When σ^2 is known

Suppose the null hypothesis under consideration is:

$$H_0 : \beta_0 = \beta_{00},$$

Where σ^2 is known, then using the result that $E(b_0) = \beta_0$, $Var(b_0) = \sigma^2\left(\dfrac{1}{n} + \dfrac{\bar{x}^2}{S_x}\right)$ and b_0 is a linear combination of normally distributed random variables, the following statistic,

$$Z_0 = \frac{b_0 - \beta_{00}}{\sqrt{\sigma^2 \dfrac{1}{n} + \dfrac{\bar{x}^2}{S_{xx}}}}$$

has a N(0,1) distribution when H_0 is true.

A decision rule to test $H_1 : \beta_0 \neq \beta_{00}$ can be framed as follows:

Reject H_0 if $|Z_0| > Z_{\alpha/2}$

where $Z_{\alpha/2}$ is the $\alpha/2$ percentage points on the normal distribution. Similarly, the decision rule for one sided alternative hypothesis can also be framed.

The 100 $(1-\alpha)$ % confidence intervals for β_0 when σ^2 are known can be derived using the Z_0 statistic as follows:

$$P\left[-z_{\alpha/2} \leq Z_0 \leq z_{\alpha/2}\right] = 1 - \alpha$$

$$P\left[-z_{\alpha/2} \leq \frac{b_0 - \beta_0}{\sqrt{\sigma^2 \frac{1}{n} + \frac{\overline{x}^2}{S_{xx}}}} \leq z_{\alpha/2}\right] = 1 - \alpha$$

$$P\left[b_0 - z_{\alpha/2}\sqrt{\sigma^2\left(\frac{1}{n} + \frac{\overline{x}^2}{S_{xx}}\right)} \leq \beta_0 \leq b_0 + z_{\alpha/2}\sqrt{\sigma^2\left(\frac{1}{n} + \frac{\overline{x}^2}{S_{xx}}\right)}\right] = 1 - \alpha$$

So the 100 $(1-\alpha)$ % of confidential interval of β_0 is:

$$\left[b_0 - z_{\alpha/2}\sqrt{\sigma^2\left(\frac{1}{n} + \frac{\overline{x}^2}{S_{xx}}\right)}, b_0 + z_{\alpha/2}\sqrt{\sigma^2\left(\frac{1}{n} + \frac{\overline{x}^2}{S_{xx}}\right)}\right]$$

Case: When σ^2 is unknown

When σ^2 is unknown, then the following statistic is constructed,

$$t_0 = \frac{b_0 - \beta_{00}}{\sqrt{\frac{SS_{res}}{n-2}\left(\frac{1}{n} + \frac{\overline{x}^2}{S_{xx}}\right)}}$$

Which follows a t-distribution with $(n-2)$ degrees of freedom, i.e., t_{n-2} when H_0 is true.

A decision rule to test $H_1 : \beta_0 \neq \beta_{00}$ is as follows:

Reject H_0 whenever $|t_0| > t_{-n2,\alpha/2}$

Where $t_{n-2,\alpha/2}$ is the $\alpha/2$ percentage point of the t-distribution with $(n-2)$ degrees of freedom. Similarly, the decision rule for one-sided alternative hypothesis can also be framed.

The 100 $(1-\alpha)$ % confidence interval of β_0 can be obtained as follows:

Consider:

$$P\left[t_{n-2,\alpha/2} \leq t_0 \leq t_{n-2,\alpha/2}\right] = 1 - \alpha$$

$$P\left[t_{n-2,\alpha/2} \leq \frac{b_o - \beta_o}{\sqrt{\frac{SS_{res}}{n-2}\left(\frac{1}{n} + \frac{\overline{x}^2}{S_{xx}}\right)}} \leq t_{n-2,\alpha/2}\right] = 1 - \alpha$$

$$P\left[b_o - t_{n-2,\alpha/2}\sqrt{\frac{SS_{res}}{n-2}\left(\frac{1}{n} + \frac{\overline{x}^2}{S_{xx}}\right)} \leq \beta_o \leq b_o + t_{n-2,\alpha/2}\sqrt{\frac{SS_{res}}{n-2}\left(\frac{1}{n} + \frac{\overline{x}^2}{S_{xx}}\right)}\right] = 1 - \alpha$$

So $100(1 - \alpha)\%$ confidence interval for β_o is

$$\left[b_o - t_{n-2,\alpha/2}\sqrt{\frac{SS_{res}}{n-2}\left(\frac{1}{n} + \frac{\overline{x}^2}{S_{xx}}\right)}, b_o + t_{n-2,\alpha/2}\sqrt{\frac{SS_{res}}{n-2}\left(\frac{1}{n} + \frac{\overline{x}^2}{S_{xx}}\right)}\right]$$

Test of Hypothesis for σ^2

We have considered two types of test statistics for testing the hypothesis about the intercept term and slope parameter- when σ^2 is known and when σ^2 is unknown. While dealing with the case of known σ^2, the value of σ^2 is known from some external sources like past experience, long association of the experimenter with the experiment, past studies etc. In such situations, the experimenter would like to test the hypothesis like $H_0 : \sigma^2 = \sigma_0^2$ against $H_0 : \sigma^2 \neq \sigma_0^2$ where σ_0^2 is specified. The test statistic is based on the result $\dfrac{SS_{res}}{\sigma^2} \sim \chi_{n-2}^2$. So the test statistic is,

$$C_o = \frac{SS_{res}}{\sigma^2} \sim \chi_{n-2}^2 \text{ Under } H_o.$$

The decision rule is to reject H_o if $C_o < \chi_{n-2,\alpha/2}^2$ or $C_o > \chi_{n-2,1-\alpha/2}^2$.

Confidence Interval for σ_2

A confidence interval for 2σ can also be derived as follows. Since $SS_{res}/\sigma^2 \sim \chi_{n-2}^2$ thus consider,

$$P\left[\chi_{n-2,\alpha/2}^2 \leq \frac{SS_{res}}{\sigma^2} \leq \chi_{n-2,1-\alpha/2}^2\right] = 1 - \alpha$$

$$P\left[\frac{SS_{res}}{\chi_{n-2,1-\alpha/2}^2} \leq \sigma^2 \leq \frac{SS_{res}}{\chi_{n-2,\alpha/2}^2}\right] = 1 - \alpha.$$

The corresponding $100(1)\% - \alpha$ confidence interval for 2σ is,

$$\left[\frac{SS_{res}}{\chi_{n-2,1-\alpha/2}^2}, \frac{SS_{res}}{\chi_{n-2,\alpha/2}^2}\right].$$

Joint Confidence Region for β_0 and β_1

A joint confidence region for β_0 and β_1 can also be found. Such a region will provide a $100(1-\alpha)$ % confidence that both the estimates of β_0 and β_1 are correct. Consider the centered version of the linear regression model,

$$y_i = \beta_0^* + \beta_1(x_i - \overline{x}) + \varepsilon_i$$

Where, $\beta_0^* = \beta_0 + \beta_1 x_i$. The least squares estimators of β_0^* and β_1 is:

$$b_0^* = \overline{y} \text{ and } b_1 = \frac{S_{xy}}{S_{xx}},$$

respectively.

Using the results that,

$$E(b_0^*) = \beta_0^*,$$

$$E(b_1) = \beta_1,$$

$$Var(b_0^*) = \frac{\sigma^2}{n},$$

$$Var(b_1) = \frac{\sigma^2}{S_{xx}},$$

When σ^2 are known, then the statistic,

$$\frac{b_0^* - \beta_0^*}{\sqrt{\frac{\sigma^2}{n}}} \sim N(0,1) \text{ and } \frac{b_1 - \beta_1}{\sqrt{\frac{\sigma^2}{n}}} \sim N(0,1).$$

Moreover, both statistics are independently distributed. Thus,

$$\left(\frac{b_0^* - \beta_0^*}{\sqrt{\frac{\sigma^2}{n}}}\right)^2 \sim \chi_1^2 \text{ and } \left(\frac{b_1 - \beta_1}{\sqrt{\frac{\sigma^2}{n}}}\right)^2 \sim \chi_1^2.$$

are also independently distributed because b_0^* and b_1 are independently distributed. Consequently, the sum of these two:

$$\frac{n(b_0^* - \beta_0^*)^2}{\sigma^2} + \frac{S_{xx}(b_1 - \beta_1)^2}{\sigma^2} \sim \chi_2^2$$

Since $\dfrac{SS_{res}}{\sigma^2} \sim \chi_{n-2}^2$

And SS_{res} is independently distributed of b_0^* and b_1, so the ratio,

$$\frac{\left(\dfrac{n\left(b_0^*-\beta_0^*\right)^2}{\sigma^2}+\dfrac{S_{xx}\left(b_1-\beta_1\right)^2}{\sigma^2}\right)/2}{\dfrac{SS_{res}}{\sigma^2}/\left(n-2\right)} \sim F_{2,n-2}.$$

Substituting $b_0^* = b_0 + b_1\bar{x}$ and $\beta_0^* = \beta_0 + \beta_1\bar{x}$, we get:

$$\frac{\left(n-2\right)}{2}\left[\frac{Q_f}{SS_{res}}\right]$$

Where,

$$Q_f = n\left(b_0-\beta_0\right)^2 + 2\sum_{i=1}^{n}x_i\left(b_0-\beta_1\right)\left(b_1-\beta_1\right) + \sum_{i=1}^{n}x_i^2\left(b_1-\beta_1\right)^2.$$

Since,

$$P\left[\left(\frac{n-2}{2}\right)\frac{Q_f}{SS_{res}} \le F_{2,n-2}\right] = 1-\alpha$$

Holds true for all values of β_0 and β_1, so the 100 $(1-\alpha)$ % confidence regions for β_0 and β_1 is,

$$\left(\frac{n-2}{2}\right).\frac{Q_f}{SS_{res}} \le F_{2,n-2;1-\alpha}$$

This confidence region is an ellipse which gives the 100 $(1-\alpha)$ % probabilities that β_0 and β_1 are contained simultaneously in this ellipse.

Analysis of Variance

The technique of analysis of variance is usually used for testing the hypothesis related to equality of more than one parameters, like population means or slope parameters. It is more meaningful in case of multiple regression model when there are more than one slope parameters. This technique is discussed and illustrated here to understand the related basic concepts and fundamentals which will be used in developing the analysis of variance in the next module in multiple linear regression model where the explanatory variables are more than two.

A test statistic for testing $H_0 : \beta_1 = 0$ can also be formulated using the analysis of variance technique as follows:

On the basis of the identity,

$$y_i - \hat{y}_i = \left(y_i - y\right) - \left(\hat{y}_i - y\right),$$

The sum of squared residuals is,

$$S(b) = \sum_{i=1}^{n}(y_i - \hat{y}_i)^2$$

$$= \sum_{i=1}^{n}(y_i - \bar{y})^2 + \sum_{i=1}^{n}(\hat{y}_i - \bar{y}_i)^2 - 2\sum_{i=1}^{n}(y_i - \bar{y})(\hat{y}_i - \bar{y})$$

Further, consider

$$\sum_{i=1}^{n}(y_i - \bar{y})(y_i - \bar{y}) = \sum_{i=1}^{n}(y_i - \bar{y})b_1(x_i - \bar{x})$$

$$= b_1^2 \sum_{i=1}^{n}(x_i - \bar{x})^2$$

$$= \sum_{i=1}^{n}(\hat{y}_i - y)^2$$

Thus we have,

$$\sum_{i=1}^{n}(y_i - \bar{y})^2 = \sum_{i=1}^{n}(y_i - \hat{y}_i)^2 + \sum_{i=1}^{n}(\hat{y}_i - \bar{y})^2.$$

The term $\sum_{i=1}^{n}(\hat{y}_i - y)^2$ is called the sum of squares about the mean, corrected sum of squares of y (i.e., $SS_{corrected}$), total sum of squares, or S_{yy}.

The term $\sum_{i=1}^{n}(\hat{y}_i - y_i)^2$ describes the deviation: observation minus predicted value, viz., the residual sum of squares, i.e., $SS_{res} = \sum_{i=1}^{n}(y_i - \hat{y}i)^2$ whereas the term $\sum_{i=1}^{n}(\hat{y}_i - y)^2$ describes the proportion of variability explained by the regression, $SS_{reg} = \sum_{i=1}^{n}(\hat{y}_i - y)^2$.

If all observations y_i are located on a straight line, then in this case $\sum_{i=1}^{n}(y_i - \hat{y}_i)^2 = 0$ and thus $SS_{corrected} = SS_{reg}$.

Note that SS_{reg} is completely determined by b_1 and so has only one degree of freedom. The total sum of squares $S_{yy} = \sum_{i=1}^{n}(y_i - \bar{y})^2$ degrees of freedom due to constraint $\sum_{i=1}^{n}(y_i - \bar{y}) = 0$ and SS_{res} has (n-2) degrees of freedom as it depends on the determination of b_0 and b_1.

All sums of squares are mutually independent and distributed as χ^2_{df} with df degrees of freedom if the errors are normally distributed.

The mean square due to regression is,

$$MS_{reg} = \frac{SS_{reg}}{1}$$

and mean square due to residuals is,

$$MSE = \frac{SS_{reS}}{n-2}.$$

The test statistic for testing $H_0 : \beta_1 = 0$

$$F_0 = \frac{M_{Sreg}}{MSE}.$$

If $H_0 : \beta_1 = 0$ is true, then MS_{reg} and MSE are independently distributed and thus,

$$F_0 \sim F_{1,n-2}.$$

The decision rule for $H_1 : \beta_1 \neq 0$ is to reject H_0 if:

$$F_0 = F_{1,n-1,1-\alpha}$$

at α level of significance. The test procedure can be described in an Analysis of variance table.

Table: Analysis of variance for testing $H_0 : \beta_1 = 0$

Source of variation	Sum of squares	Degrees of freedom	Mean square	F
Regression	SS_{reg}	1	MS_{reg}	MS_{reg}/MSE
Residual	SS_{res}	n-2	MSE	
Total	S_{yy}	n-2		

Some other forms of SS_{reg}, SS_{res}, and S_{yy} can be derived as follows:

The sample correlation coefficient then may be written as:

$$r_{xy} = \frac{S_{xy}}{\sqrt{S_{xx}}\sqrt{S_{yy}}}.$$

Moreover, we have,

$$b_1 = \frac{S_{xy}}{S_{xx}} = r_{xy}\sqrt{\frac{S_{yy}}{S_{xx}}}.$$

The estimator of σ^2 in this case may be expressed as:

$$S^2 = \frac{1}{n-2}\sum_{i=1}^{n} e_i^2$$

$$= \frac{1}{n-2} SS_{res}.$$

Various alternative formulations for SS_{res} are in use as well:

$$SS_{res} = \sum_{i=1}^{n} \left[y_i - \left(b_o + b_1 x_i \right) \right]^2$$

$$= \sum_{i=1}^{n} \left[\left(y_i - \bar{y} \right) - b_1 \left(x_i - \bar{x} \right) \right]^2$$

$$= S_{yy} + b_1^2 S_{xx} - 2b_1 S_{xy}$$

$$= S_{yy} - b_1^2 S_{xx}$$

$$= S_{yy} - \frac{\left(S_{xy} \right)^2}{S_{xx}}.$$

Using this result, we find that:

$$SS_{corrected} = S_{yy}$$

and

$$SS_{reg} = S_{yy} - SS_{res}$$

$$= \frac{\left(S_{xy} \right)2}{S_{xx}}$$

$$= b_1^2 S_{xx}$$

$$= b_1 S_{xy}.$$

Goodness of Fit of Regression

It can be noted that a fitted model can be said to be good when residuals are small. Since SS_{res} is based on residuals, so a measure of the quality of a fitted model can be based on res SS. When the intercept term is present in the model, a measure of goodness of fit of the model is given by:

$$R^2 = 1 - \frac{SS_{res}}{S_{yy}} = \frac{SS_{reg}}{S_{yy}}.$$

This is known as the coefficient of determination. This measure is based on the concept that how much variation in y 's stated by S_{yy} is explainable by SS_{reg} and how much unexplainable part is contained in SS_{res}. The ratio SS_{reg}/S_{yy} describes the proportion of variability that is explained by regression in relation to the total variability of y. The ratio SS_{reg}/S_{yy} describes the proportion of variability that is not covered by the regression.

It can be seen that:

$$R^2 = r_{xy}^2$$

where r_{xy} is the simple correlation coefficient between x and y. Clearly $0 \leq R^2 \leq 1$, so a value of 2 R closer to one indicates the better fit and value of R^2 closer to zero indicates the poor fit.

Prediction of Values of Study Variable

An important use of linear regression modeling is to predict the average and actual values of the study variable. The term prediction of the value of study variable corresponds to knowing the value of (E_y) (in case of average value) and value of y (in case of actual value) for a given value of the explanatory variable. We consider both cases.

Case: Prediction of Average Value

Under the linear regression model, $y = \beta_0 + \beta_1 x + \varepsilon$ the fitted model is $y = b_0 + b_1 x$ where b_0 and b_1 are the OLS estimators of β_0 and β_1 respectively.

Suppose we want to predict the value of E(y) for a given value of x= x_0. Then the predictor is given by:

$$\widehat{E(y|x_0)} = \hat{\mu}_{y|x_0} = b_0 + b_1 x_0$$

Predictive Bias

Then the prediction error is given as:

$$\hat{\mu}_{y|x_0} - E(y) = b_0 + b_1 x_0 - E(\beta_0 + \beta_1 x_0 + \varepsilon)$$
$$= b_0 + b_1 x_0 - (\beta_0 + \beta_1 x_0)$$
$$= (b_0 - \beta_0) + (b_1 - \beta_1) x_0$$

Then,

$$E\left[\hat{\mu}_{y|x_0} - E(y)\right] = E(b_0 - \beta_0) + E(b_1 - \beta_1) x_0$$
$$= 0 + 0 = 0$$

Thus the predictor $\mu_{y|x_0}$ is an unbiased predictor of E(y).

Predictive Variance

The predictive variance of $\hat{\mu}_{y|x_0}$ is

$$PV(\mu_{y/x_0}) = Var(b_0 + b_1 x_0)$$
$$= Var\left[y + b_1(x_0 - x)\right]$$
$$= Var(y) + (x_0 - x)^2 Var(b_1) + 2(x_0 - \bar{x}) Cov(\bar{y}, b_1)$$

$$= \frac{\sigma^2}{n} + \frac{\sigma^2(x_0 - x)^2}{S_{xx}} + 0$$

$$= \sigma^2\left[\frac{1}{n} + \frac{(x_0 - x)^2}{S_{xx}}\right]$$

Estimate of Predictive Variance

The predictive variance can be estimated by substituting σ^2 by $\hat{\sigma}^2 = MSE$ as

$$\widehat{PV}\left(\hat{\mu}_{y|x_0}\right) = \hat{\sigma}^2\left[\frac{1}{n} + \frac{(x_0 - \bar{x})^2}{S_{xx}}\right]$$

$$= MSE\left[\frac{1}{n} + \frac{(x_0 - \bar{x})^2}{S_{xx}}\right].$$

Prediction Interval Estimation

The $100(1 - \alpha)$ % prediction interval for $E(y/x_0)$ is obtained as follows:

The predictor $\hat{\mu}_{y|x_0}$ is a linear combination of normally distributed random variables, so it is also normally distributed as:

$$\hat{\mu}_{y|x_0} \sim N\left(\beta_0 + \beta_1 x_0, PV\left(\hat{\mu}_{y|x_0}\right)\right).$$

So if σ^2 is known, then the distribution of,

$$\frac{\hat{\mu}_{y|x_0} - E\left(y|x_0\right)}{\sqrt{PV\left(\hat{\mu}_{y|x_0}\right)}}$$

is $N(0,1)$. So the $100(1-\alpha)$% prediction interval is obtained as:

$$P\left[-z_{\alpha/2} \le \frac{\hat{\mu}_{y|x_0} - E\left(y|x_0\right)}{\sqrt{PV\left(\mu_{y|x_0}\right)}} \le z_{\alpha/2}\right] = 1 - \alpha$$

which gives the prediction interval for $E(y/x_0)$ as:

$$\left[\hat{\mu}_{y|x_0} - z_{\alpha/2}\sqrt{\sigma^2\left[\frac{1}{n} + \frac{(x_0 - \bar{x})^2}{S_{xx}}\right]}, \hat{\mu}_{y|x_0} + z_{\alpha/2}\sqrt{\sigma^2\left[\frac{1}{n} + \frac{(x_0 - \bar{x})^2}{S_{xx}}\right]}\right].$$

When σ^2 is unknown, it is replaced by $\hat{\sigma}^2 = MSE$ and in this case the sampling distribution of,

$$\frac{\hat{\mu}_{y|x_0} - E\left(y|x_0\right)}{\sqrt{MSE\left[\frac{1}{n} + \frac{(x_0 - \bar{x})^2}{S_{xx}}\right]}}$$

is t -distribution with $(n-2)$ degrees of freedom, i.e., t_{n-2}.

The $100(1-\alpha)\%$ prediction interval in this case is,

$$P\left[-t_{\alpha/2,n-2} \leq \frac{\hat{\mu}_{y|xo} - E\left(y|x_0\right)}{\sqrt{MSE\left[\frac{1}{n} + \frac{\left(x_0 - \bar{x}\right)^2}{S_{xx}}\right]}} \leq t_{\frac{\alpha}{2},n-2}\right] = 1-\alpha$$

which gives the prediction interval as:

$$\left[\hat{\mu}_{y|x_0} - t_{\alpha/2,n-2}\sqrt{MSE\left(\frac{1}{n} + \frac{\left(x_0 - \bar{x}\right)^2}{S_{xx}}\right)}, \hat{\mu}_{y|x_0} + t_{\alpha/2,n-2}\sqrt{MSE\left(\frac{1}{n} + \frac{\left(x_0 - \bar{x}\right)^2}{S_{xx}}\right)}\right].$$

Note that the width of the prediction interval $E(y|x_0)$ x is a function of x_0. The interval width is minimum for $x_0 = \bar{x}$ and widens as $|x_0 - \bar{x}|$ increases. This is also expected as the best estimates of y to be made at x -values lie near the center of the data and the precision of estimation to deteriorate as we move to the boundary of the x-space.

Case: Prediction of Actual Value

If x_0 is the value of the explanatory variable, then the actual value predictor for y is

$$\hat{y}_0 = b_0 + b_1 x_0.$$

The true value of y in the prediction period is given by $y_0 = \beta_0 + \beta_1 x_0 + \varepsilon_0$ where ε_0 indicates the value that would be drawn from the distribution of random error in the prediction period. Note that the form of predictor is the same as of average value predictor, but its predictive error and other properties are different. This is the dual nature of predictor.

Predictive Bias

The predictive error of $\hat{y}_0$ is given by:

$$\hat{y}_0 - y_0 = b_0 + b_1 x_0 - \left(\beta_0 + \beta_1 x_0 + \varepsilon_0\right)$$
$$= \left(b_0 - \beta_0\right) + \left(b_1 - \beta_1\right)x_0 - \varepsilon$$

Thus, we find that

$$E\left(\hat{y}_0 - y_0\right) = E\left(b_0 - \beta_0\right) + E\left(b_1 - \beta_1\right)x_0 - E\left(\varepsilon_0\right)$$
$$= 0 + 0 + 0 = 0$$

Which implies that $\hat{y}_0$ is an unbiased predictor of y_0.

Predictive Variance

Because the future observation y_0 is independent of $\hat{y}_0$ the predictive variance of $\hat{y}_0$ is,

$$PV(\hat{y}_0) = E(\hat{y}_0 - y_0)^2$$

$$= E\left[(b_0 - \beta_0) + (x_0 - \bar{x})(b_1 - \beta_1) + (b_1 - \beta_1)\bar{x} - \varepsilon_0\right]^2$$

$$= \operatorname{Var}(b_0) + (x_0 - \bar{x})^2 \operatorname{Var}(b_1) + \bar{x}^2 \operatorname{Var}(b_1) + \operatorname{Var}(\varepsilon_0) + 2(x_0 - \bar{x})\operatorname{Cov}(b_0, b_1)$$

$$+ 2\bar{x}\operatorname{Cov}(b_0, b_1) + 2(x_0 - \bar{x})\operatorname{Var}(b_1)$$

[Rest of the terms are 0 resuming the independence of ε_0 with $\varepsilon_1, \varepsilon_2, \ldots, \varepsilon_n$]

$$= \operatorname{Var}(b_0) + \left[(x_0 - \bar{x})^2 + \bar{x}^2 + 2(x_0 - \bar{x})\right]\operatorname{Var}(b_1) + \operatorname{Var}(\varepsilon) + 2\left[(x_0 - \bar{x}) + 2\bar{x}\right]\operatorname{Cov}(b_0, b_1)$$

$$= \operatorname{Var}(b_0) + x_0^2 \operatorname{Var}(b_1) + \operatorname{Var}(\varepsilon_0) + 2x_0 \operatorname{Cov}(b_0, b_1)$$

$$= \sigma^2\left[\frac{1}{n} + \frac{\bar{x}^2}{S_{xx}}\right] + x_0^2 \frac{\sigma^2}{S_{xx}} + \sigma^2 - 2x_0 \frac{\bar{x}\sigma^2}{S_{xx}}$$

$$= \sigma^2\left[1 + \frac{1}{n} + \frac{(x_0 - \bar{x})^2}{S_{xx}}\right].$$

Estimate of Predictive Variance

The estimate of predictive variance can be obtained by replacing σ^2 by its estimate $\hat{\sigma}^2 = MSE$ as:

$$\widehat{PV(\hat{y}_0)} = \hat{\sigma}^2\left[1 + \frac{1}{n} + \frac{(x_0 - \bar{x})^2}{S_{xx}}\right]$$

$$= MSE\left[1 + \frac{1}{n} + \frac{(x_0 - \bar{x})^2}{S_{xx}}\right].$$

Prediction Interval

If σ^2 is known, then the distribution of,

$$\frac{\hat{y}_0 - y_0}{\sqrt{PV(\hat{y}_0)}}$$

is $N(0,1)$. So the $100(1-\alpha)\%$ prediction interval is obtained as,

$$P\left[-z_{\alpha/2} \leq \frac{\hat{y}_0 - y_0}{\sqrt{PV(\hat{y}_0)}} \leq z_{\alpha/2}\right] = 1 - \alpha$$

which gives the prediction interval for y_0 as:

$$\left[\hat{y}_0 - z_{\alpha/2}\sqrt{\sigma^2\left(1 + \frac{1}{n} + \frac{(x_0 - \bar{x})^2}{S_{xx}}\right)}, \hat{y}_0 + z_{\alpha/2}\sqrt{\sigma^2\left(1 + \frac{1}{n} + \frac{(x_0 - \bar{x})^2}{S_{xx}}\right)}\right].$$

When σ^2 is unknown, then,

$$\frac{\hat{y}_0 - y_0}{\sqrt{\widehat{PV}(\hat{y}_0)}}$$

Follows a t -distribution with (n −2) degrees of freedom. The 100(1 - α) % prediction interval for $\hat{y}_0$ in this case is obtained as:

$$P\left[-t_{\alpha/2,n-2} \le \frac{\hat{y}_0 - y_0}{\sqrt{\widehat{PV}(\hat{y}_0)}} \le t_{\alpha/2,n-2}\right] = 1-\alpha$$

Which gives the prediction interval.

$$\left[\hat{y}_0 - t_{\alpha/2,n-2}\sqrt{MSE\left(1+\frac{1}{n}+\frac{(x_0-\overline{x})^2}{S_{xx}}\right)}, \hat{y}_0 + t_{\alpha/2,n-2}\sqrt{MSE\left(1+\frac{1}{n}+\frac{(x_0-\overline{x})^2}{S_{xx}}\right)}\right].$$

The prediction interval is of minimum width at $x_0 = \overline{x}$ and widens as $|x_0 = \overline{x}|$ increases. The prediction interval for $\hat{y}_0$ is wider than the prediction interval for $\hat{\mu}_{y/xo}$ because the prediction interval for depends on $\hat{y}_0$ both the error from the fitted model as well as the error associated with the future observations.

Reverse Regression Method

The reverse (or inverse) regression approach minimizes the sum of squares of horizontal distances between the observed data points and the line in the following scatter diagram to obtain the estimates of regression parameters.

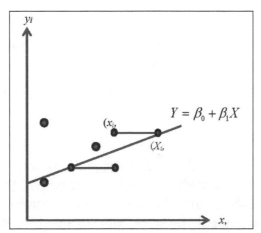

The reverse regression has been advocated in the analysis of gender (or race) discrimination in salaries. For example, if y denotes salary and x denotes qualifications, and we are interested in determining if there is gender discrimination in salaries, we can ask:

"Whether men and women with the same qualifications (value of x) are getting the same salaries (value of y). This question is answered by the direct regression."

Alternatively, we can ask:

> "Whether men and women with the same salaries (value of y) have the same qualifications (value of x). This question is answered by the reverse regression, i.e., regression of x on y."

The regression equation in case of reverse regression can be written as:

$$x_1 = \beta_o^* + \beta_1^* y_i + \delta_i \quad (i = 1, 2, \dots, n)$$

where, δ_i's are the associated random error components and satisfy the assumptions as in the case of the usual simple linear regression model. The reverse regression estimates $\hat{\beta}_{OR}$ of β_o^* and $\hat{\beta}_{IR}$ of β_1^* for the model are obtained by interchanging the x and y in the direct regression estimators of β_0 and β_1. The estimates are obtained as:

$$\hat{\beta}_{OR} = \bar{x} - \hat{\beta}_{IR} \bar{y}$$

and,

$$\hat{\beta}_{IR} = \frac{S_{yy}}{S_{xy}}$$

for β_0 and β_1 respectively. The residual sum of squares in this case is,

$$SS_{res}^* = S_{xx} - \frac{S_{xy}^2}{S_{yy}}.$$

Note that,

$$\hat{\beta}_{IR} b_1 = \frac{S_{xy}^2}{S_{xx} S_{xy}} = r_{xy}^2$$

where b_1 is the direct regression estimator of the slope parameter and r_{xy} is the correlation coefficient between x and y. Hence if r_{xy}^2 is close to 1, the two regression lines will be close to each other.

An important application of the reverse regression method is in solving the calibration problem.

Orthogonal Regression Method

The direct and reverse regression methods of estimation assume that the errors in the observations are either in x -direction or y -direction. In other words, the errors can be either in the dependent variable or independent variable. There can be situations when uncertainties are involved in dependent and independent variables both. In such situations, the orthogonal regression is more appropriate. In order to take care of errors in both the directions, the least-squares principle in orthogonal regression minimizes the squared perpendicular distance between the observed data points and the line in the following scatter diagram to obtain the estimates of regression coefficients. This is also known as the major axis regression method. The estimates obtained are called orthogonal regression estimates or major axis regression estimates of regression coefficients.

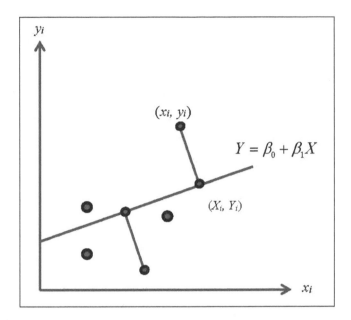

If we assume that the regression line to be fitted is $Y_i = \beta_0 + \beta_1 X_i$, then it is expected that all the observations $(x_i, y_i), (i = 1, 2, \ldots, n)$ lie on this line. But these points deviate from the line, and in such a case, the squared perpendicular distance of observed data $(x_i, y_i)(i = 1, 2, \ldots, n)$ from the line is given by:

$$d_i^2 = (X_i - x_i)^2 + (Y_i - y_i)^2$$

Where (X_i, Y_i) denotes the ith pair of observation without any error which lies on the line.

The objective is to minimize the sum of squared perpendicular distances given by $\sum_{i=1}^{n} d_i^2$ to obtain the estimates of β_0 and β_1. The observations $(x_i, y_i)(i = 1, 2, \ldots, n)$ are expected to lie on the line,

$$Y_i = \beta_0 + \beta_1 X_1$$

So let,

$$E_i = Y_i - \beta_0 - \beta_1 X_i = 0$$.

The regression coefficients are obtained by minimizing $\sum_{i=1}^{n} d_i^2$ under the constraints E_i's using the Lagrangian's multiplier method. The Lagrangian function is,

$$L_0 = \sum_{i=1}^{n} d_i^2 - 2 \sum_{i=1}^{n} \lambda_i E_i$$

Where $\lambda_1, \ldots \lambda_n$ are the Lagrangian multipliers. The set of equations are obtained by setting,

$$\frac{\partial L_0}{\partial X_i} = 0, \frac{\partial L_0}{\partial Y_i} = 0, \frac{\partial L_0}{\partial \beta_0} = 0 \text{ and } \frac{\partial L_0}{\partial \beta_1} = 0 \ (i = 1, 2, \ldots, n).$$

Thus we find:

$$\frac{\partial L_0}{\partial X_i} = (X_i - x_i) + \lambda_i \beta_1 = 0$$

$$\frac{\partial L_0}{\partial Y_i} = (Y_i - Y_i) - \lambda_i = 0$$

$$\frac{\partial L_0}{\partial \beta_0} = \sum_{i=1}^{n} \lambda_i = 0$$

$$\frac{\partial L_0}{\partial \beta_1} = \sum_{i=1}^{n} \lambda_i X_i = 0.$$

Since

$$X_i = x_i - \lambda_i \beta_1$$
$$Y_i = y_i + \lambda_i$$

so substituting these values is ε_i, we obtain:

$$\varepsilon_i = (y_i + \lambda_i) - \beta_0 - \beta_1 (x_i - \lambda_i \beta_i) = 0$$

$$\Rightarrow \lambda_i = \frac{\beta_0 + \beta_i x_i - y_i}{1 + \beta_1^2}.$$

Also using this λ_i in the equation $\sum_{i=1}^{n} \lambda_i X_i$, we get,

$$\frac{\sum_{i=1}^{n} \lambda_i (\beta_0 + \beta_1 x_i - y_i)}{1 + \beta_1^2} = 0$$

and using $(X_i - x_i) + \lambda_i \beta_1 = 0$ and $\sum_{i=1}^{n} \lambda_i X_i = 0$, we get,

$$\sum_{i=1}^{n} \lambda_i (x_i - \lambda_i \beta_1) = 0$$

Substituting λ_i in this equation, we get,

$$\frac{\sum_{i=1}^{n} (\beta_0 x_i + \beta_1 x_i^2 - y_i x_i)}{(1 + \beta_i^2)} - \frac{\beta_1 (\beta_0 + \beta_i x_i - y_i)^2}{(1 + \beta_1^2)^2} = 0.$$

Using λ_i in the equation and using the equation $\sum_{i=1}^{n} \lambda_i = 0$, we solve'

$$\frac{\sum_{i=1}^{n} (\beta_0 + \beta_i x_i - y_i)}{1 + \beta_i^2} = 0.$$

The solution provides an orthogonal regression estimate of β_0 as:

$$\hat{\beta}_{0OR} = \bar{y} - \hat{\beta}_{1OR}\bar{x}$$

Where $\hat{\beta}_{1OR}$ is an orthogonal regression estimate of β_1.

Now, substituting β_{0OR} in equation $\dfrac{\sum\limits_{i=1}^{n}\left(\beta_0 x_i + \beta_1 x_i^2 - y_i x_i\right)}{\left(1+\beta_1^2\right)} - \dfrac{\beta_1\left(\beta_0 + \beta_1 x_i - y_i\right)^2}{\left(1+\beta_1^2\right)^2} = 0.$, we get,

$$\sum_{i=1}^{n}\left(1+\beta_1^2\right)\left[\bar{y}x_i - \beta_1\bar{x}x_i + \beta_1 x_i^2 - x_i y_i\right] - \beta_1\sum_{i=1}^{n}\left(\bar{y} - \beta_1\bar{x} + \beta_1 x_i - y_i\right)^2 = 0$$

or

$$\left(1+\beta_1^2\right)\sum_{i=1}^{n}x_i\left[y_i - y - \beta_1\left(x_i - x\right)\right] + \beta_1\sum_{i=1}^{n}\left[-\left(y_i - y\right) + \beta_1\left(x^i - \bar{x}\right)\right]^2 = 0$$

or

$$\left(1+\beta_1^2\right)\sum_{i=1}^{n}\left(u_i + x\right)\left(v_i - \beta_1 u_i\right) + \beta_1\sum_{i=1}^{n}\left(-v + \beta_1 u_i\right)^2 = 0$$

where,

$$u_i = x_i - \bar{x},$$
$$v_i = y_i - \bar{y}.$$

Since $\sum\limits_{i=1}^{n}u_i = \sum\limits_{i=1}^{n}u_i = 0$, so

or

$$\sum_{i=1}^{n}\left[\beta_1^2 u_i v_i + \beta_1\left(u_i^2 - v_i^2\right) - u_i v_i\right] = 0$$

Solving this quadratic equation provides the orthogonal regression estimate of β_1 as,

$$\hat{\beta}_{1OR} = \frac{\left(S_{yy} - S_{xx}\right) + \text{sign}\left(S_{xy}\right)\sqrt{\left(S_{xx} - S_{xy}\right)^2 + 4S_{xy}^2}}{2S_{xy}}$$

where sign(S_{xy}) s denotes the sign of S_{xy} which can be positive or negative. So,

$$\text{sign}\left(S_{xy}\right) = \begin{cases} 1 & \text{if } S_{xy} > 0. \\ -1 & \text{if } S_{xy} > 0. \end{cases}$$

Notice that this gives two solutions for $\hat{\beta}_{1OR}$. We choose the solution which minimizes $\sum\limits_{i=1}^{n}d_i^2$. The other solution maximizes $\sum\limits_{i=1}^{n}d_i^2$ and is in the direction perpendicular to the optimal solution. The optimal solution can be chosen with the sign of S_{xy}.

Reduced Major Axis Regression Method

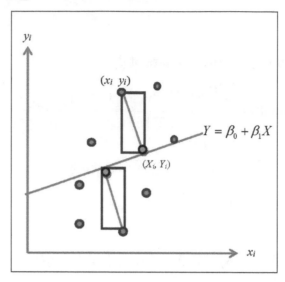

The direct, reverse and orthogonal methods of estimation minimize the errors in a particular direction which is usually the distance between the observed data points and the line in the scatter diagram. Alternatively, one can consider the area extended by the data points in a certain neighbourhood and instead of distances, the area of rectangles defined between the corresponding observed data point and the nearest point on the line in the following scatter diagram can also be minimized. Such an approach is more appropriate when the uncertainties are present in the study and explanatory variables both. This approach is termed as reduced major axis regression.

Suppose the regression line is $Y_i = \beta_0 + \beta_1 X_i$ on which all the observed points are expected to lie. Suppose the points $(x_i, y_i), i = 1, 2, \ldots, n$ are observed which lie away from the line. The area of rectangle extended between the ith observed data point and the line is:

$$A_i = (X_i \sim x_i)(Y_i \sim y_i)(i = 1, 2, \ldots, n)$$

Where (X_i, Y_i) denotes the ith pair of observation without any error which lies on the line.

The total area extended by n data points is:

$$\sum_{i=1}^{n} A_i = \sum_{i=1}^{n} (X_i \sim x_i)(Y_i \sim y_i).$$

All observed data points $(x_i, y_i), (i = 1, 2, \ldots, n)$ are expected to lie on the line,

$$Y_i = \beta_0 + \beta_1 X_i$$

and let,

$$E_i^* = Y_i - \beta_0 - \beta_1 X_i = 0.$$

So now the objective is to minimize the sum of areas under the constraints E_i^* to obtain the reduced major axis estimates of regression coefficients. Using the Lagrangian multiplier method, the Lagrangian function is,

$$L_R = \sum_{i=1}^{n} A_i - \sum_{i=1}^{n} \mu_i E_i^*$$

$$= \sum_{i=1}^{n}(X_i - x_i)(Y_i - y_i) - \sum_{i=1}^{n} \mu_i E_i^*$$

where $1,..., \mu$ μn are the Lagrangian multipliers. The set of equations are obtained by setting

$$\frac{\partial L_R}{\partial X_i} = 0, \frac{\partial L_R}{\partial Y_i} = 0, \frac{\partial L_R}{\partial \beta_0} = 0, \frac{\partial L_R}{\partial \beta_1} = 0 \quad (i = 1, 2, ..., n).$$

thus,

$$\frac{\partial L_R}{\partial X_i} = (Y_i - y_i) + \beta_i \mu_i = 0$$

$$\frac{\partial L_R}{\partial Y_i} = (X_i - x_i) - \mu_i = 0$$

$$\frac{\partial L_R}{\partial \beta_0} = \sum_{i=1}^{n} \mu_i = 0$$

$$\frac{\partial L_R}{\partial \beta_1} = \sum_{i=1}^{n} \mu_i X_i = 0$$

now,

$$X_i = x_i + \mu_i$$
$$Y_i = y_i - \beta_1 \mu_i$$
$$\beta_0 + \beta_1(x_i + \mu_i) = y_i - \beta_1 \mu_i$$

$$\Rightarrow \mu = \frac{y_i - \beta_0 - \beta_1 x_i}{2\beta_1}.$$

Substituting μ_i in $\sum_{i=1}^{n} \mu_i = 0$, the reduced major axis regression estimate of β_0 is obtained as-

$$\hat{\beta}_{0RM} = \bar{y} - \hat{\beta}_{1RM}\bar{x}$$

Where $\hat{\beta}_{1RM}$ is the reduced major axis regression estimate of β_1. Using $X_i = x_i + \mu_i, \mu_i$ and $\hat{\beta}_{0RM}$ in $\sum_{i=1}^{n} \mu_i X_i = 0$, we get:

$$\sum_{i=1}^{n}\left(\frac{y_i - \bar{y} + \beta_1\bar{x} - \beta_1 x_i}{2\beta_1}\right)\left(x_i - \frac{y_i - \bar{y} + \beta_1\bar{x} - \beta_1 x_i}{2\beta_1}\right) = 0.$$

Let $\mu_i = x_i - \overline{x}$ and $v_i = y_i - \overline{y}$ then this equation can be re-expressed as:

$$\sum_{i=1}^{n}(v_i - \beta_1\mu_i)(v_i + \beta_1\mu_i + 2\beta_1\overline{x}) = 0.$$

Using $\sum_{i=1}^{n}\mu_i = \sum_{i=1}^{n}\mu_i = 0$, we get:

$$\sum_{i=1}^{n}v_i^2 - \beta_1^2\sum_{i=1}^{n}\mu_i^2 = 0.$$

Solving this equation, the reduced major axis regression estimate of β_1 is obtained as,

$$\hat{\beta}_{1RM} = \text{sign}(s_{xy})\sqrt{\frac{S_{yy}}{S_{xx}}}$$

where $\text{sign}(S_{xy})\begin{cases} 1 & \text{if } S_{xy} > 0 \\ -1 & \text{if } S_{xy} > 0. \end{cases}$

We choose the regression estimator which has same sign as of S_{xy}.

Least Absolute Deviation Regression Method

The least-squares principle advocates the minimization of the sum of squared errors. The idea of squaring the errors is useful in place of simple errors because random errors can be positive as well as negative. So consequently their sum can be close to zero indicating that there is no error in the model and which can be misleading. Instead of the sum of random errors, the sum of absolute random errors can be considered which avoids the problem due to positive and negative random errors.

In the method of least squares, the estimates of the parameters β_0 and β_1 in the model $= \beta_0 + \beta_1 x_i + \varepsilon_i \cdot (i = 1, 2, ..., n)$ are chosen such that the sum of squares of deviations $\sum_{i=1}^{n}\varepsilon_i^2$ is minimum. In the method of least absolute deviation (LAD) regression, the parameters β_0 and β_1 are estimated such that the sum of absolute deviations $\sum_{i=1}^{n}|\varepsilon_i|$ is minimum. It minimizes the absolute vertical sum of errors as in the following scatter diagram:

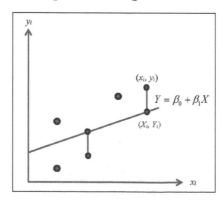

The LAD estimates $\hat{\beta}_{0L}$ and $\hat{\beta}_{1L}$ are the estimates of β_0 and β_1, respectively which minimize,

$$LAD(\beta_0, \beta_1) = \sum_{i=1}^{n} |y_i - \beta_0 - \beta_1 x_i|$$

For the given observations $(x_i, y_i) = (i = 1, 2, \ldots n)$.

Conceptually, LAD procedure is more straightforward than OLS procedure because $|e|$ (absolute residuals) is a more straightforward measure of the size of the residual than e^2 (squared residuals). The LAD regression estimates of β_0 and β_1 are not available in closed form. Instead, they can be obtained numerically based on algorithms. Moreover, this creates the problems of non-uniqueness and degeneracy in the estimates. The concept of non-uniqueness relates to that more than one best line pass through a data point. The degeneracy concept describes that the best line through a data point also passes through more than one other data points. The non-uniqueness and degeneracy concepts are used in algorithms to judge the quality of the estimates. The algorithm for finding the estimators generally proceeds in steps. At each step, the best line is found that passes through a given data point. The best line always passes through another data point, and this data point is used in the next step. When there is non-uniqueness, then there is more than one best line. When there is degeneracy, then the best line passes through more than one other data point. When either of the problems is present, then there is more than one choice for the data point to be used in the next step and the algorithm may go around in circles or make a wrong choice of the LAD regression line. The exact tests of hypothesis and confidence intervals for the LAD regression estimates can not be derived analytically. Instead, they are derived analogously to the tests of hypothesis and confidence intervals related to ordinary least squares estimates.

Estimation of Parameters when X is Stochastic

In a usual linear regression model, the study variable is supped to be random and explanatory variables are assumed to be fixed. In practice, there may be situations in which the explanatory variable also becomes random.

Suppose both dependent and independent variables are stochastic in the simple linear regression model;

$$y = \beta_0 + \beta_1 X + \varepsilon$$

Where ε is the associated random error component. The observations $(x_i, y_i), i = 1, 2, \ldots n$ are assumed to be jointly distributed. Then the statistical inferences can be drawn in such cases which are conditional on X.

Assume the joint distribution of X and y to be bivariate normal $N(\mu_x, \mu_y, \sigma_x^2, \sigma_y^2, \rho)$ where μ_x and μ_y are the means of X and y; σ_x^2 and σ_y^2 are the variances of X and; y and ρ is the correlation coefficient between X and y. Then the conditional distribution of y given X x = is the Univariate normal conditional mean:

$$E(y|X = x) = \sigma_{y|x}^2 = \sigma_y^2 (1 - \rho^2)$$

and the conditional variance of y given X= x is,

$$\text{Var}\left(y|X=x\right)=\sigma_{x|y}^2=\sigma_y^2\left(1-\rho^2\right)$$

where,

$$\beta_0=\mu_y-\mu_x\beta_1$$

and,

$$\beta_1=\frac{\sigma_y}{\sigma_x}\rho.$$

When both X and y is stochastic, then the problem of estimation of parameters can be reformulated as follows. Consider a conditional random variable $y|X=x$ having a normal distribution with mean as conditional mean $\mu\, y|x$ and variance as conditional variance $\text{Var}\left(y|X=x\right)\sigma_{y|x}^2$. Obtain n independently distributed observation $y_i|x_i, i=1,2,\dots,n$ from $N\left(\mu_{y|x},\sigma_{y|x}^2\right)$ with nonstochastic X. Now the method of maximum likelihood can be used to estimate the parameters which yield the estimates of β_0 and β_1 as earlier in the case of nonstochastic X as:

$$\tilde{b}=\bar{y}-\tilde{b}_1\bar{x}$$

and,

$$\tilde{b}=\frac{S_{xy}}{S_{xx}},$$

respectively.

Moreover, the correlation coefficient,

$$\rho=\frac{E\left(y-\mu_y\right)\left(X-\mu_x\right)}{\sigma_y\sigma_x}$$

can be estimated by the sample correlation coefficient,

$$\hat{\rho}=\frac{\sum_{i=1}^{n}\left(y_i-\bar{y}\right)\left(x_i-\bar{x}\right)}{\sqrt{\sum_{i=1}^{n}\left(x_i-\bar{x}\right)^2}\sqrt{\sum_{i=1}^{n}\left(y_i-\bar{y}\right)^2}}$$

$$=\frac{S_{xy}}{\sqrt{S_{xx}}\sqrt{S_{yy}}}$$

$$=\tilde{b}_1\sqrt{\frac{S_{xx}}{S_{xy}}}.$$

Thus,

$$\hat{\rho}^2 = \tilde{b}_1^2 \frac{S_{xx}}{S_{yy}}$$

$$= \tilde{b}_1 \frac{S_{xx}}{S_{yy}}$$

$$= \frac{syy - \sum_{i=1}^{n} \hat{\varepsilon}_i^2}{S_{yy}}$$

$$= R^2$$

Which is same as the coefficient of determination. Thus R^2 has the same expression as in the case when X is fixed. Thus R^2 again measures the goodness of the fitted model even when X is stochastic.

Probabilistic and Bayesian Approaches

Discrete Random Variable

A discrete variable is a variable which can only take a countable number of values. For a discrete random variable, its probability distribution (also called the probability distribution function) is any table, graph, or formula that gives each possible value and the probability of that value. For example, if a coin is tossed three times, the number of heads obtained can be 0, 1, 2 or 3. The probabilities of each of these possibilities can be tabulated as shown:

Number of Heads	0	1	2	3
Probability	1/8	3/8	3/8	1/8

In this example, the number of heads can only take 4 values (0, 1, 2, 3) and so the variable is discrete. The variable is said to be random if the sum of the probabilities is one. Other examples may include, a variable A = the PM of USA 2020 will be female, A = you wake up tomorrow with a headache, A = you have swine flu, etc.

Sample Space

A sample space is a set of all possible outcomes for an activity or experiment and the elements of the sample space are called outcomes. Few more examples are given in table given below:

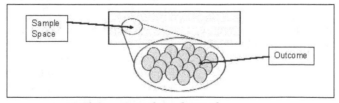

Figure: Sample and sample space.

Assume you are a doctor. This is the sample space of "patients you might see on any given day". The outcomes may be like Non-smoker, female, diabetic, headache, Smoker, male, herniated disk, back pain, mildly schizophrenic, delinquent medical bills, etc.

Activity	Sample Space
Rolling a dice:	There will be 6 outcomes in the sample space: {1, 2, 3, 4, 5, 6}.
Tossing a coin:	There will be 2 outcomes in the sample space: { Heads, Tails}.
Drawing a card from a standard deck:	There will be 52 cards in the sample space: {Spades: 2,3,4,5,6,7,8,9,10, ace, jack queen, king, Clubs: 2,3,4,5,6,7,8,9,10, ace, jack, queen, king, Diamonds: 2,3,4,5,6,7,8,9,10, ace, jack, queen, king, Hearts: 2,3,4,5,6,7,8,9,10, ace, jack, queen, king}.
Drawing one marble from the bottle:	There will be 8 marbles in the sample space: {blue marble, blue marble, blue marble, blue marble, blue marble, red marble, red marble, red marble}.
Rolling a pair of dice:	There will be 36 outcomes in the sample space: {(1,1) (1,2) (1,3) (1,4) (1,5) (1,6) (2,1) (2,2) (2,3) (2,4) (2,5) (2,6) (3,1) (3,2) (3,3) (3,4) (3,5) (3,6) (4,1) (4,2) (4,3) (4,4) (4,5) (4,6) (5,1) (5,2) (5,3) (5,4) (5,5) (5,6) (6,1) (6,2) (6,3) (6,4) (6,5) (6,6)}.
Choosing an outfit from a green blouse, a red blouse, a black skirt, a pair of sneakers, and a pair of sandals.	There will be 4 outfit combinations in the sample space: {green blouse-skirt-sneakers, green blouse-skirt-sandals, red blouse-skirt-sneakers, red blouse-skirt-sandals}.

A sample spaces can become very large. When determining a sample space, be sure to consider ALL possibilities. Oftentimes this can be a difficult task. To make this process easier, we may wish to use the Counting Principle.

The Fundamental Counting Principle: If there are a ways for one activity to occur, and b ways for a second activity to occur, then there are a • b ways for both to occur.

Examples:

- Activities: roll a die and flip a coin.

  There are 6 ways to roll a die and 2 ways to flip a coin.

  There are 6 • 2 = 12 ways to roll a die and flip a coin.

- Activities: draw two cards from a standard deck of 52 cards without replacing the cards

  There are 52 ways to draw the first card. There are 51 ways to draw the second card. There are 52 • 51 = 2,652 ways to draw the two cards.

- The Counting Principle also works for more than two activities: A coin is tossed five times and there are 2 ways to flip each coin

  There are 2 • 2 • 2 • 2 • 2 = 32 arrangements of heads and tails.

- A die is rolled four times and here are 6 ways to roll each die. There are 6 • 6 • 6 • 6 = 1,296 possible outcomes.

Events and Outcomes

Events

In probability theory, an event is a set of outcomes of an experiment (a subset of the sample space) to which a probability is assigned. When we say "Event" we mean one (or more) outcomes.

Example Events:

- Getting a Tail when tossing a coin is an event.
- Rolling a "5" is an event.
- An event can include several outcomes.
- Choosing a "King" from a deck of cards (any of the 4 Kings) is also an event.
- Rolling an "even number" (2, 4 or 6) is an event.

Events can be of the following type:

- Independent (each event is not affected by other events).
- Dependent (also called "Conditional", where an event is affected by other events).
- Mutually Exclusive (events can't happen at the same time).

Independent Events

Events can be "Independent", meaning each event is not affected by any other events. This is an important idea! A coin does not "know" that it came up heads before each toss of a coin is a perfect isolated thing.

Example: You toss a coin three times and it comes up "Heads" each time... what is the chance that the next toss will also be a "Head"?

The chance is simply 1/2, or 50%, just like any other toss of the coin. What it did in the past will not affect the current toss! Some people think "it is overdue for a Tail", but really truly the next toss of the coin is totally independent of any previous tosses. Saying "a Tail is due", or "just one more go, my luck is due" is called The Gambler's Fallacy.

Dependent Events

But some events can be "dependent"... which means they can be affected by previous events.

Example: Drawing 2 Cards from a Deck After taking one card from the deck there are less cards available, so the probabilities change! Let's look at the chances of getting a King. For the 1st card the chance of drawing a King is 4 out of 52.

But for the 2nd card: If the 1st card was a King, then the 2nd card is less likely to be a King, as only 3 of the 51 cards left are Kings.

If the 1st card was not a King, then the 2nd card is slightly more likely to be a King, as 4 of the 51 cards left are King. This is because we are removing cards from the deck:

- Replacement: When we put each card back after drawing it the chances don't change, as the events are independent.

- Without Replacement: The chances will change, and the events are dependent.

Outcomes

In probability theory, an outcome is a possible result of an experiment. Each possible outcome of a particular experiment is unique, and different outcomes are mutually exclusive (only one outcome will occur on each trial of the experiment). All of the possible outcomes of an experiment form the elements of a sample space.

Whenever we do an experiment like flipping a coin or rolling a die, we get an outcome. For example, if we flip a coin we get an outcome of heads or tails, and if we roll a die we get an outcome of 1, 2, 3, 4, 5, or 6. Unless we're rolling a 20-sided die, in which case we're likely playing Dungeons & Dragons and the outcome is that we won't go on a date for a few years yet.

We call the set of all possible outcomes of an experiment the sample space. The sample space for the experiment of flipping a coin is: {heads, tails} and the sample space for the experiment of rolling a die is {1, 2, 3, 4, 5, 6}.

When we talk about finding probabilities, we mean finding the likelihood of events. If an experiment is random/fair, the probability of an event is the number of favorable outcomes divided by the total number of possible outcomes:

No. of favorable outcomes/No. of possible outcomes

A favorable outcome is any outcome in the event whose probability you're finding (remember, an event is a set).

Conditional Probability

Let A and B be two events. Then, the conditional probability of A given that B has occurred, P(A | B), is defined as: $P(A|B) = P(A \cap B)/P(B)$.

The reasoning behind this definition is that if B has occurred, then only the "portion" of A that is contained in B, i.e., $A \cap B$ could occur; moreover, the original probability of $A \cap B$ must be recalculated to reflect the fact that the "new" sample space is B. This conditional probability is also called as Bayes Rule.

Example: Assume once more that you are a doctor. Again, this is the sample space of "patients you might see on any given day". Consider an Event: Flu (F), its probability P(F) = 0.02 and another Event: Headache (H) with probability P(H) = 0.10 as shown in below figure:

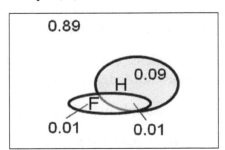

Figure: Diagrammatic representation of sample scenario and its probabilities.

Suppose we want analyze the interactions between these two events, which may be defined as:

P(H|F) = Fraction of F's outcomes which are also in H P(H|F).

= Fraction of flu in which patient has a headache.

= # with flu and headache / # with flu.

= Size of "H and F" region / Size of "F" region.

= P(H, F) / P(F).

One day you wake up with a headache. You think: "50% of flus are associated with headaches so I must have a 50-50 chance of coming down with flu", i.e., (P(H|F) = 0.50). Then,

$$P(F|H) = \frac{P(F,H)}{P(H)} = \frac{P(H|F)P(F)}{P(H)} = \frac{(0.50)(0.02)}{0.1} = 0.10$$

Example: Pick a Card from a Deck Suppose a card is drawn randomly from a deck and found to be an Ace. What is the conditional probability for this card to be Spade Ace?

A = Spade Ace

B = An Ace

A ∩ B = Spade Ace

P(A) = 1/52; P(B) = 4/52; and P A ∩ B = 1/52

Hence, P(A | B) =(1/52) /(4/52)= ¼.

Probabilistic Inference

Probabilistic inference is the task of deriving the probability of one or more random variables taking a specific value or set of values. For example, a Bernoulli (Boolean) random variable may describe the event that John has cancer. Such a variable could take a value of 1 (John has cancer) or 0 (John does not have cancer). Deep Dive uses probabilistic inference to estimate the probability that the random variable takes value 1: a probability of 0.78 would mean that John is 78% likely to have cancer.

The needs for probabilistic inference are:

- Probabilistic learning: Calculate explicit probabilities for hypothesis, among the most practical approaches to certain types of learning problems.

- Incremental: Each training example can incrementally increase/decrease the probability that a hypothesis is correct. Prior knowledge can be combined with observed data.

- Probabilistic prediction: Predict multiple hypotheses, weighted by their probabilities.

- Standard: Even when Bayesian methods are computationally intractable, they can provide a standard of optimal decision making against which other methods can be measured.

Application of Bayesian Theory

Bayesian Classification

Given training data D, posteriori probability of a hypothesis h, P(h|D) follows the Bayes theorem:

MAP (maximum posteriori) hypothesis is defined as follows:

$$h_{MAP} = \arg\max_{h \in H} P(h|D) = \arg\max_{h \in H} P(D|h)P(h).$$

Practical difficulty is that it requires initial knowledge of many probabilities, which introduces significant computational cost.

The classification problem may be formalized using a-posteriori probabilities:

P(C|X) = prob. that the sample tuple $X = <x_1, \ldots x_k>$ is of class C.

Idea is to assign to sample X the class label C such that $P(C|X)$ is maximal.

Estimating a-Posteriori Probabilities

As per Bayes theorem: $P(C|X) = P(X|C) \cdot P(C) / P(X)$

Where, $P(X)$ is constant for all classes.

> $P(C)$ = Relative freq of class C samples.
>
> C such that $P(C|X)$ is maximum = C such that $P(X|C) \cdot P(C)$ is maximum.
>
> Problem: Computing $P(X|C)$ is unfeasible!

Example – Training

Let's say we have a table that decided if we should play tennis under certain circumstances. These could be the outlook of the weather; the temperature; the humidity and the strength of the wind:

Table: Plays Tennis- Training examples.

Day	Outlook	Temperature	Humidity	Wind	Play Tennis
D1	Sunny	Hot	High	Weak	No
D2	Sunny	Hot	High	Strong	No
D3	Overcast	Hot	High	Weak	Yes
D4	Rain	Mild	High	Weak	Yes
D5	Rain	Cool	Normal	Weak	Yes
D6	Rain	Cool	Normal	Strong	No
D7	Overcast	Cool	Normal	Strong	Yes
D8	Sunny	Mild	High	Weak	No
D9	Sunny	Cool	Normal	Weak	Yes
D10	Rain	Mild	Normal	Weak	Yes
D11	Sunny	Mild	Normal	Strong	Yes
D12	Overcast	Mild	High	Strong	Yes
D13	Overcast	Hot	Normal	Weak	Yes
D14	Rain	Mild	High	Strong	No

So here we have 4 attributes. What we need to do is to create "look-up tables" for each of these attributes, and write in the probability that a game of tennis will be played based on this attribute. In these tables we have to note that there are 5 cases of not being able to play a game, and 9 cases of being able to play a game.

> $P(\text{Play=Yes}) = 9/14$.
>
> $P(\text{Play=No}) = 5/14$.

We also must note the following probabilities for P(C):

Humidity	Play= Yes	Play= No	Total
High	3/9	4/5	7/14
Normal	6/9	1/5	7/14

Wind	Play= Yes	Play= No	Total
Strong	3/9	3/5	6/14
Weak	6/9	25	8/14

Outlook	Play= Yes	Play= No	Total
Sunny	2/9	3/5	5/14
Overcast	4/9	0/5	4/17
Rain	3/9	2/5	5/14

Temperature	Play= Yes	Play= No	Total
Hot	2/9	2/5	4/14
Mild	4/9	2/5	6/17
Cold	3/9	1/5	4/14

Testing

Now, we are in the testing phase. For this, say we were given a new instance, and we want to know if we can play a game or not, then we need to look up the results from the tables above. So, this new instance is:

$$X = (\text{Outlook=Sunny, Temperature=Cool, Humidity=High, Wind=Strong})$$

Firstly we look at the probability that we can play the game, so we use the lookup tables to get:

P(Outlook=Sunny | Play=Yes) = 2/9.

P(Temperature=Cool | Play=Yes) = 3/9.

P(Humidity=High | Play=Yes) = 3/9.

P(Wind=Strong | Play=Yes) = 3/9 P(Play=Yes) = 9/14.

Next we consider the fact that we cannot play a game:

P(Outlook=Sunny | Play=No) = 3/5

P(Temperature=Cool | Play=No) = 1/5

P(Humidity=High | Play=No) = 4/5 P(Wind=Strong | Play=No) = 3/5 P(Play=No) = 5/14

Then, using those results, you have to multiple the whole lot together. So you multiple all the probabilities for Play=Yes such as:

P(X|Play=Yes)P(Play=Yes) = (2/9) * (3/9) * (3/9) * (3/9) * (9/14) = 0.0053 And this gives us a value that represents 'P(X|C)P(C)', or in this case 'P(X|Play=Yes)P(Play=Yes)'.

We also have to do the same thing for Play=No:

P(X|Play=No)P(Play=No) = (3/5) * (1/5) * (4/5) * (3/5) * (5/14) = 0.0206

Finally, we have to divide both results by the evidence, or 'P(X)'. The evidence for both equations is the same, and we can find the values we need within the 'Total' columns of the look-up tables. Therefore:

> P(X) = P(Outlook=Sunny) * P(Temperature=Cool) * P(Humidity=High) * P(Wind=Strong)
>
> P(X) = (5/14) * (4/14) * (7/14) * (6/14)
>
> P(X) = 0.02186

Then, dividing the results by this value,

> P(Play=Yes | X) = 0.0053/0.02186 = 0.2424
>
> P(Play=No | X) = 0.0206/0.02186 = 0.9421

So, given the probabilities, can we play a game or not? To do this, we look at both probabilities and see which once has the highest value, and that is our answer. Therefore:

> P(Play=Yes | X) = 0.2424
>
> P(Play=No | X) = 0.9421

Since 0.9421 is greater than 0.2424 then the answer is 'no', we cannot play a game of tennis today.

Techniques of Data Analysis

The process of collecting and analyzing data to extract useful information is called data analysis. There are various ways of analyzing data such as through support vector machines and principal component analysis. Neural networks can also be used for data analysis. All these diverse topics related to data analysis have been carefully discussed in this chapter.

Neural Network

Neural network is a computer modeling approach to computation that is loosely based upon the architecture of the brain. Many different models are available, but in general they have the following components:

- Multiple, individual "nodes" or "units" that operate at the same time (in parallel).

- A network that connects the nodes together.

- Information is stored in a distributed fashion among the links that connect the nodes.

- Learning can occur with gradual changes in connection strength.

The simplest definition of a neural network, more properly referred to as an 'artificial' neural network (ANN), is provided by the inventor of one of the first neuro computers:

> "A computing system made up of a number of simple, highly interconnected processing elements, which process information by their dynamic state response to external inputs."
> – Dr. Robert Hecht-Nielsen

An Artificial Neural Network (ANN) is an information processing paradigm that is inspired by the way biological nervous systems, such as the brain, process information. The key element of this paradigm is the novel structure of the information processing system. It is composed of a large number of highly interconnected processing elements (neurones) working in unison to solve specific problems. ANNs, like people, learn by example. An ANN is configured for a specific application, such as pattern recognition or data classification, through a learning process. Learning in biological systems involves adjustments to the synaptic connections that exist between the neurones. This is true of ANNs as well.

The artificial neural network is a computing technique designed to simulate the human brain's method in problem-solving. The similarity between artificial neural networks and the human brain is that both acquire the skills in processing data and finding solutions through training.

Neural Network's Architecture

To illustrate the structure of the artificial neural network, an anatomical and functional look must be taken on the human brain first. The human brain consists of about 10^{11} computing units "neurons" working in parallel and exchanging information through their connectors "synapses"; these neurons sum up all information coming into them, and if the result is higher than the given potential called action potential, they send a pulse via axon to the next stage. Human neuron anatomy is shown in Figure below.

In the same way, artificial neural network consists of simple computing units "artificial neurons," and each unit is connected to the other units via weight connectors; then, these units calculate the weighted sum of the coming inputs and find out the output using squashing function or activation function. Figure below shows the block diagram of artificial neuron.

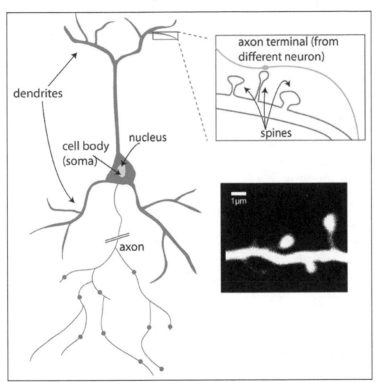

Figure: Human neuron anatomy.

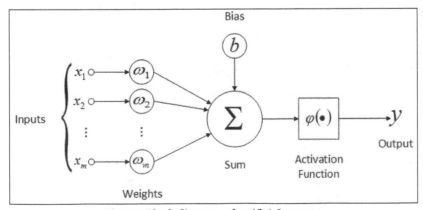

Figure: Block diagram of artificial neuron.

Based on the block diagram and function of the neural network, three basic elements of neural model can be identified:

- Synapses, or connecting links, have a weight or strength where the input signal xi connected to neuron k is multiplied by synaptic weight ww_{ki}.

- An adder for summing the weighted inputs.

- An activation function to produce the output of a neuron. It is also referred to as a squashing function, in that it squashes (limits) the amplitude range of the output signal to a finite value.

The bias b_k has the effect of increasing or decreasing the net input of the activation function, depending on whether it is positive or negative, respectively.

Mathematically, the output on the neuron k can be described as:

$$y_k = \varphi\left(\sum_{i=1}^{m} x_i w_{ki} + b_k\right)$$

Where, x_1, x_2, x_3... x_m are the input's signals.

wk_1, wk_2, wk_3,..., w_{km} are the respective weights of neuron.

b_k is the bias.

φ is the activation function.

To clarify the effect of the bias on the performance of the neuron, the output given in Eq. $y_k = \varphi\left(\sum_{i=1}^{m} x_i w_{ki} + b_k\right)$ is processed in two stages, where the first stage includes the weighted inputs and the sum which is donated as S_k:

$$S_k = \sum_{i=1}^{m} x_i w_{k_i}$$

Then, the output of adder will be given in:

$$v_k = s_k + b_k$$

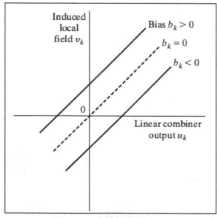

Figure: Effect of bias.

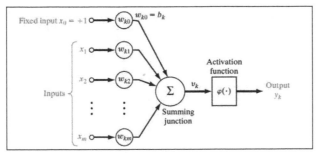

Figure: Neuron structure with considering bias as input.

Where the output of neuron will be:

$$y_k = \varphi(v_k)$$

Depending on the value of the bias, the relationship between the weighted input and adder output will be modified as shown in Figure above.

Bias could be considered as an input signal x_0 fixed at +1 with synaptic weight equal to the bias b_k as shown in Figure above.

Types of Activation Function

Activation function defines the output of neuron as the function to the adder's output v_k. The following sections describe the different activation functions.

Linear Function

Where neuron output is proportional to the input as shown in figure below:

and, it can be described by,

$$y_k = v_k$$

Threshold (Step) Function

This activation function is described in Figure below where the output of neuron is given by,

$$y_k = \begin{cases} 1 & \text{if } v_k \geq 0 \\ 0 & \text{if } v_k < 0 \end{cases}$$

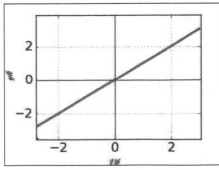

Figure: Linear activation function.

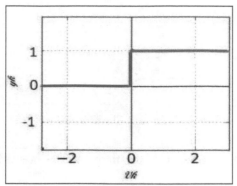

Figure: Threshold activation function.

In neural computation, such a neuron is referred to as the McCulloch-Pitts model in recognition of the pioneering work done by McCulloch and Pitts; the output of the neuron takes on the value of 1 if the induced local field of that neuron is nonnegative and 0 otherwise. This statement describes the all-or-none property of the McCulloch-Pitts model.

Sigmoid Function

The most common type of activation functions in neural network is described by,

$$yk = \frac{1}{1+e^{vk}}$$

Figure below shows the sigmoid activation function, it is clearly observed that this function has nonlinear nature and it can produce analogue output unlike threshold functions which produce output in discrete range. Also, we can note that sigmoid activation function is limited between 0 and 1 and gives an advantage over linear activation function which produces output from ∞ to +∞.

TanH Activation Function

This activation function has the advantages of sigmoid function, while it is characterized by output range between 1 and 1 as shown in figure below:

The output is described by:

$$y_k = \frac{2}{1+e^{-2vk}} - 1$$

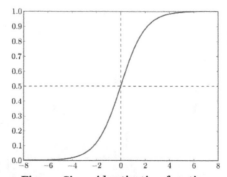

Figure: Sigmoid activation function.

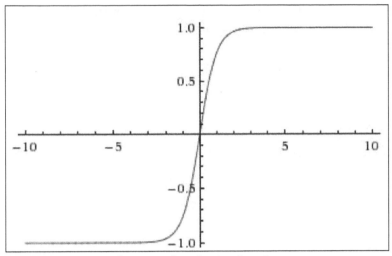

Figure: Tanh activation function.

Neural Network Models

The manner in which the neurons of a neural network are structured is intimately linked with the learning algorithm used to train the network. Three main models can be identified for the neural network.

Single-Layer Feed Forward Neural Network

In a layered neural network, the neurons are organized in the form of layers. The simplest structure is the single-layer feed forward network that consists of input nodes connected directly to the single layer of neurons. The node outputs are based on the activation function as shown in Figure below:

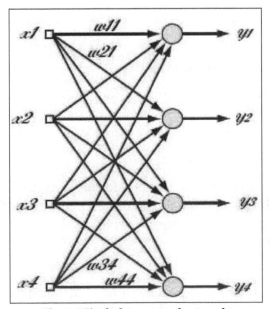

Figure: Single-layer neural network.

Mathematically, the inputs will be presented as vectors with dimensions of $1 \times i$, while the weights will be presented as a matrix with dimensions of i× k, and outputs will be presented as a vector with dimensions of 1× k as given in equation below:

$$\left[y_1, y_2, \ldots, y_k\right] = \left[x_1, x_2, \ldots x_i\right] \left[\begin{bmatrix} W_{11} & W_{21} & \cdots & W_{k1} \\ & \vdots & \ddots & \vdots \\ W_{1k} & W_{2k} & \cdots & W_{ik} \end{bmatrix}\right]$$

Multilayer Feed Forward Neural Network

The second class of a feed forward neural network distinguishes itself by the presence of one or more hidden layers, whose computation nodes are correspondingly called hidden neurons as shown in figure below.

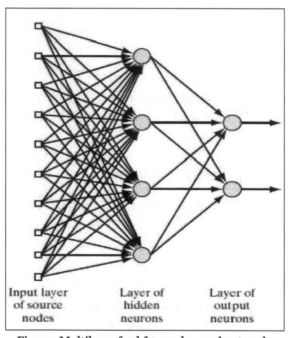

Figure: Multilayer feed forward neural network.

By adding one or more hidden layers, the network is enabled to extract higher-order statistics from its input.

Neural Network Training

The process of calibrating the values of weights and biases of the network is called training of neural network to perform the desired function correctly. Learning methods or algorithms can be classified into supervised learning and unsupervised learning.

Supervised Learning

In supervised learning, the data will be presented in a form of couples (input, desired output), and then the learning algorithm will adapt the weights and biases depending on the error signal between the real output of network and the desired output as shown in figure.

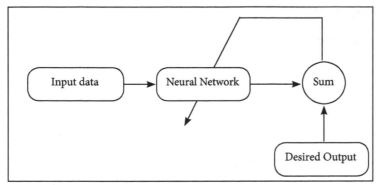

Figure: Supervised learning.

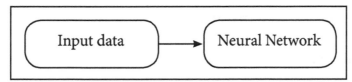

Figure: Unsupervised learning.

As a performance measure for the system, we may think in terms of the mean squared error or the sum of squared errors over the training sample defined as a function of the free parameters (i.e., synaptic weights) of the system.

Unsupervised Learning

To perform unsupervised learning, a competitive learning rule is used. For example, we may use a neural network that consists of two layers—an input layer and a competitive layer. The input layer receives the available data. The competitive layer consists of neurons that compete with each other (in accordance with a learning rule) for the "opportunity" to respond to features contained in the input data.

Types of Neural Networks

Neural networks can be broadly classified as: Dynamic neural network, Static neural network, Memory network and other types. Few examples for each type is given below:

Dynamic Neural Network

- Feed forward neural network (FNN).

- Recurrent neural network (RNN).

  ○ Hopfield network.

  ○ Boltzmann machine.

  ○ Simple recurrent networks.

  ○ Echo state network.

  ○ Long short-term memory.

- ° Bi-directional RNN.

- ° Hierarchical RNN.

- ° Stochastic neural networks.

- Kohonen Self-Organizing Maps.

- Auto encoder.

- Probabilistic neural network (PNN).

- Time delay neural network (TDNN).

- Regulatory feedback network (RFNN).

Static Neural Network

- Neocognitron.

- McCulloch-Pitts cell.

- Radial basis function network (RBF).

- Learning vector quantization.

- Perceptron:

  - ° Adaline model.

  - ° Convolutional neural network (CNN).

- Modular neural networks:

  - ° Committee of machines (COM).

  - ° Associative neural network (ASNN).

Memory Network

- Google/Deep Mind.

- Facebook/MemNN.

- Holographic associative memory.

- One-shot associative memory.

- Neural Turing Machine.

- Adaptive resonance theory.

- Hierarchical temporal memory.

Other Types of Networks

- Instantaneously trained neural networks (ITNN).

- Spiking neural network (SNN):

  ○ Pulse Coded Neural Networks (PCNN).

- Cascading neural networks.

- Neuro-fuzzy networks.

- Growing Neural Gas (GNG).

- Compositional pattern-producing networks.

- Counter propagation network.

- Oscillating neural network.

- Hybridization neural network.

- Physical neural network:

  ○ Optical neural network.

Network Pruning and Rule Extraction

Network pruning:

- Fully connected network will be hard to articulate.

- N input nodes, h hidden nodes and m output nodes lead to h(m+N) weights.

- Pruning: Remove some of the links without affecting classification accuracy of the network.

Extracting rules from a trained network:

- Discretize activation values; replace individual activation value by the cluster average maintaining the network accuracy.

- Enumerate the output from the discretized activation values to find rules between activation value and output.

- Find the relationship between the input and activation value.

- Combine the above two to have rules relating the output to input.

Applications of Network Pruning and Rule Extraction

In Science and medicine domain NN is used for modeling, prediction, diagnosis, pattern recognition, e.g. effects and undesirable effects of drugs early tumor recognition. It is used for process modeling and analysis manufacturing industries. In Marketing and Sales used for analysis, classification, customer targeting, e.g. turnover prognosis for individual articles/stores.

In Finance NN is used for portfolio trading, investment support type of decision making. For Banking & Insurance, credit and policy approval, e.g. credit-scoring (Basel II), finance time series prediction, valuation of derivates, risk minimized trading strategies; client valuation e.g. risk and cost prediction for individual clients, probability of contract cancellation, fraud recognition, justice in tariffs. Also it is used in Security applications like bomb, iceberg, and fraud detection. In Engineering it is used for dynamic load scheduling, pattern recognition.

Support Vector Machines

Support Vector Machine (SVM) was first heard in 1992, introduced by Boser, Guyon, and Vapnik in COLT-92. Support vector machines (SVMs) are a set of related supervised learning methods used for classification and regression. They belong to a family of generalized linear classifiers. In another terms, Support Vector Machine (SVM) is a classification and regression prediction tool that uses machine learning theory to maximize predictive accuracy while automatically avoiding over-fit to the data. Support Vector machines can be defined as systems which use hypothesis space of a linear functions in a high dimensional feature space, trained with a learning algorithm from optimization theory that implements a learning bias derived from statistical learning theory. Support vector machine was initially popular with the NIPS community and now is an active part of the machine learning research around the world. SVM becomes famous when, using pixel maps as input; it gives accuracy comparable to sophisticated neural networks with elaborated features in a handwriting recognition task. It is also being used for many applications, such as hand writing analysis, face analysis and so forth, especially for pattern classification and regression based applications. The foundations of Support Vector Machines (SVM) have been developed by Vapnik and gained popularity due to many promising features such as better empirical performance. The formulation uses the Structural Risk Minimization (SRM) principle, which has been shown to be superior, to traditional Empirical Risk Minimization (ERM) principle, used by conventional neural networks. SRM minimizes an upper bound on the expected risk, whereas ERM minimizes the error on the training data. It is this difference which equips SVM with a greater ability to generalize, which is the goal in statistical learning. SVMs were developed to solve the classification problem, but recently they have been extended to solve regression problems.

Statistical Learning Theory

The statistical learning theory provides a framework for studying the problem of gaining knowledge, making predictions, making decisions from a set of data. In simple terms, it enables the choosing of the hyper plane space such a way that it closely represents the underlying function in the target space.

Support Vector Machines are based on the concept of decision planes that define decision boundaries. A decision plane is one that separates between a set of objects having different class memberships. A schematic example is shown in figure below. In this example, the objects belong either to class GREEN or RED. The separating line defines a boundary on the right side of which all objects are GREEN and to the left of which all objects are RED. Any new object (white circle) falling to the right is labeled, i.e., classified, as GREEN (or classified as RED should it fall to the left of the separating line).

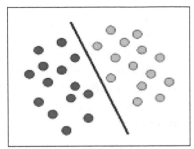

Figure: Linear Plane as decision boundary.

The above is a classic example of a linear classifier, i.e., a classifier that separates a set of objects into their respective groups (GREEN and RED in this case) with a line. Most classification tasks, however, are not that simple, and often more complex structures are needed in order to make an optimal separation, i.e., correctly classify new objects (test cases) on the basis of the examples that are available (train cases). This situation is depicted in the illustrated in figure given below. Compared to the previous schematic, it is clear that a full separation of the GREEN and RED objects would require a curve (which is more complex than a line). Classification tasks based on drawing separating lines to distinguish between objects of different class memberships are known as hyperplane classifiers. Support Vector Machines are particularly suited to handle such tasks.

Figure: Non-Linear Plane as decision boundary.

The illustration in figure below shows the basic idea behind Support Vector Machines. Here we see the original objects (left side of the schematic) mapped, i.e., rearranged, using a set of mathematical functions, known as kernels. The process of rearranging the objects is known as mapping (transformation). Note that in this new setting, the mapped objects (right side of the schematic) is linearly separable and, thus, instead of constructing the complex curve (left schematic), all we have to do is to find an optimal line that can separate the GREEN and the RED objects.

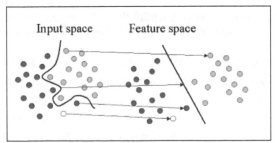

Figure: Basic Idea behind Support Vector Machines.

Early machine learning algorithms aimed to learn representations of simple functions. Hence, the goal of learning was to output a hypothesis that performed the correct classification of the training data and early learning algorithms were designed to find such an accurate fit to the data. The ability of a hypothesis to correctly classify data not in the training set is known as its generalization. SVM performs better in term of not over generalization when the neural networks might end up over generalizing easily. Another thing to observe is to find where to make the best trade-off in trading complexity with the number of epochs.

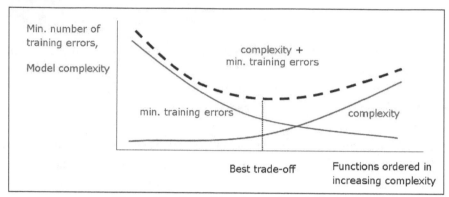

Figure: Number of Epochs vs. Complexity.

SVM

Firstly working with neural networks for supervised and unsupervised learning showed good results while used for such learning applications. MLP's uses feed forward and recurrent networks. Multilayer perceptron (MLP) properties include universal approximation of continuous nonlinear functions and include learning with input-output patterns and also involve advanced network architectures with multiple inputs and outputs.

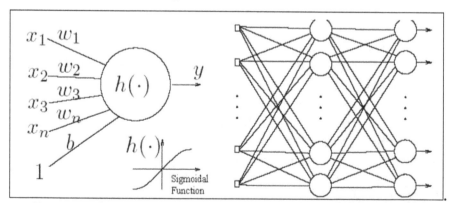

Figure: Simple Neural Network b]Multilayer Perceptron. These are simple visualizations just to have an overview as how neural network looks like.

There can be some issues noticed. Some of them are having many local minima and also finding how many neurons might be needed for a task is another issue which determines whether optimality of that NN is reached. Another thing to note is that even if the neural network solutions used tends to converge, this may not result in a unique solution. Now let us look at another example where we plot the data and try to classify it and we see that there are many hyper planes which can classify it. But which one is better?

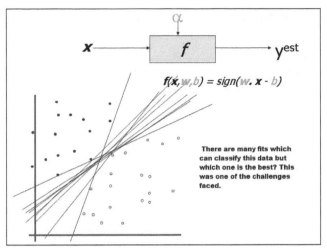

Figure: Here we see that there are many hyper planes which can be fit in to classify the data but which one is the best is the right or correct solution. The need for SVM arises. Note the legend is not described as they are sample plotting to make understand the concepts involved.

From above illustration, there are many linear classifiers (hyper planes) that separate the data. However, only one of these achieves maximum separation. The reason we need it is because if we use a hyper plane to classify, it might end up closer to one set of datasets compared to others and we do not want this to happen and thus we see that the concept of maximum margin classifier or hyper plane as an apparent solution. The next illustration gives the maximum margin classifier example which provides a solution to the above mentioned problem.

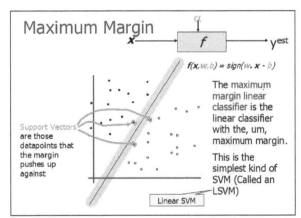

Figure: Illustration of Linear SVM. Note the legend is not described as they are sample plotting to make understand the concepts involved.

Expression for Maximum margin is given as:

$$\text{margin} = \arg\min_{x \in D} d(x) = \arg\min_{x \in D} \frac{|x \cdot w + b|}{\sqrt{\sum_{i=1}^{d} w_i^2}}$$

The above illustration is the maximum linear classifier with the maximum range. In this context it is an example of a simple linear SVM classifier. Another interesting question is why maximum margin? There are some good explanations which include better empirical performance. Another reason is that even if we've made a small error in the location of the boundary this gives us least chance of causing a misclassification. The other advantage would be avoiding local minima and better classification. Now we try to express the SVM mathematically and for this tutorial we try to present a linear SVM. The goals of SVM are separating the data with hyper plane and extend this to non-linear boundaries using kernel trick. For calculating the SVM we see that the goal is to correctly classify all the data. For mathematical calculations we have:

[a] If $Y_i = +1$.

[b] If $Y_i = -1$; $wx_i + b \leq 1$.

[c] For all i; $y_i(w_i + b) \geq 1$.

In this equation x is a vector point and w is weight and is also a vector. So to separate the data [a] should always be greater than zero. Among all possible hyper planes, SVM selects the one where the distance of hyper plane is as large as possible. If the training data is good and every test vector is located in radius r from training vector. Now if the chosen hyper plane is located at the farthest possible from the data. This desired hyper plane which maximizes the margin also bisects the lines between closest points on convex hull of the two datasets. Thus we have [a], [b] & [c].

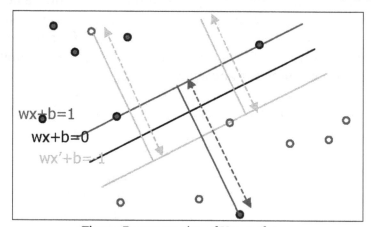

Figure: Representation of Hyper planes.

Distance of closest point on hyper plane to origin can be found by maximizing the x as x is on the hyper plane. Similarly for the other side points we have a similar scenario. Thus solving and subtracting the two distances we get the summed distance from the separating hyper plane to nearest points. Maximum Margin $= M = 2/\|W\|$.

Now maximizing the margin is same as minimum. Now we have a quadratic optimization problem and we need to solve for w and b. To solve this we need to optimize the quadratic function with linear constraints. The solution involves constructing a dual problem and where a Langlier's multiplier α_i is associated. We need to find w and b such that $\Phi(w) = \frac{1}{2}|w'||w|$ is minimized;

And for all $\{(x_i, y_i)\}$: $y_i(w * x_i + b) \geq 1$.

Now solving: we get that $w = \Sigma\alpha_i * x_i$; $b = y_k - w * x_k$ for any x_k such that $\alpha k \neq 0$

Now the classifying function will have the following form: $f(x) = \Sigma\alpha_i y_i x_i * x + b$

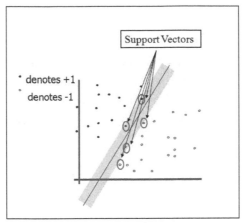

Figure: Representation of Support Vectors.

SVM Representation

In this we present the QP formulation for SVM classification. This is a simple representation only.
SV classification:

$$\min_{f,\xi_i} \|f\|_k^2 + C\sum_{i=1}^{l}\xi_i \quad y_if(x_i) \geq 1-\xi_i, \text{for all } i\, \xi_i \geq 0$$

SVM classification, Dual formulation:

$$\min\sum_{i=1}^{l}\alpha_i - \frac{1}{2}\sum_{i=1}^{l}\sum_{j=1}^{l}\alpha_i\alpha_j y_i y_j K(x_i,x_j) \quad 0 \leq \alpha_i \leq C, \text{for all } i; \quad \sum_{i=1}^{l}\alpha_i y_i = 0$$

Variables ξ_i are called slack variables and they measure the error made at point (x_i,y_i). Training SVM becomes quite challenging when the number of training points is large. A number of methods for fast SVM training have been proposed.

Soft Margin Classifier

In real world problem it is not likely to get an exactly separate line dividing the data within the space. And we might have a curved decision boundary. We might have a hyper plane which might exactly separate the data but this may not be desirable if the data has noise in it. It is better for the smooth boundary to ignore few data points than be curved or go in loops, around the outliers. This is handled in a different way; here we hear the term slack variables being introduced. Now we have,. $y_i(w'x + b) \geq 1-S_k$. This allows a point to be a small distance S_k on the wrong side of the hyper plane without violating the constraint. Now we might end up having huge slack variables which allow any line to separate the data, thus in such scenarios we have the Lagrangian variable introduced which penalizes the large slacks.

$$\min L = \tfrac{1}{2}w'w - \sum\lambda_k\left(y_k(w'x_k+b)+s_k-1\right)+\alpha\sum s_k$$

Where reducing α allows more data to lie on the wrong side of hyper plane and would be treated as outliers which give smoother decision boundary.

Kernal Trick

Let's first look at few definitions as what is a kernel and what does feature space mean? Kernel: If data is linear, a separating hyper plane may be used to divide the data. However it is often the case that the data is far from linear and the datasets are inseparable. To allow for this kernels are used to non-linearly map the input data to a high-dimensional space. The new mapping is then linearly separable. A very simple illustration of this is shown below in figure.

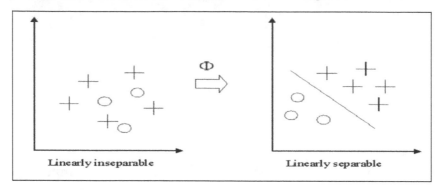

This mapping is defined by the Kernel:

$$K(x,y) = \Phi(x) \cdot \Phi(y)$$

Feature Space: Transforming the data into feature space makes it possible to define a similarity measure on the basis of the dot product. If the feature space is chosen suitably, pattern recognition can be easy.

$$\langle x_1 \cdot x_2 \rangle \leftarrow K(x_1, x_2) = \langle \Phi(x_1) \cdot \Phi(x_2) \rangle$$

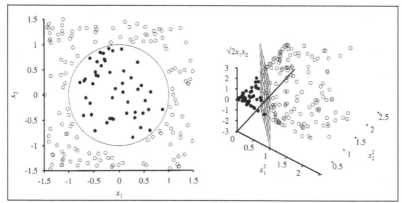

Figure: Feature Space Representation. Note the legend is not described as they are sample plotting to make understand the concepts involved.

Now getting back to the kernel trick, we see that when w,b is obtained the problem is solved for a simple linear scenario in which data is separated by a hyper plane. The Kernal trick allows SVM's to form nonlinear boundaries. Steps involved in kernel trick are given below:

- The algorithm is expressed using only the inner products of data sets. This is also called as dual problem.

- Original data are passed through nonlinear maps to form new data with respect to new dimensions by adding a pair wise product of some of the original data dimension to each data vector.

- Rather than an inner product on these new, larger vectors, and store in tables and later do a table lookup, we can represent a dot product of the data after doing nonlinear mapping on them. This function is the kernel function.

Kernal Trick: Dual Problem

First we convert the problem with optimization to the dual form in which we try to eliminate w, and a Lagrangian now is only a function of λ_i. There is a mathematical solution for it but this can be avoided here as this tutorial has instructions to minimize the mathematical equations, I would describe it instead. To solve the problem we should maximize the LD with respect to λ_i. The dual form simplifies the optimization and we see that the major achievement is the dot product obtained from this.

Inner Product summarization Here we see that we need to represent the dot product of the data vectors used. The dot product of nonlinearly mapped data can be expensive. The kernel trick just picks a suitable function that corresponds to dot product of some nonlinear mapping instead. Some of the most commonly chosen kernel functions are given below in later part of this tutorial. A particular kernel is only chosen by trial and error on the test set, choosing the right kernel based on the problem or application would enhance SVM's performance.

Kernel Functions

The idea of the kernel function is to enable operations to be performed in the input space rather than the potentially high dimensional feature space. Hence the inner product does not need to be evaluated in the feature space. We want the function to perform mapping of the attributes of the input space to the feature space. The kernel function plays a critical role in SVM and its performance. It is based upon reproducing Kernel Hilbert Spaces.

$$K\left(x_1,x'\right)=\left\langle \Phi\left(x\right)\cdot\Phi\left(x'\right)\right\rangle$$

If K is a symmetric positive definite function, which satisfies Mercer's Conditions,

$$K\left(x,x'\right)=\sum_{m}^{\infty}a_m\phi_m\left(x\right)\phi_m\left(x'\right),\quad a_m\geq 0,$$

$$\iint K\left(x,x'\right)g\left(x\right)g\left(x'\right)dxdx'>0,\quad g\in L_2$$

Then the kernel represents a legitimate inner product in feature space. The training set is not linearly separable in an input space. The training set is linearly separable in the feature space. This is called the "Kernel trick".

The different kernel functions are listed below:

1. Polynomial: A polynomial mapping is a popular method for non-linear modeling. The second kernel is usually preferable as it avoids problems with the hessian becoming Zero.

$$K(x,x') = \langle x,x' \rangle^d .$$

$$K(x,x') = (\langle x,x'+1 \rangle)^d .$$

2. Gaussian Radial Basis Function: Radial basis functions most commonly with a Gaussian form:

$$K(x,x') = \exp\left(-\frac{\|x-x'\|^2}{2\sigma^2} \right)$$

3. Exponential Radial Basis Function: A radial basis function produces a piecewise linear solution which can be attractive when discontinuities are acceptable.

$$K(x,x') = \exp\left(-\frac{\|x-x'\|}{2\sigma^2} \right)$$

4. Multi-Layer Perceptron: The long established MLP, with a single hidden layer, also has a valid kernel representation.

$$K(x,x') = \tanh(\rho(x,x') + \varrho)$$

There are many more including Fourier, splines, B-splines, additive kernels and tensor products.

Controlling Complexity in SVM: Trade-offs

SVM is powerful to approximate any training data and generalizes better on given datasets. The complexity in terms of kernel affects the performance on new datasets. SVM supports parameters for controlling the complexity and above all SVM does not tell us how to set these parameters and we should be able to determine these Parameters by Cross-Validation on the given datasets. The diagram given below gives a better illustration.

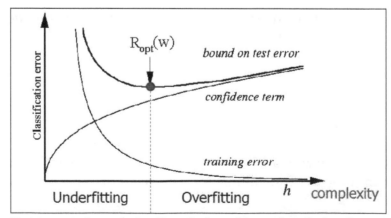

Figure: How to control complexity. Note the legend is not described as they are sample plotting to make understand the concepts involved.

SVM for Classification

SVM is a useful technique for data classification. Even though it's considered that Neural Networks are easier to use than this, however, sometimes unsatisfactory results are obtained. A classification task usually involves with training and testing data which consist of some data instances. Each instance in the training set contains one target values and several attributes. The goal of SVM is to produce a model which predicts target value of data instances in the testing set which are given only the attributes.

Classification in SVM is an example of Supervised Learning. Known labels help indicate whether the system is performing in a right way or not. This information points to a desired response, validating the accuracy of the system, or be used to help the system learn to act correctly. A step in SVM classification involves identification as which are intimately connected to the known classes. This is called feature selection or feature extraction. Feature selection and SVM classification together have a use even when prediction of unknown samples is not necessary. They can be used to identify key sets which are involved in whatever processes distinguish the classes.

SVM for Regression

SVMs can also be applied to regression problems by the introduction of an alternative loss function. The loss function must be modified to include a distance measure. The regression can be linear and nonlinear. Linear models mainly consist of the following loss functions, e-intensive loss functions, quadratic and Huber loss function. Similarly to classification problems, a non-linear model is usually required to adequately model data. In the same manner as the non-linear SVC approach, a non-linear mapping can be used to map the data into a high dimensional feature space where linear regression is performed. The kernel approach is again employed to address the curse of dimensionality. In the regression method there are considerations based on prior knowledge of the problem and the distribution of the noise. In the absence of such information Huber's robust loss function, has been shown to be a good alternative.

Applications of SVM

SVM has been found to be successful when used for pattern classification problems. Applying the Support Vector approach to a particular practical problem involves resolving a number of questions based on the problem definition and the design involved with it. One of the major challenges is that of choosing an appropriate kernel for the given application. There are standard choices such as a Gaussian or polynomial kernel that are the default options, but if these prove ineffective or if the inputs are discrete structures more elaborate kernels will be needed. By implicitly defining a feature space, the kernel provides the description language used by the machine for viewing the data. Once the choice of kernel and optimization criterion has been made the key components of the system are in place. Let's look at some examples.

The task of text categorization is the classification of natural text documents into a fixed number of predefined categories based on their content. Since a document can be assigned to more than one category this is not a multi-class classification problem, but can be viewed as a series of binary classification problems, one for each category. One of the standard representations of text for the purposes of information retrieval provides an ideal feature mapping for constructing a Mercer kernel. Indeed, the kernels somehow incorporate a similarity measure between instances, and it is reasonable to assume that experts working in the specific application domain have already identified valid similarity measures, particularly in areas such as information retrieval and generative models.

Traditional classification approaches perform poorly when working directly because of the high dimensionality of the data, but Support Vector Machines can avoid the pitfalls of very high dimensional representations. A very similar approach to the techniques described for text categorization can also be used for the task of image classification, and as in that case linear hard margin machines are frequently able to generalize well. The first real-world task on which Support Vector Machines were tested was the problem of hand-written character recognition. Furthermore, multi-class SVMs have been tested on these data. It is interesting not only to compare SVMs with other classifiers, but also to compare different SVMs amongst themselves. They turn out to have approximately the same performance, and furthermore to share most of their support vectors, independently of the chosen kernel. The fact that SVM can perform as well as these systems without including any detailed prior knowledge is certainly remarkable.

Strength and Weakness of SVM

The major strengths of SVM are the training is relatively easy. No local optimal, unlike in neural networks. It scales relatively well to high dimensional data and the trade-off between classifier complexity and error can be controlled explicitly. The weakness includes the need for a good kernel function.

Principle Component Analysis

PCA is a linear transformation method. PCA yields the directions (principal components) that maximize the variance of the data. In other words, PCA projects the entire dataset onto a different feature (sub) space. Often, the desired goal is to reduce the dimensions of a d-dimensional dataset by projecting it onto a (k<d) in order to increase the computational efficiency while retaining most of the information.

PCA Approach

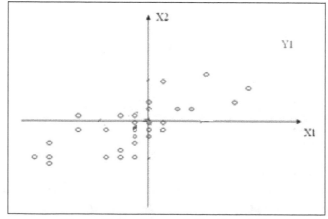

Figure: Data with 2 variables X_1 and X_2.

- Given N data vectors from k-dimensions, find c <= k orthogonal vectors that can be best used to represent data.

- The original data set is reduced to one consisting of N data vectors on c principal components (reduced dimensions).

- Each data vector is a linear combination of the c principal component vectors.

- Works for numeric data only V. Used when the number of dimensions is large.

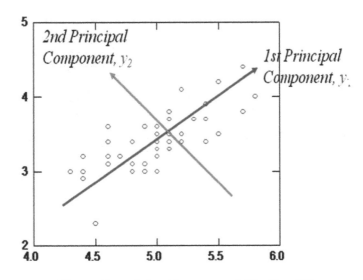

Figure: Same data with 2 new variables Y_1 and Y_2.

From k original variables: $x_1, x_2, ..., x_k,$ (as shown in figure above produce k new variables: $y_1, y_2, ..., y_k$:

$$y_1 = a_{11}x_1 + a_{12}x_2 + ... + a_{1k}x_k$$

$$y_2 = a_{21}x_1 + a_{22}x_2 + ... + a_{2k}x_k$$

$$y_k = a_{k1}x_1 + a_{k2}x_2 + ... + a_{kk}x_k$$

such that:

y_k 's are uncorrelated (orthogonal) Principal Components.

y_1 Explains as much as possible of original variance in data set.

y_2 Explains as much as possible of remaining variance etc.

and

$\{a_{11}, a_{12}, ..., a_{1k}\}$ is 1st Eigenvector of correlation/covariance matrix, and coefficients of first principal component.

$\{a_{21}, a_{22}, ..., a_{2k}\}$ is 2nd Eigenvector of correlation/covariance matrix, and coefficients of 2nd principal component.

$\{a_{k1}, a_{k2}, ..., a_{kk}\}$ is k^{th} Eigenvector of correlation/covariance matrix, and coefficients of kth principal component.

In summary, PCA rotates multivariate dataset into a new configuration which is easier to interpret for two major reasons:

- Simplify data.

- Look at relationships between variables.

- Look at patterns of units.

Fundamentals

To get to PCA, we're going to quickly define some basic statistical ideas – mean, standard deviation, variance and covariance – so we can weave them together later. Their equations are closely related. Mean is simply the average value of all x's in the set X, which is found by dividing the sum of all data points by the number of data points, n.

$$\bar{} \quad \frac{\sum_{i} 1}{}$$

Variance (s^2) is the measure of the data's spread.

$$s^2 = \frac{\sum_{i=1}^{n} (X_i - X)^2}{(n-1)}$$

Standard deviation is simply the square root of the average square distance of data points to the mean. In the equation below, the numerator contains the sum of the differences between each data point and the mean, and the denominator is simply the number of data points (minus one), producing the average distance.

$$s = \sqrt{\frac{\sum_{1}^{n} (Xi - \bar{X})^2}{(n-1)}}$$

Variance is the spread, or the amount of difference that data expresses.

Covariance (cov(X, Y)) is the joint variability between two random variables X and Y, and covariance is always measured between 2 or more dimensions. If you calculate the covariance between one dimension and itself, you get the variance.

$$cov(X, Y) = \frac{\sum_{i=1}^{n} (X_i - \bar{X})(Y_i - \bar{Y})}{(n-1)}$$

For both variance and standard deviation, squaring the differences between data points and the mean makes them positive, so that values above and below the mean don't cancel each other out.

Input to various regression techniques can be in the form of correlation or covariance matrix. Covariance Matrix is a matrix whose element in the i, j position is the covariance between the ith and j^{th} elements of a random vector. A random vector is a random variable with multiple dimensions.

Correlation Matrix is a table showing correlation coefficients between sets of variables.

Covariance Matrix vs. Correlation Matrix

Covariance Matrix	Correlation Matrix
• Variables must be in same units • Emphasizes variables with most variance • Mean eigenvalue ≠1.0	• Variables are standardized (mean 0.0, SD 1.0) • Variables can be in different units • All variables have same impact on analysis • Mean eigenvalue = 1.0

Some Important Theorems

First let's look at some theorems:

Theorem: The inverse of an orthogonal matrix is its transpose, why?

Let A be an m*n orthogonal matrix where a_i is the ith column vector. The Ij^{th} element of $A^T A$ is:

$$\left(A^T A\right)_{ij} = a_i^T a_j =$$
$$\begin{cases} 1 \text{ if } i = j \\ 0 \text{ otherwise} \end{cases}$$

Therefore, because $A^T A = I$, it follows that $A^{-1} = A^T$.

Theorem: Let A be a real symmetric matrix and $\lambda_1, \lambda_2, \ldots, \lambda_k$ be distinct Eigen values of A.

Let $u_i \in R^n$ be nonzero such that, $1 \leq i \leq k$.

Then, $\{u_1, u_2, \ldots, u_k\}$ forms an orthogonal set.

Proof:

For $i \neq j$, $1 \leq i, j \leq k$, since $A^T = A$, we have:

$$\lambda_i\left(u_i, u_j\right) = \left\langle \lambda_i u_i, u_j \right\rangle$$

$$= \left\langle Au_i, u_j \right\rangle = \left\langle u_i, A^T u_j \right\rangle = \left\langle u_i, Au_j \right\rangle$$

$$= \lambda_j \left\langle u_i, u_j \right\rangle$$

Since, $i \neq j$ we have $\lambda_i \neq \lambda_j$ and hence $\left\langle u_i, u_j \right\rangle = 0$

Theorem: Let A be n*n real symmetric matrix such that all its Eigen values are distinct. Then, there exists an orthogonal matrix P such that, $P^{-1}AP=D$, where D is a diagonal matrix with diagonal entries being the Eigen values of A.

Proof: Let A has Eigen values $\lambda_1, \lambda_2, \ldots, \lambda_n$ with $u_i \in R^n$ such that $|u_i| = 1$ and $Au_i = \lambda_i u_i, 1 \le i \le n$.

By corollary, the matrix

$P = [u_1, u_2, \ldots u_n]$ is invertible and $P^{-1}AP = D$, is diagonal with diagnosis entries.

Further by previous theorem $(u_1, u_1, \ldots, u_n)$ is an orthogonal set. Hence P is in fact an orthogonal matrix.

Having these theorems, we can say that, A symmetric matrix is diagonalized by a matrix of its orthonormal eigenvectors. Orthonormal vectors are just normalized orthogonal vectors.

PCA Steps

- Consider a Data.

- Subtract the mean - from each of the data dimensions.

- Calculate the covariance matrix.

- Calculate the eigenvalues and eigenvectors of the covariance matrix.

- Reduce dimensionality and form feature vector:

  ○ Order the eigenvectors by eigenvalues, highest to lowest. This gives you the components in order of significance and ignores the components of lesser significance

  ○ Feature Vector = $(eig_1\ eig_2\ eig_3 \ldots eig_n)$.

- Deriving the new data:

  Final Data = Row Feature Vector × Row Zero Mean Data

  ○ Row Feature Vector is the matrix with the eigenvectors in the rows, with the most significant eigenvector at the top.

  ○ Row Zero Mean Data is the mean-adjusted data transposed, i.e. the data items are in each column, with each row holding a separate dimension.

PCA Steps Explained with Examples

Step 1: Get some data.

Consider a data with just 2 dimensions, and its 2D plots of the data to show what the PCA analysis is doing at each step. The data used is found in Figure below, along with a plot of that data in figure.

Step 2: Subtract the mean.

For PCA to work properly, you have to subtract the mean from each of the data dimensions. The mean subtracted is the average across each dimension. So, all the x values have x̄ (the mean of the < values of all the data points) subtracted, and all the y values have ȳ subtracted from them. This produces a data set whose mean is zero as shown in figure below:

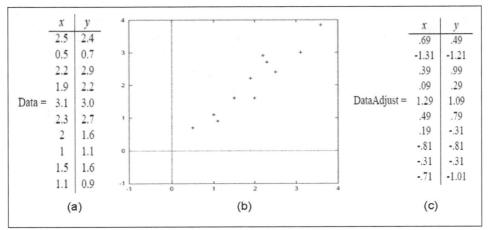

Figure: PCA Steps 1 and 2.

Step 3: Calculate the covariance matrix.

Since the data is 2 dimensional, the covariance matrix will be 2 × 2 as given below:

$$\text{cov} = \begin{pmatrix} .616555556 & .615444444 \\ .615444444 & .716555556 \end{pmatrix}$$

So, since the non-diagonal elements in this covariance matrix are positive, we should expect that both the x and y variable increase together.

Step 4: Calculate the eigenvectors and eigenvalues of the covariance matrix.

Since the covariance matrix is square, we can calculate the eigenvectors and eigenvalues for this matrix. These are rather important, as they tell us useful information about our data. The eigenvectors and eigenvalues are given below:

$$\text{eigen values} = \begin{pmatrix} .0490833989 \\ 1.28402771 \end{pmatrix}$$

$$\text{eigen vectors} = \begin{pmatrix} -.735178656 & -.677873399 \\ .677873399 & -.735178656 \end{pmatrix}$$

It is important to notice that these eigenvectors are both unit eigenvectors ie. their lengths are both 1. So, by this process of taking the eigenvectors of the covariance matrix, we have been able to extract lines that characterize the data. The rest of the steps involve transforming the data so that it is expressed in terms of them lines.

Step 5: Choosing components and forming a feature vector.

Here is where the notion of data compression and reduced dimensionality comes into it. If you look at the eigenvectors and eigenvalues from the previous step, you will notice that the eigenvalues are quite different values. In fact, it turns out that the eigenvector with the highest eigenvalue is the principle component of the data set.

In our example, the eigenvector with the larges eigenvalue was the one that pointed down the middle of the data. It is the most significant relationship between the data dimensions. Once eigenvectors are found from the covariance matrix, the next step is to order them by eigenvalue, highest to lowest. This gives you the components in order of significance. To be precise, if you originally have n dimensions in your data, and so you calculate n eigenvectors and eigenvalues, and then you choose only the first p eigenvectors, then the final data set has only p dimensions. What needs to be done now is you need to form a feature vector:

$$\text{feature vector} = \left(\text{eig}_1, \text{eig}_2, \text{eig}_3, \ldots \text{eig}_n\right)$$

Given our example set of data, and the fact that we have 2 eigenvectors, we have two choices. We can either form a feature vector with both of the eigenvectors or we can choose to leave out the smaller, less significant component and only have a single column:

$$\begin{pmatrix} -.677873399 & -.735178656 \\ -.735178656 & -.677873399 \end{pmatrix} \text{ OR } \begin{pmatrix} -.677873399 \\ -.735178656 \end{pmatrix}$$

Step 6: Deriving the new data set.

This is the final step in PCA, and is also the easiest. Once we have chosen the components (eigenvectors) that we wish to keep in our data and formed a feature vector, we simply take the transpose of the vector and multiply it on the left of the original data set, transposed.

Final Data= Row Feature Vector × Row Data Adjust

Where Row Feature Vector is the matrix with the eigenvectors in the columns transposed so that the eigenvectors are now in the rows, with the most significant eigenvector at the top, and Row Data Adjust is the mean-adjusted data transposed, i.e. the data items are in each column, with each row holding a separate dimension. Final Data is the final data set, with data items in columns, and dimensions along rows.

Our original data set had two axes, x and y, so our data was in terms of them. It is possible to express data in terms of any two axes that you like. If these axes are perpendicular, then the expression is the most efficient. This was why it was important that eigenvectors are always perpendicular to each other. We have changed our data from being in terms of the axes x and y, and now they are in terms of our 2 eigenvectors.

In the case of keeping both eigenvectors for the transformation, we get the data and the plot found in figure. This plot is basically the original data, rotated so that the eigenvectors are the axes. This is understandable since we have lost no information in this decomposition.

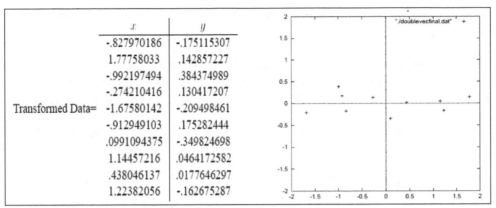

	x	y
	-.827970186	-.175115307
	1.77758033	.142857227
	-.992197494	.384374989
	-.274210416	.130417207
Transformed Data=	-1.67580142	-.209498461
	-.912949103	.175282444
	.0991094375	-.349824698
	1.14457216	.0464172582
	.438046137	.0177646297
	1.22382056	-.162675287

Figure: Transformed Data and New Plot.

Basically we have transformed our data so that is expressed in terms of the patterns between them, where the patterns are the lines that most closely describe the relationships between the data. This is helpful because we have now classified our data point as a combination of the contributions from each of those lines.

Interpretation of PCs

Consider Places Rated Almanac data which rates 329 communities according to nine criteria:

- Climate and Terrain (C1).

- Housing (C2).

- Health Care & Environment (C3).

- Crime (C4).

- Transportation (C5).

- Education (C6).

- The Arts (C7).

- Recreation (C8).

- Economics (C9).

Step 1: Examine the eigenvalues to determine how many principal components should be considered:

- If you take all of these eigenvalues and add them up and you get the total variance of 0.5223.

- The proportion of variation explained by each eigenvalue is given in the third column. For example, 0.3775 divided by the 0.5223 equals 0.7227, or, about 72% of the variation is explained by this first eigenvalue.

- The cumulative percentage explained is obtained by adding the successive proportions of variation explained to obtain the running total. For instance, 0.7227 plus 0.0977 equals

0.8204, and so forth. Therefore, about 82% of the variation is explained by the first two eigenvalues together.

- Next we need to look at successive differences between the eigenvalues. Subtracting the second eigenvalue 0.051 from the first eigenvalue, 0.377 we get a difference of 0.326. The difference between the second and third eigenvalues is 0.0232; the next difference is 0.0049.

- A sharp drop from one eigenvalue to the next may serve as another indicator of how many eigenvalues to consider.

- The first three principal components explain 87% of the variation. This is an acceptably large percentage.

Table: Eigenvalues and the proportion of variation explained by the principal components.

Component	Eigenvalue	Proportion	Cumulative
1	0.3775	0.7227	0.7227
2	0.0511	0.0977	0.8204
3	0.0279	0.0535	0.8739
4	0.0230	0.0440	0.9178
5	0.0168	0.0321	0.9500
6	0.0120	0.0229	0.9728
7	0.0085	0.0162	0.9890
8	0.0039	0.0075	0.9966
9	0.0018	0.0034	1.0000
Total	0.5225		

Step 2: Next, compute the principal component scores:

- For example, the first principal component can be computed using the elements of the first eigenvector:

$$Y_1 = 0.0351 \times (c\lim ate) + 0.0933 \times (hou\sin g) + 0.4078 \times (health)$$
$$+ 0.1004 \times (crime) + 0.1501 \times (transportation) + 0.0321 \times (education)$$
$$+ 0.08743 \times (arts) + 0.1590 \times (recreation) + 0.0195 \times (economy)$$

Step 3: To interpret each component, compute the correlations between the original data for each variable and each principal component.

First Principal Component Analysis - PCA1

The first principal component is a measure of the quality of Health and the Arts, and to some extent Housing, Transportation and Recreation. Health increases with increasing values in the Arts. If any of these variables goes up, so do the remaining ones. They are all positively related as they all have positive signs.

Second Principal Component Analysis - PCA2

The second principal component is a measure of the severity of crime, the quality of the economy, and the lack of quality in education. Crime and Economy increase with decreasing Education. Here we can see that cities with high levels of crime and good economies also tend to have poor educational systems.

Variable	Principal component		
	1	2	3
Climate	0.190	0.017	0.207
Housing	0.544	0.020	0.204
Health	0.782	-0.605	0.144
Crime	0.365	0.294	0.585
Transportation	0.585	0.085	0.234
Education	0.394	-0.273	0.027
Arts	0.985	0.126	-0.111
Recreation	0.520	0.402	0.519
Economy	0.142	0.150	0.239

Third Principal Component Analysis - PCA3

The third principal component is a measure of the quality of the climate and poorness of the economy. Climate increases with decreasing Economy. The inclusion of economy within this component will add a bit of redundancy within our results. This component is primarily a measure of climate, and to a lesser extent the economy.

Example of PCA on Fossil Teeth Data

PCA has been applied and found useful in very many disciplines. The first examines a dataset consisting of nine measurements on 88 fossil teeth from the early mammalian insectivore Kuehneotherium, while the second is from atmospheric science.

Kuehneotherium is one of the earliest mammals and remains have been found during quarrying of limestone in South Wales, UK. The bones and teeth were washed into fissures in the rock, about 200 million years ago, and all the lower molar teeth used in this analysis are from a single fissure. However, it looked possible that there were teeth from more than one species of Kuehneotherium in the sample.

Of the nine variables, three measure aspects of the length of a tooth, while the other six are measurements related to height and width. A PCA was performed using the prcomp command of the R statistical software. The first two PCs account for 78.8% and 16.7%, respectively, of the total variation in the dataset, so the two-dimensional scatter-plot of the 88 teeth given by figure below is a very good approximation to the original scatter-plot in nine-dimensional space. It is, by definition, the best variance-preserving two-dimensional plot of the data, representing over 95% of total variation. All of the loadings in the first PC have the same sign, so it is a weighted average of all variables, representing 'overall size'. In figure below, large teeth are on the left and small teeth on the right. The second PC has negative loadings for the three length variables and positive loadings for the other six variables, representing an aspect of the 'shape' of teeth. Fossils near the top of figure below have smaller lengths, relative to their heights and widths, than those towards the bottom. The relatively compact cluster of points in the bottom half of figure below is thought to correspond to a species of Kuehneotherium, while the broader group at the top cannot be assigned to Kuehneotherium, but to some related, but as yet unidentified, animal.

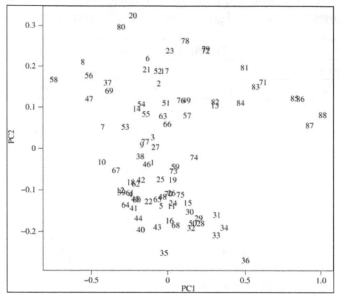

Figure: The two-dimensional principal subspace for the fossil teeth data. The coordinates in either or both PCs may switch signs when different software is used.

Some Key Issues

Covariance and Correlation Matrix Principal Component Analysis

So far, PCs have been presented as linear combinations of the (centered) original variables. However, the properties of PCA have some undesirable features when these variables have different units of measurement. While there is nothing inherently wrong, from a strictly mathematical point of view, with linear combinations of variables with different units of measurement (their use is widespread in, for instance, linear regression), the fact that PCA is defined by a criterion (variance) that depends on units of measurement implies that PCs based on the covariance matrix S will change if the units of measurement on one or more of the variables change (unless all$p$ variables undergo a common change of scale, in which case the new covariance matrix is merely a scalar multiple of the old one, hence with the same eigenvectors and the same proportion of total variance explained by each PC). To overcome this undesirable feature, it is common practice to begin by standardizing the variables. Each data value x_{ij} is both centered and divided by the standard deviation s_j of the n observations of variable j,

$$z_{ij} = \frac{x_{ij} - \overline{x}_j}{s_j}$$

Thus, the initial data matrix X is replaced with the standardized data matrix Z, whose jth column is vector z_j with the n standardized observations of variable j ($z_{ij} = \frac{x_{ij} - \overline{x}_j}{s_j}$). Standardization is useful because most changes of scale are linear transformations of the data, which share the same set of standardized data values.

Since the covariance matrix of a standardized dataset is merely the correlation matrix R of the original dataset, a PCA on the standardized data is also known as a correlation matrix PCA. The eigenvectors a_k of the correlation matrix R define the uncorrelated maximum-variance linear combinations $Z_{ak} = \sum_{j=1}^{p} a_{jk} z_j$ of the standardized variables $z_1,...,z_p$. Such correlation matrix PCs are not the same as, nor are they directly related to, the covariance matrix PCs defined previously. Also, the percentage variance accounted for by each PC will differ and, quite frequently, more correlation matrix PCs than covariance matrix PCs is needed to account for the same percentage of total variance. The trace of a correlation matrix R is merely the number p of variables used in the analysis, hence the proportion of total variance accounted for by any correlation matrix PC is just the variance of that PC divided by p. The SVD approach is also valid in this context. Since $(n-1)$ R=Z'Z, an SVD of the standardized data matrix Z amounts to a correlation matrix PCA of the dataset.

Correlation matrix PCs are invariant to linear changes in units of measurement and are therefore the appropriate choice for datasets where different changes of scale are conceivable for each variable. Some statistical software assumes by default that a PCA means a correlation matrix PCA and, in some cases, the normalization used for the vectors of loadings $\mathbf{a}_k$ of correlation matrix PCs is not the standard $a'_k a_k = 1$. In a correlation matrix PCA, the coefficient of correlation between the jth variable and the kth PC is given by:

$$r_{varj}, PC_k = \sqrt{\lambda_k a_{jk}}.$$

Thus, if the normalization $\bar{a}_k' \bar{a}_k = \lambda_k$ is used instead of $a'_k a = 1$, the coefficients of the new loading vectors $\bar{a}_k$ are the correlations between each original variable and the kth PC.

All nine measurements are in the same units, so a covariance matrix PCA makes sense. A correlation matrix PCA produces similar results, since the variances of the original variable do not differ very much. The first two correlation matrix PCs account for 93.7% of total variance. For other datasets, differences can be more substantial.

Biplots

One of the most informative graphical representations of a multivariate dataset is via a biplot, which is fundamentally connected to the SVD of a relevant data matrix, and therefore to PCA. A rank q approximation X^*_q of the full column-centered data matrix X^*, defined by ($Y_q = U_q L_q A'_q$), is written as $X^*_q = GH'$, where $G = U_q$ and $H = A_q L_q$ (although other options are possible. The n rows g_i of matrix G defines graphical markers for each individual, which are usually represented by points. The p rows h_j of matrix H define markers for each variable and are usually represented by vectors. The properties of the biplot are best discussed assuming that q=p, although the biplot is defined on a low-rank approximation (usually q=2), enabling a graphical representation of the markers. When q=p the biplot has the following properties:

- The cosine of the angle between any two vectors representing variables is the coefficient of correlation between those variables; this is a direct result of the fact that the matrix of inner products between those markers is $HH' = AL^2A' = (n-1)S$ ($(n-1)S = X^*'X^* = (ULA')'(ULA') = ALU'ULA' = AL^2A'$), so that inner products between vectors are proportional to covariances (variances for a common vector).

- Similarly, the cosine of the angle between any vector representing a variable and the axis representing a given PC is the coefficient of correlation between those two variables.

- The inner product between the markers for individual i and variable j gives the (centered) value of individual i on variable j. This is a direct result of the fact that GH′=X*. The practical implication of this result is that orthogonally projecting the point representing individual i onto the vector representing variable j recover the (centered) value x_{ij} $\bar{x}_j$.

- The Euclidean distance between the markers for individuals i and i′ is proportional to the Mahalanobis distance between them.

As stated above, these results are only exact if all q=p dimensions are used. For q<p, the results are merely approximate and the overall quality of such approximations can be measured by the percentage of variance explained by the q largest variance PCs, which were used to build the marker matrices G and H.

Figure below gives the biplot for the correlation matrix PCA of the fossil teeth data. The variable markers are displayed as arrows and the tooth markers as numbers. The group of three nearly horizontal and very tightly knit variable markers for two width variables and one height variable, WIDTH, HTMDT and TRIWIDTH, suggests a group of highly correlated variables, which are also strongly correlated with the first PC (represented by the horizontal axis). The very high proportion of variability explained by the two-dimensional principal subspace provides solid grounds for these conclusions. In fact, the smallest of the three true coefficients of correlation between these three variables is 0.944 (HTMDT and TRIWIDTH), and the smallest magnitude correlation between PC1 and any of these variables is 0.960 (TRIWIDTH). The sign difference in PC2 loadings between the three length variables (towards the bottom left of the plot) and the other variables is clearly visible. Projecting the marker for individual 58 onto the positive directions of all variable markers suggests that fossil tooth 58 (on the left of the biplot) is a large tooth. Inspection of the data matrix confirms that it is the largest individual on six of the nine variables, and close to largest on the remaining three. Likewise, individuals 85–88 (on the right) are small-sized teeth. Individuals whose markers are close to the origin have values close to the mean for all variables.

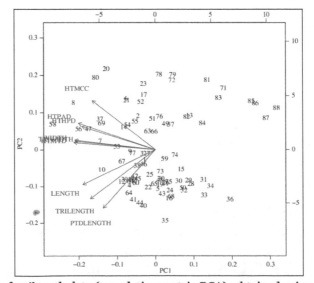

Figure: Biplot for the fossil teeth data (correlation matrix PCA), obtained using R's biplot command.

Centrings

PCA amounts to an SVD of a column-centered data matrix. In some applications, centring the columns of the data matrix may be considered inappropriate. In such situations, it may be preferred to avoid any pre-processing of the data and to subject the uncentred data matrix to an SVD or, equivalently, to carry out the Eigen decomposition of the matrix of non-centered second moments, T, whose eigenvectors define linear combinations of the uncentred variables. This is often referred to as an uncentred PCA and there has been an unfortunate tendency in some fields to equate the name SVD only with this uncentred version of PCA.

Uncentred PCs are linear combinations of the uncentred variables which successively maximize non-central second moments, subject to having their crossed non-central second moments equal to zero. Except when the vector of column means $\bar{x}$ (i.e. the center of gravity of the original n-point scatterplot in p-dimensional space) is near zero (in which case centered and uncentred moments are similar), it is not immediately intuitive that there should be similarities between both variants of PCA. Cadima & Jolliffe have explored the relations between the standard (column-centered) PCA and uncentred PCA and found them to be closer than might be expected, in particular when the size of vector $\bar{x}$ is large. It is often the case that there are great similarities between many eigenvectors and (absolute) eigenvalues of the covariance matrix S and the corresponding matrix of non-centered second moments, T.

In some applications, row centrings, or both row- and column-centring (known as double-centring) of the data matrix, have been considered appropriate. The SVDs of such matrices give rise to row-centered and doubly centered PCA, respectively.

Datasets where there are fewer observed entities than variables (n<p) are becoming increasingly frequent, thanks to the growing ease of observing variables, together with the high costs of repeating observations in some contexts (such as microarrays. For example in genomics in which n=59 and p=21.

In general, the rank of an n×p data matrix is $r \leq \min\{n,p\}$. If the data matrix has been column-centered, it is $r \leq \min\{n-1,p\}$. When n<p, it is the number of observed individuals, rather than the number of variables, that usually determines the matrix rank. The rank of the column-centered data matrix X* (or its standardized counterpart Z) must equal the rank of the covariance (or correlation) matrix. The practical implication of this is that there are only r non-zero eigenvalues; hence r PCs explains all the variability in the dataset. Nothing prevents the use of PCA in such contexts, although some software, as is the case with R's princomp (but not the prcomp) command, may balk at such datasets. PCs can be determined as usual, by either an SVD of the (centered) data matrix or the eigenvectors/values of the covariance (or correlation) matrix.

Fuzzy Logic

Set Theory

The classical set theory simply designates the branch of mathematics that studies sets. For example, 5, 10, 7, 6, 9 is a set of integers. 0, 1, 2, 3, 4, 5, 6, 7, 8, 9, 10 is the set of integers between 0 and 10. "s" 'd'; 'z', 'a' is a set of characters. "Site", "of", "zero" is a set of words. We can also create sets of functions, assumptions, definitions, sets of individuals (that is to say, a population), etc. and even sets of sets.

Note that in a set, the order does not matter: 7, 6, 9 denotes the same set as 9, 7, 6. However, to improve readability, it is convenient to classify the elements in ascending order, i.e. 6, 7, 9. Usually, a set is denoted by a capital letter: thus, we write A = 6, 7, 9. The empty set is denoted Ø: it is a remarkable since it contains no element. This seems unnecessary at first glance, but in fact, we will often use it. Sets are often represented in graphic form, typically by circles, as figure illustrates below.

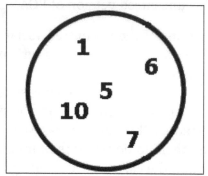

Figure: Graphical representation of the set.

The concept of belonging is important in set theory: it refers to the fact that an element is part of a set or not. For example, the integer 7 belongs to the set 6, 7, 9. In contrast, the integer 5 does not belong to the set 6, 7, and 9. Membership is symbolized by the character in the non-membership and by the same symbol, but barred possible. Thus, we have $7 \in \{6, 7, 9\}$ and $5 \notin \{6, 7, 9\}$.

A membership function (also called indicator function or characteristic function) is a function that explicit membership or not a set E. Let f be the characteristic function of the set E = {6, 7, 9}, and x is any integer:

TODO Math Formula

This concept of membership is very important for this course because fuzzy logic is based on the concept of fuzzy membership. This simply means that we can belong to a set to 0.8, in contrast to classical set theory where as we have just seen membership is either 0 (not owned) or 1 (part).

In order to manipulate classical ensembles and make something interesting, we define a set of operations, which are very intuitive.

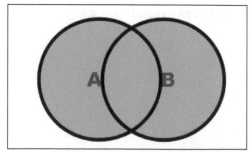

Figure: Union of two sets, denoted A ∪ B = {x ∈ Aextorx inB}. A ∪ B corresponds to the blue area.
For example if A = {6; 7; 9} et B = {1; 5; 6; 7; 10}, then A ∪ B = {1; 5; 6; 7; 9; 10}.

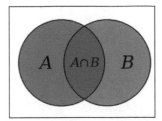

Figure: Intersection of two sets, denoted A ∩ B = {x ∈ Aetx ∈ B}. For example,
if A = {6; 7; 9} and B = {1; 5; 6; 7; 10}, then

A ∩ B = {6; 7}.

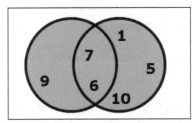

Figure: Here is the graphical representation of the sets A = {6, 7, 9} and B = {1, 5, 6, 7, 10}.
We see immediately that A ∪ B = {1, 5, 6, 7, 9, 10} and A B = {6, 7}.

But classical set theory is not the subject of this course, so we stop here. However, as fuzzy logic is based on the concept of fuzzy, we see now the kind of problems that we face: how to define such a union if memberships are not either 0 or 1?

Fuzzy Logic was initiated in 1965, by Dr. Lotfi A. Zadeh, professor for computer science at the University of California in Berkley. Basically, Fuzzy Logic is a multivalued logic that allows intermediate values to be defined between conventional evaluations like true/false, yes/no, high/low, etc. Fuzzy Logic starts with and builds on a set of user–supplied human language rules. Fuzzy Systems convert these rules to their mathematical equivalents.

Fuzzy Sets

Fuzzy logic is based on the theory of fuzzy sets, which is a generalization of the classical set theory. Saying that the theory of fuzzy sets is a generalization of the classical set theory means that the latter is a special case of fuzzy sets theory. To make a metaphor in set theory speaking, the classical set theory is a subset of the theory of fuzzy sets, as figure below illustrates.

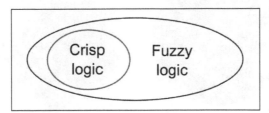

Figure: The classical set theory is a subset of the theory of fuzzy sets".

Fuzzy logic is based on fuzzy set theory, which is a generalization of the classical set theory. By abuse of language, following the habits of the literature, we will use the terms fuzzy sets instead of fuzzy subsets. The classical sets are also called clear sets, as opposed to vague, and by the same token classical logic is also known as Boolean logic or binary.

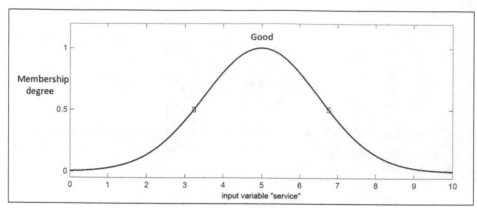

Figure: Membership function characterizing the subset of 'good' quality of service.

The figure above shows the membership function chosen to characterize the subset of 'good' quality of service.

Let X be a set. A fuzzy subset A of X is characterized by a membership function. $f^a : X \rightarrow [0, 1]$. (In theory, it is possible that the output is greater than 1, but in practice it is almost never used.) Note: This membership function is equivalent to the identity function of a classical set.

In our tip example, we will redefine membership functions for each fuzzy set of each of our three variables:

- Input 1: Quality of service. Subsets: poor, good and excellent.

- Input 2: Quality of food. Subsets: awful and delicious.

- Output: Tip amount. Subsets: low, medium and high.

The shape of the membership function is chosen arbitrarily by following the advice of the expert or by statistical studies: sigmoid, hyperbolic, tangent, exponential, Gaussian or any other form can be used. The figure below shows the difference between a conventional set and a fuzzy set corresponding to a delicious food and compares the two membership functions corresponding to the previous set.

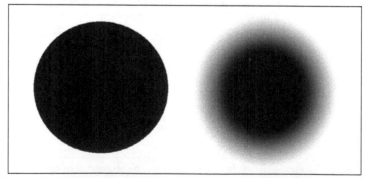

Figure: Graphical representation of a conventional set and a fuzzy set.

In order to define the characteristics of fuzzy sets, we are redefining and expanding the usual characteristics of classical sets. Fuzzy set have a number of properties. Here are definitions of the most important properties, but they are not necessary for understanding of the course.

Let X be a set and A a fuzzy subset of X and μ_A the membership function characterizing it. $\mu_A(x)$ is called the membership degree of x in A.

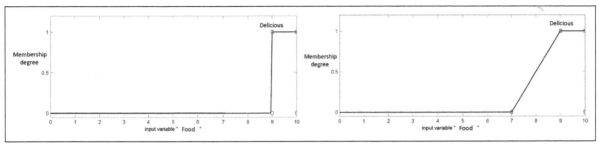

Figure: Comparison between an identity function of a conventional set and a membership function of fuzzy set.

The height of A, denoted h(A), corresponds to the upper bound of the codomain of its membership function: h(A) = sup{μA(x) | x ∈ X}.

A is said to be normalized if and only if h(A) = 1. In practice, it is extremely rare to work on non-normalized fuzzy sets.

The support of A is the set of elements of X belonging to at least some A (i.e. the membership degree of x is strictly positive). In other words, the support is the set $supp(A) = \{x \in X \,|\, \mu_A(x) > 0\}$.

The kernel of A is the set of elements of X belonging entirely to A. In other words, the kernel noy $(A) = \{x \in X \,|\, \mu_A(x) = 1\}$. By construction, noy(A) ⊆ supp(A).

A α-cut of A is the classical subset of elements with a membership degree greater than or equal toα: α-cut (A) = $\{x \in X \,|\, \mu_A(x) \geq \alpha\}$.

Another membership function for an average tip through which we have included the above properties is presented in Figure below.

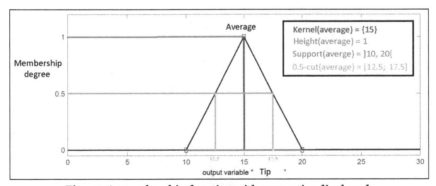

Figure: A membership function with properties displayed.

We can see that if A was a conventional set, we would simply have supp(A) = noy(A) and h(A) = 1 (ou h(A) = 0 si A = ∅). Our definitions can therefore recover the usual properties of classical sets.

The Linguistic Variables

The concept of membership function discussed above allows us to define fuzzy systems in natural language, as the membership function couple fuzzy logic with linguistic variables that we will define now.

Let V be a variable (quality of service, tip amount, etc.), X the range of values of the variable and TV a finite or infinite set of fuzzy sets. A linguistic variable corresponds to the triplet (V, X, T_v).

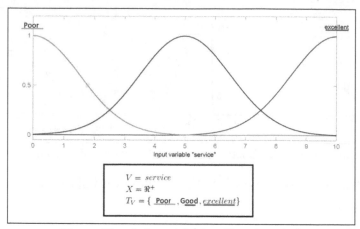

Figure: Linguistic variable 'quality of service'.

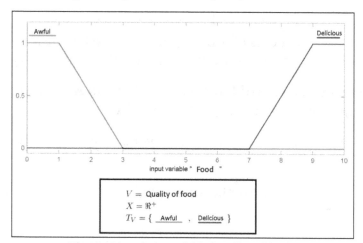

Figure: Linguistic variable 'quality of food'.

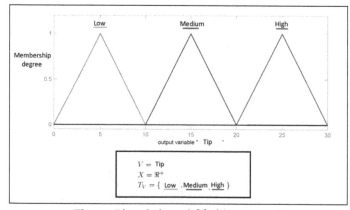

Figure: Linguistic variable 'tip amount'.

When we define the fuzzy sets of linguistic variables, the goal is not to exhaustively define the linguistic variables. Instead, we only define a few fuzzy subsets that will be useful later in definition of the rules that we apply it. This is for example the reason why we have not defined subset "average" for the quality of the food. Indeed, this subset will not be useful in our rules. Similarly, it is also the reason why (for example) 30 is a higher tip than 25, while 25 however belongs more to the fuzzy set "high" as 30: this is due to the fact that 30 is seen not as high but very high (or exorbitant if you want to change adjective). However, we have not created of fuzzy set "very high" because we do not need it in our rules.

The Fuzzy Operators

In order to easily manipulate fuzzy sets, we are redefining the operators of the classical set theory to fit the specific membership functions of fuzzy logic for values strictly between 0 and 1.

Unlike the definitions of the properties of fuzzy sets that are always the same, the definition of operators on fuzzy sets is chosen, like membership functions. Here are the two sets of operators for the complement (NOT), the intersection (AND) and union (OR) most commonly used:

Name	Intersection AND: $\mu_{A \cap B}(x)$	Union OU: $\mu_{A \cup B}(x)$	Complement NOT: $\mu_{\bar{A}}(x)$
Zadeh Operators MIN/MAX	$\min(\mu_A(x), \mu_B(x))$	$\max(\mu_A(x), \mu B(x))$	$1 - \mu_A(x)$
Probabilistic PROD/PRO-BOR	$\mu_A(x) \times \mu_B(x)$	$\mu_A(x) + \mu_B(x) - \mu_A(x) \times \mu_B(x)$	$1 - \mu_A(x)$

With the usual definitions of fuzzy operators, we always find the properties of commutativity, distributivity and associativity classics. However, there are two notable exceptions:

- In fuzzy logic, the law of excluded middle is contradicted: $A \cup A^- 6= X$, i.e. $\mu_{A \cap \bar{A}}(x) \neq 1$.

- In fuzzy logic, an element can belong to A and not A at the same time: $A \cap \bar{A} 6= \emptyset$, i.e. $\mu_{A \cap \bar{A}}(x) \neq 0$. Note that these elements correspond to the set supp(A) − noy(A).

Reasoning in Fuzzy Logic

In classical logic, the arguments are of the form:

$$\begin{cases} \text{If p then q} \\ \text{p true then q true} \end{cases}$$

In fuzzy logic, fuzzy reasoning, also known as approximate reasoning, is based on fuzzy rules that are expressed in natural language using linguistic variables which we have given the definition above. A fuzzy rule has the form:

If $x \in A$ and $y \in B$ then $z \in C$, with A, B and C fuzzy sets.

For example: 'If (the quality of the food is delicious), then (tip is high)'.

The variable 'tip' belongs to the fuzzy set 'high' to a degree that depends on the degree of validity of the premise, i.e. the membership degree of the variable 'food quality' to the fuzzy set 'delicious '. The underlying idea is that the more propositions in premise are checked, the more the suggested output actions must be applied. To determine the degree of truth of the proposition fuzzy 'tip will be high'; we must define the fuzzy implication.

Like other fuzzy operators, there is no single definition of the fuzzy implication: the fuzzy system designer must choose among the wide choice of fuzzy implications already defined, or set it by hand. Here are two definitions of fuzzy implication most commonly used:

Name	Truth
Mamdani	$\min\bigl(f_a(x), f_b(x)\bigr)$
Larsen	$f_a(x), f_b(x)$

Notably, these two implications do not generalize the classical implication. There are other definitions of fuzzy implication generalizing the classical implication, but are less commonly used.

If we choose the Mamdani implication, here is what we get for the fuzzy rule 'If (the food quality is delicious), then (tip is high)' where the food quality is rated 8.31 out of 10:

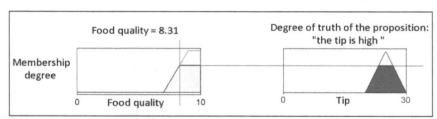

Figure: Example of fuzzy implication.

The result of the application of a fuzzy rule thus depends on three factors: 1. the definition of fuzzy implication chosen, 2. the definition of the membership function of the fuzzy set of the proposition located at the conclusion of the fuzzy rule, 3. the degree of validity of propositions located premise. As we have defined the fuzzy operators AND, OR and NOT, the premise of a fuzzy rule may well be formed from a combination of fuzzy propositions. All the rules of a fuzzy system is called the decision matrix. Here is the decision matrix for our tip example:

If the service is bad or the food is awful	Then the tip is low
If the service is good	Then the tip is average
If the service is excellent or the food is delicious	Then the tip is high

The figure below shows what we get for fuzzy rule 'If (the service is excellent and the food is delicious), then (tip is high)' where the quality of service is rated 7.83 out of 10 and the quality of food 7.32 out of 10 if we choose the Mamdani implication and the translation of OR by MAX.

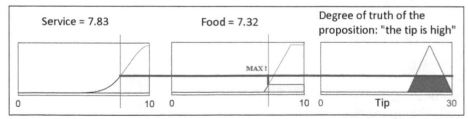

Figure: Example of fuzzy implication with conjunction OR translated into a MAX.

We will now apply all the 3 rules of our decision matrix. However, we will obtain three fuzzy sets for the tip: we will aggregate them by the operator MAX which is almost always used for aggregation. The figure below shows this aggregation.

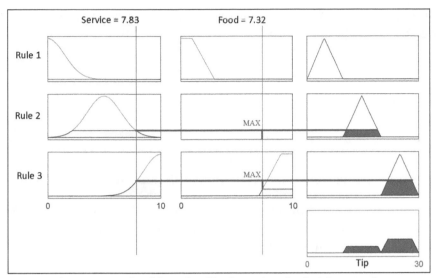

Figure: Example of fuzzy implication using the decision matrix.

As we see, we now has to make the final decision, namely decide how much the tip will be knowing that the quality of service is rated 7.83 out of 10 and quality of food 7.32 out of 10. This final step, which allows switching from the fuzzy set resulting from the aggregation of results to a single decision, is called the defuzzification.

The Defuzzification

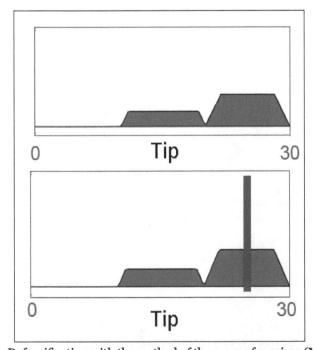

Figure: Defuzzification with the method of the mean of maxima (MeOM).

As with all fuzzy operators, the fuzzy system designer must choose among several possible definitions of defuzzification. We will briefly present the two main methods of defuzzification: the method of the mean of maxima (MeOM) and the method of center of gravity (COG). The MeOM defuzzification sets the output (decision of the tip amount) as the average of the abscissas of the maxima of the fuzzy set resulting from the aggregation of the implication results.

$$\text{Decision} = \frac{\int_s y \cdot dy}{\int_s dy}$$

where $S = \left\{ y_m \in R, \; \mu(y_m) = SUP_{y \in R}(\mu(y)) \right\}$

and R is the fuzzy set resulting from the aggregation of the implication results.

The COG defuzzification is more commonly used. It defines the output as corresponding to the abscissa of the center of gravity of the surface of the membership function characterizing the fuzzy set resulting from the aggregation of the implication results.

$$\text{Decision} = \frac{\int_s y \cdot \mu(\mu) \cdot dy}{\int_s \mu(\mu) \cdot dy}$$

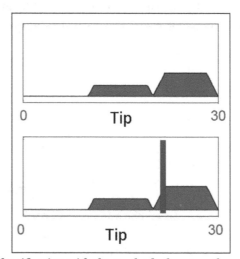

Figure: Defuzzification with the method of center of gravity (COG).

This definition avoids the discontinuities could appear in the MeOM defuzzification, but is more complex and has a greater computational cost. As we see in the two figures showing the MeOM and COG defuzzifications applied to our example, the choice of this method can have a significant effect on the final decision.

Fuzzifier

The fuzzifier is the input interface which maps a numeric input to a fuzzy set so that it can be matched with the premises of the fuzzy rules defined in the application-specific rule base.

Rule Base

The rule base contains a set of fuzzy if-then rules which defines the actions of the controller in terms of linguistic variables and membership functions of linguistic terms.

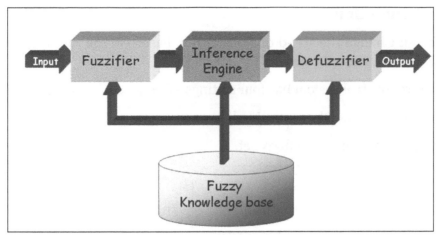

Figure: Basic configuration of a fuzzy logic controller.

Fuzzy Inference Engine

The fuzzy inference engine applies the inference mechanism to the set of rules in the fuzzy rule base to produce a fuzzy output set. This involves matching the input fuzzy set with the premises of the rules, activation of the rules to deduce the conclusion of each rule that is fired, and combination of all activated conclusions using fuzzy set union to generate fuzzy set output.

Defuzzifier

The defuzzifier is an output mapping which converts fuzzy set output to a crisp output. Based on the crisp output, the fuzzy logic controller can drive the system under control. The fuzzy rule base contains a set of linguistic rules. These linguistic rules are expressed using linguistic values and linguistic variables. Different linguistic values can be assigned to a linguistic variable. These linguistic values are modeled as fuzzy sets. Based on the linguistic values, their corresponding membership functions can be expressed based on application requirements. So, we can say that the job of a fuzzy logic controller is to carry out the following three steps:

- To receive one or a large number, of measurement or other assessment of conditions existing in some system we wish to analyze or control.

- Processing all these inputs according to human based, fuzzy "If-Then" rules, which can be expressed in plain language words.

- Averaging and weighting the resulting outputs from all the individual rules into one single output decision or signal which decides what to do or tells a controlled system what to do. The output signal eventually arrived at is a precise appearing, defuzzified, value.

Fuzzy Logic in Control Systems

Fuzzy Logic provides a more efficient and resourceful way to solve Control Systems. Some Examples:

- Temperature Controller.

- Anti – Lock Brake System (ABS).

Temperature Controller

- The problem: Change the speed of a heater fan, based off the room temperature and humidity as given in figure below.

- A temperature control system has four settings - Cold, Cool, Warm, and Hot.

- Humidity can be defined by - Low, Medium, and High.

- Using this we can define - the fuzzy set.

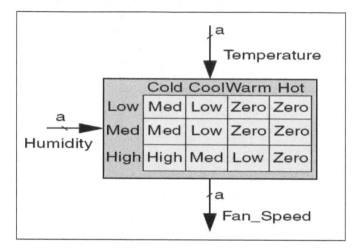

Anti – Lock Brake System (ABS)

ABS is nonlinear and dynamic in nature with inputs for Intel Fuzzy ABS which is derived from:

- Brake
- 4 WD
- Feedback
- Wheel speed
- Ignition

The outputs are pulse width and error lamp.

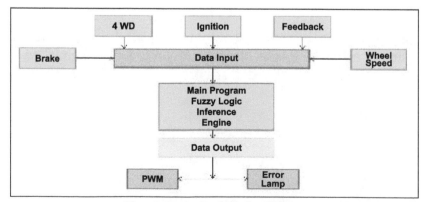

Figure: Anti – Lock Brake System.

Fuzzy Classification

Fuzzy classification is the process of grouping elements into a fuzzy set whose membership function is defined by the truth value of a fuzzy propositional function. Goal of fuzzy classification is create fuzzy "category memberships" function, to convert objectively measurable parameters to "category memberships" and which are then used for classification:

- In fuzzy classification, a sample can have membership in many different classes to different degrees. Typically, the membership values are constrained so that all of the membership values for a particular sample sum to 1.

- Now the expert knowledge for this variable can be formulated as a rule like.

- IF Entropy high AND α high THEN Class = class 4.

- The rules can be combined in a table, called as rule base.

Entropy	α	Class
Very low	Low	Class A
Low	Medium	Class B
Medium	High	Class C
High	High	Class D

Fuzzy Logic in other Fields

- Aerospace: Altitude control of spacecraft, satellite altitude control, flow and mixture regulation in aircraft deicing vehicles.

- Automotive: Trainable fuzzy systems for idle speed control, shift scheduling method for automatic transmission, intelligent highway systems, traffic control, improving efficiency of automatic transmissions.

- Business: Decision-making support systems, personnel evaluation in a large company.

- Chemical Industry: Control of pH, drying, chemical distillation processes, polymer extrusion production, gas cooling plant.

- Defense: Underwater target recognition, automatic target recognition of thermal infrared images, naval decision support aids, control of a hypervelocity interceptor.

- Electronics: Control of automatic exposure in video cameras, humidity in a clean room, air conditioning systems, washing machine timing, microwave ovens, vacuum cleaners.

- Financial: Banknote transfer control, fund management, stock market predictions.

- Industrial: Cement kiln controls, heat exchanger control, activated sludge wastewater treatment process control, water purification plant control, quantitative pattern analysis for industrial quality assurance, control of constraint satisfaction problems in structural design, control of water purification plants.

- Manufacturing: Optimization of cheese production.

- Marine: Autopilot for ships, optimal route selection, control of autonomous underwater vehicles, ship steering.

- Medical: Medical diagnostic support system, control of arterial pressure during anesthesia, multivariable control of anesthesia, modeling of neuropathological findings in Alzheimer's patients, radiology diagnoses, fuzzy inference diagnosis of diabetes and prostate cancer.

- Mining and Metal Processing: Sinter plant control, decision making in metal forming.

- Robotics: Fuzzy control for flexible-link manipulators, robot arm control.

- Securities: Decision systems for securities trading.

- Signal Processing and Telecommunications: Adaptive filter for nonlinear channel equalization control of broadband noise.

- Transportation: Automatic underground train operation, train schedule control, railway acceleration, braking, and stopping.

Data Clustering

The task of segregating groups with similar traits and assigning them into clusters is called clustering. It plays an important role in analyzing high dimensional data. The topics elaborated in this chapter will help in gaining a better perspective about clustering as well as the methods used in it.

High Dimensional Data

Clustering in high-dimensional spaces is a difficult problem which is recurrent in many domains, for example in image analysis. The difficulty is due to the fact that high dimensional data usually live in different low-dimensional subspaces hidden in the original space. For example, given a cloud of data points as shown in figure below and we want to understand its structure, it may be very difficult even for a very advance level tool. The only think which we can visually find is the organization of points in a two dimensional space.

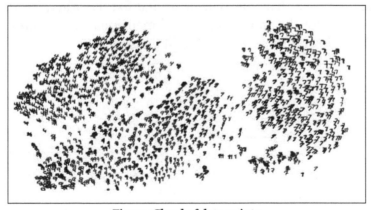

Figure: Cloud of data points.

Clustering High-Dimensional Data

Clustering high-dimensional data has many applications such as text documents, DNA micro-array data and so on. Major challenges are:

- Many irrelevant dimensions may mask clusters and hence the cluster properties can be mined exactly.

- Distance measure becomes meaningless, due to equidistance.

- Clusters may exist only in some subspaces and hence identification and representation suitable subspaces become very much essential.

Clustering Methods for High-Dimensional Data

Clustering of high dimensional data needs feature transformation, feature selection and subspace clustering. Feature transformation will be effective only if most dimensions are relevant and methods like PCA & SVD are useful only when features are highly correlated/ redundant.

Feature selection is done using wrapper or filter approaches for finding a subspace where the data have nice clusters. Subspace-clustering is essential for finding clusters in all the possible subspaces. Methods like CLIQUE, ProClus, and frequent pattern based clustering are common among them.

Challenges with High Dimensions

- Data in only one dimension is relatively packed.

- Adding a dimension "stretch" the points across that dimension, making them further apart.

- Adding more dimensions will make the points further apart—high dimensional data is extremely sparse.

- Distance measure becomes meaningless—due to equidistance.

The Problems of Clustering Sparsity in High-Dimensional Data

Given a set of points, with a notion of distance between points, group the points into some number of clusters; so that Members of a cluster are close/ similar to each other, Members of different clusters are dissimilar. Usually, for the Points in a high-dimensional space, Similarity is defined using a distance measure (Euclidean, Cosine, Jaccard, edit distance, etc).

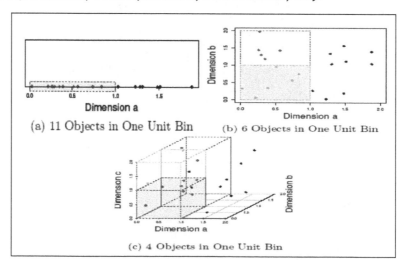

Figure: Clusters of data visualized in 1, 2 and 3 Dimensions.

The representation of data points in figure above are in 1, 2 and 3 dimensions respectively. From the illustration it can be understood that as the dimensions increases the data becomes more and more sparse.

Clustering is a hard problem: Clustering in two dimensions looks easy. Clustering small amounts of data looks easy and in most cases, looks are not deceiving. In many applications involve not 2, but 10 or 10,000 dimensions. High-dimensional spaces look different. Almost all pairs of points are at about the same distance. The human eye can pretty easily separate these data into three groups, but the clustering algorithms fail pretty hard.

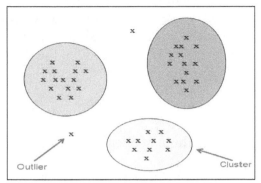

Figure: Sample Clusters and Outliers.

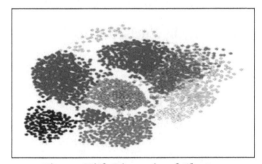

Figure: High Dimensional Cluster.

Every clustering algorithm makes structural assumptions about the dataset that need to be considered. This can produce undesirable results when the clusters are elongated in certain directions particularly when the between-cluster distance is smaller than the maximum within-cluster distance. Single-linkage clustering, in contrast, can perform well in these cases, since points are clustered together based on their nearest neighbor, which facilitates clustering along 'paths' in the dataset.

Clustering Problem

Galaxies

A catalog of 2 billion "sky objects" represents objects by their radiation in 7 dimensions (frequency bands). The problem is Cluster into similar objects, e.g., galaxies, nearby stars, quasars, etc.

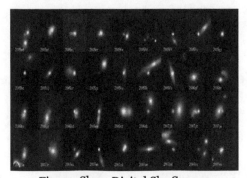

Figure: Sloan Digital Sky Survey.

Music CDs

Intuitively, Music divides into categories, and customers prefer a few categories. Represent a CD by a set of customers who bought it and similar CDs have similar sets of customers, and vice-versa. Space of all CDs can be visualized as a space with one dimension for each customer. The values in a dimension may be 0 or 1 only and a CD might be considered as a point in this space $(x_1, x_2,...,x_k)$, where $x_i = 1$ if the ith customer bought the CD. For Amazon, the dimension is tens of millions and the task is to find the clusters of similar CDs.

Distance Metrics

As with CDs we have a choice when we think of documents as sets of words or shingles:

- Sets as vectors: Measure similarity by the cosine distance.

- Sets as sets: Measure similarity by the Jaccard distance.

- Sets as points: Measure similarity by Euclidean distance.

Documents

Finding topics, it represent a document by a vector $(x_1, x_2,...,x_k)$, where $x_i = 1$ if the ith word (in some order) appears in the document. It actually doesn't matter if k is infinite; i.e., we don't limit the set of words. Documents with similar sets of words may be about the same topic.

Distance Measures

Since clustering is the grouping of similar instances/objects, some sort of measure that can determine whether two objects are similar or dissimilar is required. There are two main type of measures used to estimate this relation: distance measures and similarity measures. Many clustering methods use distance measures to determine the similarity or dissimilarity between any pair of objects. It is useful to denote the distance between two instances xi and xj as: d(xi,xj). A valid distance measure should be symmetric and obtains its minimum value (usually zero) in case of identical vectors. The distance measure is called a metric distance measure if it also satisfies the following properties:

1. Triangle inequality $d(x_i, x_k) \le d(x_i, x_j) + d(x_j, x_k)$ $\forall x_i, x_j, x_j \in S$.

2. $d(x_i, x_j) = 0 \Rightarrow x_i = x_j$ $\forall x_i, x_j \in S$.

Minkowski: Distance Measures for Numeric Attributes

Given two p-dimensional instances, $x_i = (x_{i1}, x_{i2}, \ldots, x_{ip})$ and $x_j = (x_{j1}, x_{j2}, \ldots, x_{jp})$, the distance between the two data instances can be calculated using the Minkowski metric:

$$d(x_i, x_j) = \left(|x_{i1} - x_{j1}|^g + |x_{i2} - x_{j2}|^g + \ldots + |x_{ip} - x_{jp}|^g \right)^{1/g}$$

The commonly used Euclidean distance between two objects is achieved when g = 2. Given g = 1, the sum of absolute paraxial distances (Manhattan metric) is obtained, and with g = ∞ one gets the greatest of the paraxial distances (Chebychev metric).

The measurement unit used can affect the clustering analysis. To avoid the dependence on the choice of measurement units, the data should be standardized. Standardizing measurements attempts to give all variables an equal weight. However, if each variable is assigned with a weight according to its importance, then the weighted distance can be computed as:

$$d(x_i, x_j) = \left(w_1 \left| x_{i1} - x_{j1} \right|^g + w_2 \left| x_{i2} - x_{j2} \right|^g + \ldots + w_p \left| x_{ip} - x_{jp} \right|^g \right)^{1/g}$$

Where $w_i \in [0, \infty)$.

Distance Measures for Binary Attributes

The distance measure described in the last section may be easily computed for continuous-valued attributes. In the case of instances described by categorical, binary, ordinal or mixed type attributes, the distance measure should be revised.

In the case of binary attributes, the distance between objects may be calculated based on a contingency table. A binary attribute is symmetric if both of its states are equally valuable. In that case, using the simple matching coefficient can assess dissimilarity between two objects:

$$d(x_i, x_j) = \frac{r+s}{q+r+s+t}$$

Where q is the number of attributes that equal 1 for both objects; t is the number of attributes that equal 0 for both objects; and s and r are the number of attributes that are unequal for both objects.

A binary attribute is asymmetric, if its states are not equally important (usually the positive outcome is considered more important). In this case, the denominator ignores the unimportant negative matches (t). This is called the Jaccard coefficient:

$$d(x_i, x_j) = \frac{r+s}{q+r+s}$$

Distance Measures for Nominal Attributes

When the attributes are nominal, two main approaches may be used:

- Simple matching:

$$d(x_i, x_j) = \frac{p-m}{p}$$

Where p is the total number of attributes and m is the number of matches.

- Creating a binary attribute for each state of each nominal attribute and computing their dissimilarity as described above.

Distance Metrics for Ordinal Attributes

When the attributes are ordinal, the sequence of the values is meaningful. In such cases, the attributes can be treated as numeric ones after mapping their range onto [0, 1]. Such mapping may be carried out as follows:

$$z_{in} = \frac{r_{i,n} - 1}{M_n - 1}$$

Where $z_{i,n}$ is the standardized value of attribute an of object i. r_i,n is that value before standardization, and M_n is the upper limit of the domain of attribute an (assuming the lower limit is 1).

Distance Metrics for Mixed-Type Attributes

In the cases where the instances are characterized by attributes of mixed type, one may calculate the distance by combining the methods mentioned above. For instance, when calculating the distance between instances i and j using a metric such as the Euclidean distance, one may calculate the difference between nominal and binary attributes as 0 or 1 ("match" or "mismatch", respectively), and the difference between numeric attributes as the difference between their normalized values. The square of each such difference will be added to the total distance. Such calculation is employed in many clustering algorithms presented below.

The dissimilarity d(x_i, x_j) between two instances, containing p attributes of mixed types, is defined as:

$$d\left(x_i, x_j\right) = \frac{\sum_{n=1}^{p} \delta_{ij}^{(n)} d_{ij}^{(n)}}{\sum_{n=1}^{p} \delta_{ij}^{(n)}}$$

Where the indicator $\delta_{ij}^{(n)} = 0$ if one of the values is missing. The contribution of attribute n to the distance between the two objects $d^{(n)}\left(x_i, x_j\right) = 0$ is computed according to its type:

- If the attribute is binary or categorical, $d^{(n)}\left(x_i, x_j\right) = 0$ if $x_{in} = x_{jn}$, otherwise $d^{(n)}\left(x_i, x_j\right) = 1$.

- If the attribute is continuous-valued $d_{ij}^{(n)} = \frac{\left|x_{in} - x_{jn}\right|}{\max_h x_{hn} - \min_n x_{hn}}$, where h runs over all non-missing objects for attribute n.

- If the attribute is ordinal, the standardized values of the attribute are computed first and then, $z_{i,n}$ is treated as continuous-valued.

Similarity Functions

An alternative concept to that of the distance is the similarity function s(xi, xj) that compares the two vectors x_i and x_j. This function should be symmetrical (namely s(x_i, x_j) = s(x_j, x_i)) and have a large value when x_i and x_j are somehow "similar" and constitute the largest value for identical vectors.

A similarity function where the target range is [0, 1] is called a dichotomous similarity function.

In fact, the methods described in the previous sections for calculating the "distances" in the case of binary and nominal attributes may be considered as similarity functions, rather than distances.

Cosine Measure

When the angle between the two vectors is a meaningful measure of their similarity, the normalized inner product may be an appropriate similarity measure:

$$s\left(x_i, x_j\right) = \frac{x_i^{T} \cdot x_j}{\|x_i\| \cdot \|x_j\|}$$

Pearson Correlation Measure

The normalized Pearson correlation is defined as:

$$s\left(x_i, x_j\right) = \frac{\left(x_i - \overline{x}_i\right)^{T} \cdot \left(x_j - \overline{x}_j\right)}{\|x_i - \overline{x}_i\| \cdot \|x_j - \overline{x}_j\|}$$

Where $\overline{x}_i$ denotes the average feature value of x over all dimensions.

Extended Jaccard Measure

The extended Jaccard measure was presented by and it is defined as:

$$s\left(x_i, x_j\right) = \frac{x_i^{T} \cdot x_j}{\|x_i\|^2 + \|x_j\|^2 - x_i^{T} \cdot x_j}$$

Dice Coefficient Measure

The dice coefficient measure is similar to the extended Jaccard measure and it is defined as:

$$s\left(x_i, x_j\right) = \frac{2x_i^{T} \cdot x_j}{\|x_i\|^2 + \|x_j\|^2}$$

Evaluation Criteria Measures

Evaluating if a certain clustering is good or not, then it is a problematic and controversial issue. In fact Bonner was the first to argue that there is no universal definition for what is a good clustering. The evaluation remains mostly in the eye of the beholder. Nevertheless, several evaluation criteria have been developed in the literature. These criteria are usually divided into two categories: Internal and External.

Internal Quality Criteria

Internal quality metrics usually measure the compactness of the clusters using some similarity measure. It usually measures the intra-cluster homogeneity, the inter-cluster separability or a combination of these two. It does not use any external information beside the data itself.

Sum of Squared Error (SSE)

SSE is the simplest and most widely used criterion measure for clustering. It is calculated as:

$$SSE = \sum_{k=1}^{K} \sum_{\forall x_i \in C_k} \|x_i - \mu_k\|^2$$

where C_k is the set of instances in cluster k; μ_k is the vector mean of cluster k. The components of μ_k are calculated as:

$$\mu_{k \cdot j} = \frac{1}{N_k} \sum_{\forall x_i \in C_k} x_{i,j}$$

Where $N_k = |C_k|$ is the number of instances belonging to cluster k.

Clustering methods that minimize the SSE criterion are often called minimum variance partitions, since by simple algebraic manipulation the SSE criterion may be written as:

$$SSE = \frac{1}{2} \sum_{k=1}^{K} N_k \bar{S}_k$$

Where,

$$\bar{S}_k = \frac{1}{N_k^2} \sum_{x_i, x_j \in C_k} \|x_i - x_j\|^2$$

(C_k=cluster k)

The SSE criterion function is suitable for cases in which the clusters form compact clouds that are well separated from one another.

Other Minimum Variance Criteria

Additional minimum criteria to SSE may be produced by replacing the value of S_k with expressions such as:

$$\bar{S}_k = \frac{1}{N_k^2} \sum_{x_i, x_j \in C_k} s(x_i, x_j)$$

Or

$$\bar{S}_k = \min_{x_i, x_j \in C_k} s(x_i, x_j)$$

Scatter Criteria

The scalar scatter criteria are derived from the scatter matrices, reflecting the within-cluster scatter, the between-cluster scatter and their summation — the total scatter matrix. For the kth cluster, the scatter matrix may be calculated as:

$$\overline{S}_k = \sum_{x \in C_k} (x - \mu_k)(x - \mu_k)^T$$

The within-cluster scatter matrix is calculated as the summation of the last definition over all clusters:

$$S_w = \sum_{k-1}^{K} S_k$$

The between-cluster scatter matrix may be calculated as:

$$S_B = \sum_{k=1}^{K} N_k (\mu_k - \mu)(\mu_k - \mu)^T$$

Where μ is the total mean vector and is defined as:

$$\mu = \frac{1}{m} \sum_{k-=1}^{K} N_k \mu_k$$

The total scatter matrix should be calculated as:

$$S_T - \sum_{X \in C_1, C_2 \ldots C_K} (x - \mu)(x - \mu)^T$$

Three scalar criteria may be derived from S_w, S_B and S_T:

The trace criterion: The sum of the diagonal elements of a matrix. Minimizing the trace of SW is similar to minimizing SSE and is therefore acceptable. This criterion, representing the within-cluster scatter, is calculated as:

$$J_e = tr[S_w] = \sum_{k=1}^{K} \sum_{x \in C_k} \|x - \mu_k\|^2$$

Another criterion, which may be maximized, is the between cluster criterion:

$$tr[SB] = \sum_{k=1}^{K} N_k \|\mu k - \mu\|^2$$

The determinant criterion: The determinant of a scatter matrix roughly measures the square of the scattering volume. Since S_B will be singular if the number of clusters is less than or equal to the dimensionality, or if m – c is less than the dimensionality, its determinant is not an appropriate criterion. If we assume that SW is nonsingular, the determinant criterion function using this matrix may be employed:

$$J_d = |S_w| = \left| \sum_{k=1}^{K} S_k \right|$$

The invariant criterion — the eigenvalues $\lambda_1, \lambda_2 \ldots \lambda_d$ of $S_W^{-1} S_B$

are the basic linear invariants of the scatter matrices. Good partitions are ones for which the non-zero eigenvalues are large. As a result, several criteria may be derived including the eigenvalues. Three such criteria are:

- $\operatorname{tr}\left[S_w^{-1}S_B\right] = \sum_{i=1}^{d}\lambda_i$

- $J_f = \operatorname{tr}\left[S_T^{-1}S_w\right] = \sum_{i=1}^{d}\frac{1}{1+\lambda_i}$

- $\dfrac{S_w}{S_T} = \prod_{i=1}^{d}\dfrac{1}{1+\lambda_i}$

Condorcet's Criterion

Another appropriate approach is to apply the Condorcet's solution (1785) to the ranking problem. In this case the criterion is calculated as following:

$$\sum_{C_i \in C}\ \sum_{\substack{x_j,x_k \in C_i \\ x_j \neq x_k}} s\left(x_j,x_k\right) + \sum_{C_i \in C}\ \sum_{x_j \in C_i ; x_k \notin C_i} d\left(x_j,x_k\right)$$

Where $s(x_j, x_k)$ and $d(x_j, x_k)$ measure the similarity and distance of the vectors x_j and x_k.

The C-Criterion

The C-criterion is an extension of Condorcet's criterion and is defined as:

$$\sum_{C_i \in C}\ \sum_{\substack{x_j,x_k \in C_i \\ x_j \neq x_k}} \left(s\left(x_j,x_k\right) - \gamma\right) + \sum_{C_i \in C}\ \sum_{x_j \in C_i ; x_k \notin C_i} \left(\gamma - s\left(x_j,x_k\right)\right)$$

where γ is a threshold value.

Category Utility Metric

The category utility is defined as the increase of the expected number of feature values that can be correctly predicted given a certain clustering. This metric is useful for problems that contain a relatively small number of nominal features each having small cardinality.

Edge Cut Metrics

In some cases it is useful to represent the clustering problem as an edge cut minimization problem. In such instances the quality is measured as the ratio of the remaining edge weights to the total precut edge weights. If there is no restriction on the size of the clusters, finding the optimal value is easy. Thus the min-cut measure is revised to penalize imbalanced structures.

External Quality Criteria

External measures can be useful for examining whether the structure of the clusters match to some predefined classification of the instances.

Mutual Information Based Measure

The mutual information criterion can be used as an external measure for clustering. The measure for m instances clustered using $C = \{C_1... C_g\}$ and referring to the target attribute y whose domain is $dom(y) = \{c_1... c_k\}$ is defined as follows:

$$C = \frac{2}{m}\sum_{l=1}^{g}\sum_{h=1}^{k} m_{l,h} \log_{g.k}\left(\frac{m_{l,h} \cdot m}{m_{.,l} \cdot m_{l,.}}\right)$$

where $m_{l,h}$ indicate the number of instances that are in cluster C_l and also in class c_h. $m_{.,h}$ denotes the total number of instances in the class c_h. Similarly, $m_{l,.}$ indicates the number of instances in cluster C_l.

Precision-Recall Measure

The precision-recall measure from information retrieval can be used as an external measure for evaluating clusters. The cluster is viewed as the results of a query for a specific class. Precision is the fraction of correctly retrieved instances, while recall is the fraction of correctly retrieved instances out of all matching instances. A combined F measure can be useful for evaluating a clustering structure.

Rand Index

The Rand index is a simple criterion used to compare an induced clustering structure (C_1) with a given clustering structure (C_2). Let a be the number of pairs of instances that are assigned to the same cluster in C_1 and in the same cluster in C_2; b be the number of pairs of instances that are in the same cluster in C_1, but not in the same cluster in C_2; c be the number of pairs of instances that are in the same cluster in C_2, but not in the same cluster in C_1; and d be the number of pairs of instances that are assigned to different clusters in C_1 and C_2. The quantities a and d can be interpreted as agreements, and b and c as disagreements. The Rand index is defined as:

$$RAND = \frac{a+d}{a+b+c+d}$$

The Rand index lies between 0 and 1. When the two partitions agree perfectly, the Rand index is 1.

A problem with the Rand index is that its expected value of two random clustering does not take a constant value (such as zero).

Clustering Methods

The main reason for having many clustering methods is the fact that the notion of "cluster" is not precisely defined. Consequently many clustering methods have been developed, each of which uses a different induction principle. Researchers suggest dividing the clustering methods into two main groups: hierarchical and partitioning methods. Categorizing the methods into additional three main categories: density-based methods, model-based clustering and grid based methods.

Hierarchical Methods

These methods construct the clusters by recursively partitioning the instances in either a top-down or bottom-up fashion. These methods can be subdivided as following:

- Agglomerative hierarchical clustering: Each object initially represents a cluster of its own. Then clusters are successively merged until the desired cluster structure is obtained.

- Divisive hierarchical clustering: All objects initially belong to one cluster. Then the cluster is divided into sub-clusters, which are successively divided into their own sub-clusters. This process continues until the desired cluster structure is obtained.

The result of the hierarchical methods is a dendrogram, representing the nested grouping of objects and similarity levels at which groupings change. A clustering of the data objects is obtained by cutting the dendrogram at the desired similarity level.

The merging or division of clusters is performed according to some similarity measure, chosen so as to optimize some criterion (such as a sum of squares). The hierarchical clustering methods could be further divided according to the manner that the similarity measure is calculated:

- Single-link clustering (also called the connectedness, the minimum method or the nearest neighbor method): Methods that consider the distance between two clusters to be equal to the shortest distance from any member of one cluster to any member of the other cluster. If the data consist of similarities, the similarity between a pair of clusters is considered to be equal to the greatest similarity from any member of one cluster to any member of the other cluster.

- Complete-link clustering (also called the diameter, the maximum method or the furthest neighbor method): Methods that consider the distance between two clusters to be equal to the longest distance from any member of one cluster to any member of the other cluster.

- Average-link clustering (also called minimum variance method): Methods that consider the distance between two clusters to be equal to the average distance from any member of one cluster to any member of the other cluster.

The disadvantages of the single-link clustering and the average-link clustering can be summarized as follows:

- Single-link clustering has a drawback known as the "chaining effect": A few points that form a bridge between two clusters cause the single-link clustering to unify these two clusters into one.

- Average-link clustering may cause elongated clusters to split and for portions of neighboring elongated clusters to merge.

The complete-link clustering methods usually produce more compact clusters and more useful hierarchies than the single-link clustering methods, yet the single-link methods are more versatile. Generally, hierarchical methods are characterized with the following strengths:

- Versatility: The single-link methods, for example, maintain good performance on data sets containing non-isotropic clusters, including well separated, chain-like and concentric clusters.

- Multiple partitions: Hierarchical methods produce not one partition, but multiple nested partitions, which allow different users to choose different partitions, according to the desired similarity level. The hierarchical partition is presented using the dendrogram.

The main disadvantages of the hierarchical methods are:

- Inability to scale well: The time complexity of hierarchical algorithms is at least $O(m^2)$ (where m is the total number of instances), which is non-linear with the number of objects. Clustering a large number of objects using a hierarchical algorithm is also characterized by huge I/O costs.

- Hierarchical methods can never undo what was done previously. Namely there is no back-tracking capability.

Partitioning Methods

Partitioning methods relocate instances by moving them from one cluster to another, starting from an initial partitioning. Such methods typically require that the number of clusters will be pre-set by the user. To achieve global optimality in partitioned-based clustering, an exhaustive enumeration process of all possible partitions is required. Because this is not feasible, certain greedy heuristics are used in the form of iterative optimization. Namely, a relocation method iteratively relocates points between the k clusters.

Error Minimization Algorithms

These algorithms, which tend to work well with isolated and compact clusters, are the most intuitive and frequently used methods. The basic idea is to find a clustering structure that minimizes a certain error criterion which measures the "distance" of each instance to its representative value. The most well-known criterion is the Sum of Squared Error (SSE), which measures the total squared Euclidian distance of instances to their representative values. SSE may be globally optimized by exhaustively enumerating all partitions, which is very time-consuming, or by giving an approximate solution (not necessarily leading to a global minimum) using heuristics. The latter option is the most common alternative.

The simplest and most commonly used algorithm, employing a squared error criterion is the K-means algorithm. This algorithm partitions the data into K clusters (C_1, C_2. C_K) represented by their centers or means. The center of each cluster is calculated as the mean of all the instances belonging to that cluster.

The algorithm starts with an initial set of cluster centers, chosen at random or according to some heuristic procedure. In each iteration, each instance is assigned to its nearest cluster center according to the Euclidean distance between the two. Then the cluster centers are re-calculated.

The center of each cluster is calculated as the mean of all the instances belonging to that cluster:

$$\mu_k = \frac{1}{N_k} \sum_{q=1}^{N_k} x_q$$

Where N_k is the number of instances belonging to cluster k and μ_k is the mean of the cluster k.

A number of convergence conditions are possible. For example, the search may stop when the partitioning error is not reduced by the relocation of the centers. This indicates that the present partition is locally optimal. Other stopping criteria can be used also such as exceeding a pre-defined number of iterations.

'K-means Algorithm'

```
Input: S (instance set), K (number of cluster)

Output: clusters

    1. Initialize K cluster centers.

    2. while termination condition is not satisfied do

    3. Assign instances to the closest cluster center.

    4. Update cluster centers based on the assignment.

    5. end while
```

The K-means algorithm may be viewed as a gradient-decent procedure, which begins with an initial set of K cluster-centers and iteratively updates it so as to decrease the error function.

The complexity of T iterations of the K-means algorithm performed on a sample size of m instances, each characterized by N attributes, is: O (T * K * m * N).

This linear complexity is one of the reasons for the popularity of the K-means algorithms. Even if the number of instances is substantially large (which often is the case nowadays), this algorithm is computationally attractive. Thus, the K-means algorithm has an advantage in comparison to other clustering methods (e.g. hierarchical clustering methods), which have non-linear complexity.

Other reasons for the algorithm's popularity are its ease of interpretation, simplicity of implementation, speed of convergence and adaptability to sparse data.

The Achilles heel of the K-means algorithm involves the selection of the initial partition. The algorithm is very sensitive to this selection, which may make the difference between global and local minimum.

Being a typical partitioning algorithm, the K-means algorithm works well only on data sets having isotropic clusters, and is not as versatile as single link algorithms, for instance.

In addition, this algorithm is sensitive to noisy data and outliers (a single outlier can increase the squared error dramatically); it is applicable only when mean is defined (namely, for numeric attributes); and it requires the number of clusters in advance, which is not trivial when no prior knowledge is available.

The use of the K-means algorithm is often limited to numeric attributes. Haung presented the K-prototypes algorithm, which is based on the K-means algorithm but removes numeric data limitations while preserving its efficiency. The algorithm clusters objects with numeric and categorical attributes in a way similar to the K-means algorithm. The similarity measure on numeric attributes is the square Euclidean distance; the similarity measure on the categorical attributes is the number of mismatches between objects and the cluster prototypes.

Another partitioning algorithm, which attempts to minimize the SSE, is the K-medoids or PAM (partition around medoids. This algorithm is very similar to the K-means algorithm. It differs from the latter mainly in its representation of the different clusters. Each cluster is represented by the most centric object in the cluster, rather than by the implicit mean that may not belong to the cluster.

The K-medoids method is more robust than the K-means algorithm in the presence of noise and outliers because a medoid is less influenced by outliers or other extreme values than a mean. However, its processing is more costly than the K-means method. Both methods require the user to specify K, the number of clusters.

Other error criteria can be used instead of the SSE. Estivill-Castro analyzed the total absolute error criterion. Namely, instead of summing up the squared error, he suggests to summing up the absolute error. While this criterion is superior in regard to robustness, it requires more computational effort.

Graph-Theoretic Clustering

Graph theoretic methods are methods that produce clusters via graphs. The edges of the graph connect the instances represented as nodes. A well-known graph-theoretic algorithm is based on the Minimal Spanning Tree — MST. Inconsistent edges are edges whose weight (in the case of clustering-length) is significantly larger than the average of nearby edge lengths. Another graph-theoretic approach constructs graphs based on limited neighborhood sets.

There is also a relation between hierarchical methods and graph theoretic clustering:

- Single-link clusters are sub graphs of the MST of the data instances. Each sub graph is a connected component, namely a set of instances in which each instance is connected to at least one other member of the set, so that the set is maximal with respect to this property. These sub graphs are formed according to some similarity threshold.

- Complete-link clusters are maximal complete sub graphs, formed using a similarity threshold. A maximal complete sub graph is a sub graph such that each node is connected to every other node in the sub graph and the set is maximal with respect to this property.

Density-Based Methods

Density-based methods assume that the points that belong to each cluster are drawn from a specific probability distribution. The overall distribution of the data is assumed to be a mixture of several distributions. The aim of these methods is to identify the clusters and their distribution parameters. These methods are designed for discovering clusters of arbitrary shape which are not necessarily convex, namely:

$$x_i, x_j \in C_k$$

This does not necessarily imply that:

$$\alpha \cdot x_i + (1-\alpha) \cdot x_j \in C_k$$

The idea is to continue growing the given cluster as long as the density (number of objects or data points) in the neighborhood exceeds some threshold. Namely, the neighborhood of a given radius has to contain at least a minimum number of objects. When each cluster is characterized by local mode or maxima of the density function, these methods are called mode-seeking.

Much work in this field has been based on the underlying assumption that the component densities are multivariate Gaussian (in case of numeric data) or multinominal (in case of nominal data).

An acceptable solution in this case is to use the maximum likelihood principle. According to this principle, one should choose the clustering structure and parameters such that the probability of the data being generated by such clustering structure and parameters is maximized. The expectation maximization algorithm — EM —, which is a general-purpose maximum likelihood algorithm for missing-data problems, has been applied to the problem of parameter estimation. This algorithm begins with an initial estimate of the parameter vector and then alternates between two steps: an "E-step", in which the conditional expectation of the complete data likelihood given the observed data and the current parameter estimates is computed, and an "M-step", in which parameters that maximize the expected likelihood from the E-step are determined. This algorithm was shown to converge to a local maximum of the observed data likelihood.

The K-means algorithm may be viewed as a degenerate EM algorithm, in which:

$$p(k/x) = \begin{cases} 1 & k = \arg\max\{\hat{p}(k/x)\} \\ 0 & \text{otherwise} \end{cases}$$

Assigning instances to clusters in the K-means may be considered as the E-step; computing new cluster centers may be regarded as the M-step.

The DBSCAN algorithm (density-based spatial clustering of applications with noise) discovers clusters of arbitrary shapes and is efficient for large spatial databases. The algorithm searches for clusters by searching the neighborhood of each object in the database and checks if it contains more than the minimum number of objects.

AUTOCLASS is a widely-used algorithm that covers a broad variety of distributions, including Gaussian, Bernoulli, Poisson, and log-normal distributions. Other well-known density-based methods include: SNOB and MCLUST.

Density-based clustering may also employ nonparametric methods, such as searching for bins with large counts in a multidimensional histogram of the input instance space.

Model-Based Clustering Methods

These methods attempt to optimize the fit between the given data and some mathematical models. Unlike conventional clustering, which identifies groups of objects; model-based clustering methods also find characteristic descriptions for each group, where each group represents a concept or class. The most frequently used induction methods are decision trees and neural networks.

Decision Trees

In decision trees, the data is represented by a hierarchical tree, where each leaf refers to a concept and contains a probabilistic description of that concept. Several algorithms produce classification trees for representing the unlabeled data. The most well-known algorithms are:

- COBWEB: This algorithm assumes that all attributes are independent (an often too naive assumption). Its aim is to achieve high predictability of nominal variable values, given a cluster. This algorithm is not suitable for clustering large database data. CLASSIT, an extension of COBWEB for continuous-valued data, unfortunately has similar problems as the COBWEB algorithm.

Neural Networks

This type of algorithm represents each cluster by a neuron or "prototype". The input data is also represented by neurons, which are connected to the prototype neurons. Each such connection has a weight, which is learned adaptively during learning.

A very popular neural algorithm for clustering is the self-organizing map (SOM). This algorithm constructs a single-layered network. The learning process takes place in a "winner-takes-all" fashion:

- The prototype neurons compete for the current instance. The winner is the neuron whose weight vector is closest to the instance currently presented.

- The winner and its neighbors learn by having their weights adjusted.

The SOM algorithm is successfully used for vector quantization and speech recognition. It is useful for visualizing high-dimensional data in 2D or 3D space. However, it is sensitive to the initial selection of weight vector, as well as to its different parameters, such as the learning rate and neighborhood radius.

Grid-Based Methods

These methods partition the space into a finite number of cells that form a grid structure on which all of the operations for clustering are performed. The main advantage of the approach is its fast processing time.

Soft-Computing Methods

Fuzzy Clustering

Traditional clustering approaches generate partitions; in a partition, each instance belongs to one and only one cluster. Hence, the clusters in a hard clustering are disjointed. Fuzzy clustering extends this notion and suggests a soft clustering schema. In this case, each pattern is associated with every cluster using some sort of membership function, namely, each cluster is a fuzzy set of all the patterns. Larger membership values indicate higher confidence in the assignment of the pattern to the cluster. A hard clustering can be obtained from a fuzzy partition by using a threshold of the membership value.

The most popular fuzzy clustering algorithm is the fuzzy c-means (FCM) algorithm. Even though it is better than the hard K-means algorithm at avoiding local minima, FCM can still converge to local minima of the squared error criterion. The design of membership functions is the most important problem in fuzzy clustering; different choices include those based on similarity decomposition and centroids of clusters. A generalization of the FCM algorithm has been proposed through a family of objective functions. A fuzzy c-shell algorithm and an adaptive variant for detecting circular and elliptical boundaries have been presented.

Evolutionary Approaches for Clustering

Evolutionary techniques are stochastic general purpose methods for solving optimization problems. Since clustering problem can be defined as an optimization problem, evolutionary approaches may be appropriate here. The idea is to use evolutionary operators and a population of clustering structures to converge into a globally optimal clustering. Candidate clustering are encoded as chromosomes. The most commonly used evolutionary operators are: selection, recombination, and mutation. A fitness function evaluated on a chromosome determines a chromosome's likelihood of surviving into the next generation. The most frequently used evolutionary technique in clustering problems is genetic algorithms (GAs). A fitness value is associated with each clusters structure. A higher fitness value indicates a better cluster structure. A suitable fitness function is the inverse of the squared error value. Cluster structures with a small squared error will have a larger fitness value.

GA for Clustering

```
Input: S (instance set), K (number of clusters), n (population size)

Output: clusters

    1. Randomly create a population of n structures; each corresponds to valid
    K-clusters of the data.

    2. repeat

    3. Associate a fitness value ∀structure ∈ population.

    4. Regenerate a new generation of structures.

    5. until some termination condition is satisfied
```

The most obvious way to represent structures is to use strings of length m (where m is the number of instances in the given set). The ith entry of the string denotes the cluster to which the ith instance belongs. Consequently, each entry can have values from 1 to K. An improved representation scheme is proposed where an additional separator symbol is used along with the pattern labels to represent a partition. Using this representation permits them to map the clustering problem into a permutation problem such as the travelling salesman problem, which can be solved by using the permutation crossover operators. This solution also suffers from permutation redundancy.

In GAs, a selection operator propagates solutions from the current generation to the next generation based on their fitness. Selection employs a probabilistic scheme so that solutions with higher fitness have a higher probability of getting reproduced.

There are a variety of recombination operators in use; crossover is the most popular. Crossover takes as input a pair of chromosomes (called parents) and outputs a new pair of chromosomes (called children or offspring). In this way the GS explores the search space. Mutation is used to make sure that the algorithm is not trapped in local optimum.

More recently investigated is the use of edge-based crossover to solve the clustering problem. Here, all patterns in a cluster are assumed to form a complete graph by connecting them with edges. Offspring are generated from the parents so that they inherit the edges from their parents. In a hybrid approach that has been proposed, the GAs is used only to find good initial cluster centers and the K-means algorithm is applied to find the final partition. This hybrid approach performed better than the GAs.

A major problem with GAs is their sensitivity to the selection of various parameters such as population size, crossover and mutation probabilities, etc. Several researchers have studied this problem and suggested guidelines for selecting these control parameters. However, these guidelines may not yield good results on specific problems like pattern clustering. It was reported that hybrid genetic algorithms incorporating problem-specific heuristics are good for clustering. A similar claim is made about the applicability of GAs to other practical problems. Another issue with GAs is the selection of an appropriate representation which is low in order and short in defining length.

There are other evolutionary techniques such as evolution strategies (ESs), and evolutionary programming (EP). These techniques differ from the GAs in solution representation and the type of mutation operator used; EP does not use a recombination operator, but only selection and mutation. Each of these three approaches has been used to solve the clustering problem by viewing it as a minimization of the squared error criterion. Some of the theoretical issues, such as the convergence of these approaches, were studied. GAs performs a globalized search for solutions whereas most other clustering procedures per- form a localized searches. In a localized search, the solution obtained at the 'next iteration' of the procedure is in the vicinity of the current solution. In this sense, the K-means algorithm and fuzzy clustering algorithms are all localized search techniques. In the case of GAs, the crossover and mutation operators can produce new solutions that are completely different from the current ones.

It is possible to search for the optimal location of the centroids rather than finding the optimal partition. This idea permits the use of ESs and EP, because centroids can be coded easily in both these approaches, as they support the direct representation of a solution as a real-valued vector. ESs were used on both hard and fuzzy clustering problems and EP has been used to evolve fuzzy min-max clusters. It has been observed that they perform better than their classical counterparts, the K-means algorithm and the fuzzy c-means algorithm. However, all of these approaches are over sensitive to their parameters. Consequently, for each specific problem, the user is required to tune the parameter values to suit the application.

Proclus

Projected cluster: Subset of data points, together with a subset of dimensions, such that the points are closely clustered in the corresponding subspace.

PROCLUS (Projected Clustering) is a projected clustering algorithm which is partitioned in nature. In a high dimensional data, all dimensions are not relevant to each cluster. The problem of handling very high dimensional data can be solved by picking the projected dimensions and discovering clusters in those projected sub spaces. The main goal of their algorithm is to pick up the relevant dimensions on which data points are mostly correlated. Pruning the irrelevant dimensions from the data set greatly reduces the noise. Alternatively, feature selection methods can also be used for selecting relevant dimensions, but, sometimes it will lead to loss of information. The concept of discovering 29 clusters in a sub set of dimensions has been observed for the first time by Aggarwal et al. The output of the PROCLUS algorithm will be k+1 partition of the data such as C1, C2.. Ck and O. The partitions are called projected clusters and O is called as outlier.

Objective of Proclus

- PROCLUS (Projected Clustering).

  ○ Algorithm to find out the clusters and the dimensions for the corresponding clusters.

  ○ Splits out those Outliers (points that do not cluster well) from the clusters.

Input and Output for Proclus

Input:

- The set of data points.

- Number of clusters, denoted by k.

- Average number of dimensions for each cluster, denoted by L.

Output:

- The clusters found, and the respective dimensions to such clusters.

Three Phases for PROCLUS:

- Initialization Phase.

- Iterative Phase.

- Refinement Phase.

- The best set of mediods is found by a hill climbing process. Hill climbing simply means process of improving the set of mediods.

Initialization Phase

The purpose of initialization phase is to select representative points from each cluster. In full dimensional space, piercing set of mediods is identified with the help of greedy method which is proposed in. In PROCLUS, greedy technique is used to find the good superset of the piercing set of mediods. Initialization phase also reduces the size of the original data set.

- Choose a sample set of data point randomly.

- Choose a set of data point which is probably the medoids of the clusters.

Choosing Mediods of Clusters

Medoids are representative objects of a data set or a cluster with a data set whose average dissimilarity to all the objects in the cluster is minimal. Medoids are similar in concept to means or centroids, but medoids are always members of the data set. Medoids are most commonly used on data when a mean or centroid cannot be defined such as 3-D trajectories or in the gene expression context. The term is used in computer science in data clustering algorithms.

For some data sets there may be more than one medoid, as with medians. A common application of the medoid is the k-medoids clustering algorithm, which is similar to the k-means algorithm but works when a mean or centroid is not definable. This algorithm basically works as follows. First, a set of medoids is chosen at random. Second, the distances to the other points are computed. Third, data are clustered according to the medoid they are most similar to. Fourth, the medoid set is optimized via an iterative process.

Data Visualization

The graphical representation of data in the form of graphs, charts, tables and maps to understand the information easily is called data visualization. This chapter discusses in detail the theories and methodologies related to visualization in 2 variables, visualization in 3 or more variables, and big data visualization.

Data visualization is a general term that describes any effort to help people understand the significance of data by placing it in a visual context. Patterns, trends and correlations that might go undetected in text-based data can be exposed and recognized easier with data visualization software. It is the process of converting raw data into easily understood pictures of information that enable fast and effective decisions.

Visualization is the practice of mapping data to visual form for exploration and analysis and for presentation. Leverage existing scientific methods by providing new scientific insight through visual methods is the goal of visualization. Data visualization is important. Because of the way the human brain processes information, using charts or graphs to visualize large amounts of complex data is easier than poring over spreadsheets or reports. Data visualization is a quick, easy way to convey concepts in a universal manner and you can experiment with different scenarios by making slight adjustments.

Data visualization can also identify areas that need attention or improvement, clarify which factors influence behavior, help you understand which products customer to place where and predict sales volumes.

Usage

- Comprehend Information Quickly: By using graphical representations of business information, businesses are able to see large amounts of data in clear, cohesive ways and draw conclusions from that information. And since it's significantly faster to analyze information in graphical format (as opposed to analyzing information in spreadsheets), businesses can address problems or answer questions in a more timely manner.

- Identify Relationships and Patterns: Even extensive amounts of complicated data start to make sense when presented graphically; businesses can recognize parameters that are highly correlated. Some of the correlations will be obvious, but others won't. Identifying those relationships helps organizations focus on areas most likely to influence their most important goals.

- Pinpoint Emerging Trends: Using data visualization to discover trends both in the business and in the market can give businesses an edge over the competition, and ultimately affect the bottom line. It's easy to spot outliers that affect product quality or customer churn, and address issues before they become bigger problems.

- Communicate the Story to others: Once a business has uncovered new insights from visual analytics, the next step is to communicate those insights to others. Using charts, graphs or other visually impactful representations of data is important in this step because it's engaging and gets the message across quickly.

Stages in Transformation from Data to Visual Output

Jacques Bertin who wrote the classic works of graphical visualization "Semiology of Graphics" states that the "transformation from numbers to insight requires two stages."

- Stage 1: Data → Image

- Stage 2: Image→ Insight

Stage one indicates that using a suitable algorithm the data can be visualized as patterns or image. The second stage allows the used to analyze the image or visual patterns in different perspective.

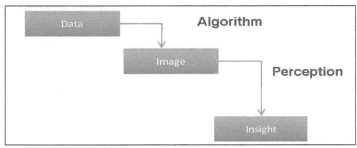

Figure: Transformation from numbers to insight.

Goals of Visualization

Today there is the need to manage a huge amount of data, and computer systems help us in this task. The purpose of visualization is to convey information. The main goal of Data Image Insight Algorithm Perception data visualization is effectively, efficiently, elegantly, accurately as well as meaningfully communicating information. It fulfills its objectives only if it encodes the given input in such a manner that our eyes can recognize and our brain can comprehend. One of the main goals of data visualization is to give support in making decision through appropriately designed graphically represented information. Sophistically-designed data visualization systems can greatly assist users with proper reasoning and decision making. Usually, visually presented data is easier to understand.

Benefits of Data Visualization

Data visualization helps to deal with the flood of information, integrating the human in the data analysis process. Visualizing data allows the user to gain insight into the data, drawing conclusions and directly interacting with the data. The following points summarize some relevant benefits of data visualization:

- Data visualization allows users see several different perspectives of the data.

- Data visualization makes it possible to interpret vast amounts of data.

- Data visualization offers the ability to note exceptions in the data.

- Data visualization allows the user to analyze visual patterns in the data.

- Exploring trends within a database through visualization by letting analysts navigate through data and visually orient themselves to the patterns in the data.

- Data visualization can help translate data patterns into insights, making it a highly effective decision-making tool.

- Data visualization equips users with the ability to see influences that would otherwise be difficult to find.

- By simplifying the presentation, Data Visualization can reduce the time and difficulty it takes to move from data to decision making.

Advantages of Visualization Techniques

A huge amount of data is being generated every single moment, at unbelievably rapid speeds across the globe. The data must be gathered, organized, made interpretable, and then analyzed and acted on to provide any meaningful value. This is where data- visualization steps in, and allows the organizational leaders to access and interpret data in real-time so that they can make highly informed decisions quickly. Data visualization tools and techniques offer executives and other knowledge workers new approaches to dramatically improve their ability to grasp information hiding in their data. Some of the advantages of visualization techniques are given below:

- Visual data exploration can easily deal with very large, highly non homogeneous and noisy amount of data.

- Visual data exploration requires no understanding of complex mathematical or statistical algorithms.

- Visualization techniques provide a qualitative overview useful for further quantitative analysis.

Approach Methodologies

Confirmative Analysis

It is a special form of factor analysis, most commonly used in social research. It is used to test whether measures of a construct are consistent with a researcher's understanding of the nature of that construct (or factor).

- Starting point: Hypotheses about the data.

- Result: Visualization of the data allowing confirmation or rejection of the hypotheses.

Presentation Analysis

It is the process of organizing data into logical, sequential and meaningful categories and classifications to make them amenable to study and interpretation:

- Starting point: Facts to be presented are fixed a priori.

- Result: High-quality visualization of the data presenting the facts.

Explorative Analysis

It is an approach to analyzing data sets to summarize their main characteristics, often with visual methods.

- Starting point: Data without hypotheses.

- Result: Visualization of the data, which can provide hypotheses about data distribution.

Impact of Visualization

Many studies have shown that between 30% and 40% of business decisions are solely driven by data (the remainder is coming from decision maker's own knowledge and gut feeling plus advice from collaborators). We also know that the way data is visualized affects the viewer's ability to make good decisions. Data visualization has huge impact on policy, planning and disaster avoidance.

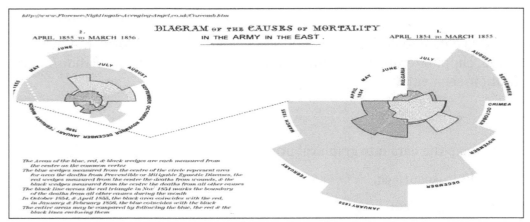

Figure: Florence Nightingale's visualization of casualties during the Crimean War.

- John Snow's Cholera Map.

- Snow used a spot map to illustrate how cases of cholera clustered around the pump.

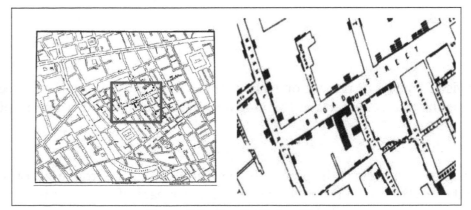

Figure: John Snow's Cholera Map.

Visualization Process

Data is transformed to some graphic form and rendered.

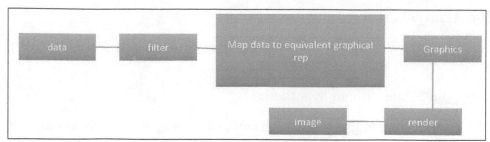

Figure: Visualization process.

Data

Obtain the data, whether from a file on a disk or a source over a network. data filter Map data to equivalent graphical rep Graphics image render.

Filter

This step converts data into desired format.ie, data -> data of desired format. It includes data format conversion, clipping/cropping/ denoising, slicing, resampling, interpolation/approximation, and classification/segmentation.

Mapping

These steps will map the data into graphical primitives. It includes:

- Scalar field ->isosurface.
- 2D field ->height field.
- Vector field ->vectors.
- Tensor field ->glyphs.
- 3D field -> volume.
- highD -> 2D.

Graphics

Graphics are visual images or designs on some surface, such as a wall, canvas, screen, paper, or stone to inform, illustrate, or entertain. This step will convert the data into some graphical format.

Render

Rendering or image synthesis is the process of generating an image from a 2D or 3D model (or models in what collectively could be called a scene file) by means of computer programs. Also, the results of such a model can be called a rendering.

Image

An image is a visual representation of data. This step will generate a required image.

Visualization of Data

- Try to envision the domain in your mind. Each pixel has a value of intensity.

1.3	1.6	2.2	2.6	3.0	3.3	3.6	3.9	4.1	4.3	4.4	4.5
1.3	1.6	2.2	2.5	2.9	3.2	3.4	3.6	3.8	4.0	4.1	4.1
1.4	1.6	2.1	2.5	2.7	3.0	3.2	3.4	3.5	3.7	3.7	3.6
1.4	1.7	2.1	2.4	2.6	2.8	3.0	3.2	3.3	3.3	3.4	3.4
1.4	1.7	2.0	2.3	2.5	2.7	2.9	2.9	3.0	3.0	3.0	3.0
1.4	1.7	2.0	2.2	2.4	2.6	2.6	2.7	2.7	2.7	2.7	2.6
1.5	1.7	1.9	2.1	2.3	2.4	2.4	2.5	2.5	2.4	2.3	2.2
1.5	1.7	1.9	2.0	2.1	2.2	2.2	2.2	2.2	2.1	2.0	1.9
1.5	1.7	1.8	1.9	2.0	2.1	2.0	2.0	1.9	1.8	1.7	1.5
1.5	1.7	1.8	1.9	1.9	1.9	1.9	1.8	1.7	1.5	1.3	1.1
1.6	1.7	1.7	1.8	1.8	1.7	1.7	1.5	1.4	1.2	1.0	0.7
1.6	1.7	1.7	1.7	1.7	1.6	1.5	1.3	1.1	0.9	0.6	0.3

Figure: Pixel intensity.

- But, with some modifications to the images average deviation of each datum from the average value.

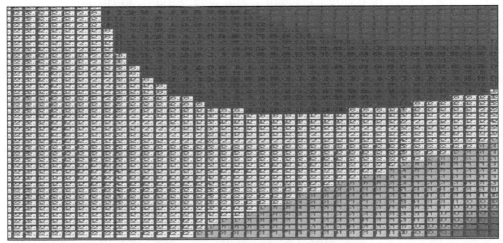

Figure: Corresponding color of pixels.

- Interpolated vs. Non-interpolated: In the mathematical field of numerical analysis, interpolation is a method of constructing new data points within the range of a discrete set of known data points. Linear interpolation is a way to fill in the ``holes'' in tables. Multivariate interpolation is the interpolation of functions of more than one variable. Methods include bilinear interpolation and bicubic interpolation in two dimensions, and trilinear interpolation in three dimensions. They can be applied to gridded or scattered data.

- Multivariate interpolation is the interpolation of functions of more than one variable.

- Methods include bilinear interpolation and bicubicinterpolation in two dimensions, and trilinear interpolation in three dimensions.

- They can be applied to gridded or scattered data.

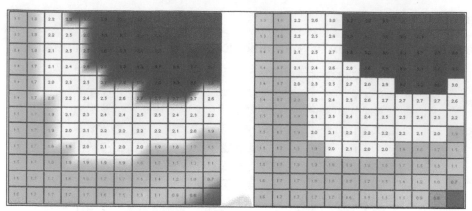

Figure: Interpolated vs. Non-interpolated.

The Groundwork for Data Visualization

Some initial preparations are required for data visualization process:

- Understand the data you're trying to visualize, including its size and cardinality (the uniqueness of data values in a column).

- Determine what you're trying to visualize and what kind of information you want to communicate.

- Know your audience and understand how it processes visual information.

- Use a visual that conveys the information in the best and simplest form for your audience.

Once you've answered those initial questions about the type of data you have and the audience who'll be consuming the information, you need to prepare for the amount of data you'll be working with. Big data brings new challenges to visualization because large volumes, different varieties and varying velocities must be taken into account. Plus, data is often generated faster that it can be managed and analyzed.

There are factors you should consider, such as the cardinality of columns you're trying to visualize. High cardinality means there's a large percentage of unique values (e.g., bank account numbers, because each item should be unique). Low cardinality means a column of data contains a large percentage of repeat values (as might be seen in a "gender" column).

Doing Visualization

There are some points of advice for visualization (1) Do not forget the metadata. Data about data can be very revealing. (2) Participation matters. Visualization tools should be interactive, and user engagement is very important. (3) Encourage interactivity. Static data tools don't lead to discovery as well as interactive tools do.

Make Decisions Related to:

- Data Sources.

- Data Variables.

- Representation Types.

- Visualization Techniques.

- Interactive or Batch.

- Data Types and Topologies.

Visualization Techniques

Direct visualization of big data sources is often not possible or effective. Analytics plays a key role by helping reduce the size and complexity of big data. The visualization and analytics can be integrated so that they work best.

- Geometric techniques: Tables and Stacked plots, scatterplots matrices, Hyperslice, parallel coordinates.

- Pixel-oriented techniques: simple line-by-line, spiral and circle segments.

- Hierarchical techniques: Treemap, cone trees.

- Graph-based techniques: 2D and 3D graph.

- Contour Lines/Iso-surfaces.

- Color Shading.

- Vector Fields: Arrows, Streamlines, Particle Tracing.

- Distortion techniques: hyperbolic tree, fisheye view, perspective wall.

- User interaction: brushing, linking, dynamic projections and rotations, dynamic queries

- Adding Textures.

- Animation.

- Virtual Reality.

- Data Sonification.

Data Variables

- Scalar: The data types like char, int, short long, float, and double are called scalar (or base) data types because they hold a single data item.

  - Temperature, pressure, velocity.

- Vector: Vector data provide a way to represent real world features. Vector features have attributes, which consist of text or numerical information that describe the features.

  - Magnetic field, speed.

- Tensor: In mathematics, tensors are geometric objects that describe linear relations between geometric vectors, scalars, and other tensors. Elementary examples of such relations include the dot product, the cross product, and linear maps.

  ◦ Stress, strain.

- Multivariate: Multivariate analysis is essentially the statistical process of simultaneously analyzing multiple independent variables with multiple dependent variables.

  ◦ Weather characteristics, water quality factors.

Visualization in Two Variables

Presentation of data and information is not simply about picking any data visualization design. Matching data to the right information visualization begins by answering 5 key questions:

- What relationship we are trying to understand between our data sets?

- Do we want to understand the distribution of data and look for outliers?

- Are we looking to compare multiple values or looking to analyze a single value over time?

- Are we interested in analyzing trends in our data sets?

- Is this visualization an important part of our overarching data story?

With those questions (and your answers) in mind, we'll dive into the 11 most common graph types you can mix and match to the best data visualization to bring your data story to life. We'll provide you with the data viz 101 and best practices, so feel free to navigate to the one you want to explore the most.

Bar Chart

At some point or another, you've either seen, interacted with, or built a bar chart before. Bar charts are such popular graph visualization because of how easy you can scan them for quick information. Bar charts organize data into rectangular bars that make it a breeze to compare related data sets.

When do we use Bar Chart Visualization?

Use a bar chart for the following reasons:

- You want to compare two or more values in the same category.

- You want to compare parts of a whole.

- You don't have too many groups (less than 10 works best).

- You want to understand how multiple similar data sets relate to each other.

Don't use a bar chart for the following reasons:

- The category you're visualizing only has one value associated with it.

- You want to visualize continuous data.

Best Practices for a Bar Chart Visualization

If you use a bar chart, here are the key design best practices:

- Use consistent colors and labeling throughout so that you can identify relationships more easily.

- Simplify the length of the y-axis labels and don't forget to start from 0 so you can keep your data in order.

Line Chart

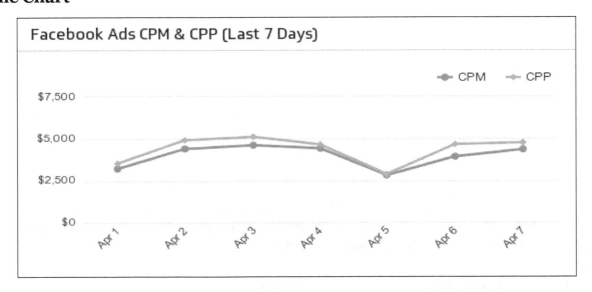

Like bar charts, line charts help to visualize data in a compact and precise format which makes it easy to rapidly scan information in order to understand trends. Line charts are used to show resulting data relative to a continuous variable - most commonly time or money. The proper use of color in this visualization is necessary because different colored lines can make it even easier for users to analyze information.

When do we use Line Chart Visualization?

Use a line chart for the following reasons:

- You want to understand trends, patterns, and fluctuations in your data.

- You want to compare different yet related data sets with multiple series.

- You want to make projections beyond your data.

Don't use a line chart for the following reason:

- You want to demonstrate an in-depth view of your data.

Best Practices for a Line Chart Visualization

If you use a line chart, here are the key design best practices:

- Along with using a different color for each category you're comparing, make sure you also use solid lines to keep the line chart clear and concise.

- To avoid confusion, try not to compare more than 4 categories in one line chart.

Scatterplot

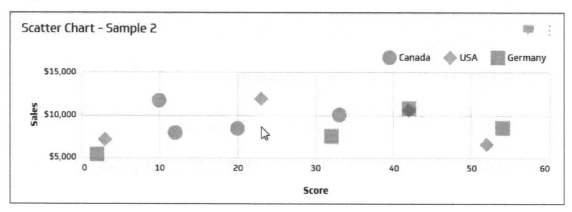

Scatterplots are the right data visualizations to use when there are many different data points, and you want to highlight similarities in the data set. This is useful when looking for outliers or for understanding the distribution of your data.

If the data forms a band extending from lower left to upper right, there most likely a positive correlation between the two variables. If the band runs from upper left to lower right, a negative correlation is probable. If it is hard to see a pattern, there is probably no correlation.

When do we use Scatter Plot Visualization?

Use a scatterplot for the following reasons:

- You want to show the relationship between two variables.

- You want compact data visualization.

Don't use a scatterplot for the following reasons:

- You want to rapidly scan information.

- You want clear and precise data points.

Best Practices for a Scatter Plot Visualization

If you use a scatterplot, here are the key design best practices:

- Although trend lines are a great way to analyze the data on a scatterplot, ensure you stick to 1 or 2 trend lines to avoid confusion.

- Don't forget to start at **0** for the y-axis.

Sparkline

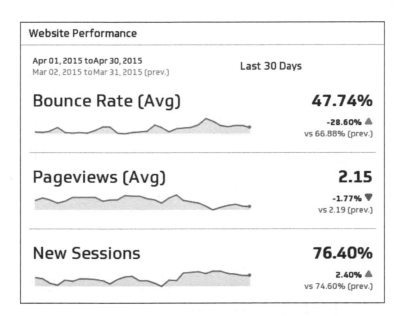

Sparklines are arguably the best data visualization for showing trends because of how compact they are. They get the job done when it comes to painting a picture for your audience fast. Though, it is important to make sure your audience understands how to read sparklines correctly to optimize their use.

When do we use Sparkline Visualization?

Use a Sparkline for the following reasons:

- You can pair it with a metric that has a current status value tracked over a specific time period.

- You want to show a specific trend behind a metric.

Don't use a Sparkline for the following reasons:

- You want to plot multiple series.

- You want to illustrate precise data points (i.e. individual values).

Best Practices for a Sparkline Visualization

If you use a Sparkline, here are the key design best practices:

- To assist with readability, consider adding indicators on the side that give a better glimpse into the data, like in the example above.

- Stick to one color for your sparklines to keep them consistent on your dashboard.

Pie Chart

Pie charts are interesting graph visualization. At a high-level, they're easy to read and understand because the parts-of-a-whole relationship is made very obvious. But top data visual experts agree that one of their disadvantages is that the percentage of each section isn't obvious without adding numerical values to each slice of the pie.

So, what's the point? As long as you stick to best practices, pie charts can be a quick way to scan information.

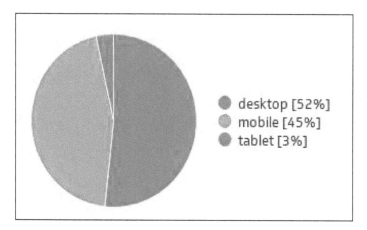

When do we use Pie Chart Visualization?

Use a pie chart for the following reasons:

- You want to compare relative values.

- You want to compare parts of a whole.

- You want to rapidly scan metrics.

Don't use a pie chart for the following reason:

- You want to precisely compare data.

Best Practices for a Pie Chart Visualization

If you use a pie chart, here are the key design best practices:

- Make sure that the pie slices add up to 100%. To make this easier, add the numerical values and percentages to your pie chart.

- Order the pieces of your pie according to size.

- Use a pie chart if you have only up to 5 categories to compare. If you have too many categories, you won't be able to differentiate between the slices.

Gauge

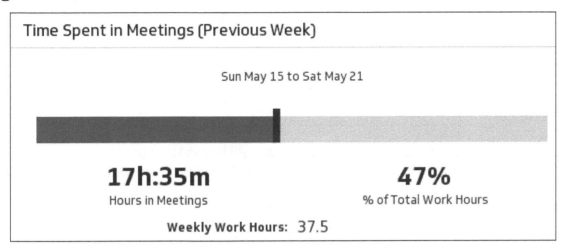

Gauges typically only compare two values on a scale: they compare a current value and a target value, which often indicates whether your progress is either good or bad, in the green or in the red.

When do we use Gauge Visualization?

Use a gauge for the following reason:

- You want to track single metrics that have a clear, in the moment objective.

Don't use a gauge for the following reasons:

- You want to track multiple metrics.

- You're looking to visualize precise data points.

Best Practices for a Gauge Visualization

If you use a gauge, here are the key design best practices:

- Feel free to play around with the size and shape of the gauge. Whether it's an arc, a circle or a line, it'll get the same job done.

- Keep the colors consistent with what means "good" or "bad" for you and your numbers.

- Use consistent colors and labeling throughout so that you can identify relationships more easily.

- Simplify the length of the y-axis labels and don't forget to start from 0 so you can keep your data in order.

Waterfall Chart

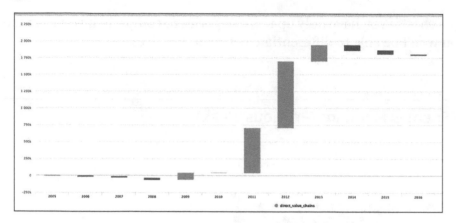

A waterfall chart is an information visualization that should be used to show how an initial value is affected by intermediate values and resulted in a final value. The values can be either negative or positive.

When do we use Waterfall Chart Visualization?

Use a waterfall chart for the following reason:

- To reveal the composition or makeup of a number.

Don't use a waterfall chart for the following reason:

- You want to focus on more than one number or metric.

Best Practices for a Waterfall Chart Visualization

If you use a waterfall chart, here are the key design best practices:

- Use contrasting colors to highlight differences in data sets.

- Choose warm colors to indicate increases and cool colors to indicate decreases.

Funnel Chart

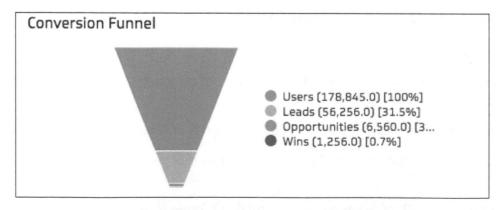

A funnel chart is your data visualization of choice if you want to display a series of steps and the completion rate for each step. This can be used to track the sales process, a marketing funnel or the conversion rate across a series of pages or steps. Funnel charts are most often used to represent how something moves through different stages in a process. A funnel chart displays values as progressively decreasing proportions amounting to 100 percent in total.

When do we use Funnel Chart Visualization?

Use a funnel chart for the following reason:

- To display a series of steps and each step's completion rate.

Don't use a funnel chart for the following reason:

- To visualize individual, unconnected metrics.

Best Practices for a Funnel Chart Visualization

If you use a funnel chart, here are the key design best practices:

- Scale the size of each section to accurately reflect the size of its data set.

- Use contrasting colors or one color in gradating hues, from darkest to lightest as the size of the funnel decreases.

Heat Map

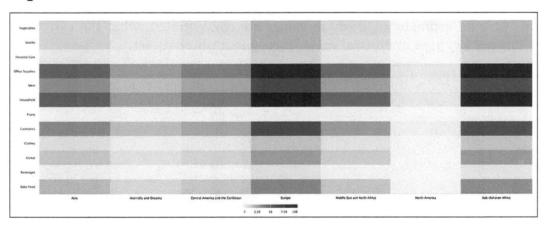

A heat map or choropleth map is a data visualization that shows the relationship between two measures and provides rating information. The rating information is displayed using varying colors or saturation and can exhibit ratings such as high to low or bad to awesome, and needs improvement to working well.

It can also be a thematic map in which the area inside recognized boundaries is shaded in proportion to the data being represented.

When do we use Heat Map Visualization?

Use a heat map for the following reasons:

- To show a relationship between two measures.

- To illustrate an important detail.

- To use a rating system.

Don't use a heat map for the following reason:

- To visualize individual, unconnected metrics.

Best Practices for a Heat Map Visualization

If you use a heat map, here are the key design best practices:

- Use a simple map outline to avoid distracting from the data.

- Use a single color in varying shades to show changes in data.

- Avoid using multiple patterns.

Histogram

A histogram is a data visualization that shows the distribution of data over a continuous interval or certain time period. It's basically a combination of a vertical bar chart and a line chart. The continuous variable shown on the X-axis is broken into discrete intervals and the number of data you have in that discrete interval determines the height of the bar.

Histograms give an estimate as to where values are concentrated, what the extremes are and whether there are any gaps or unusual values throughout your data set.

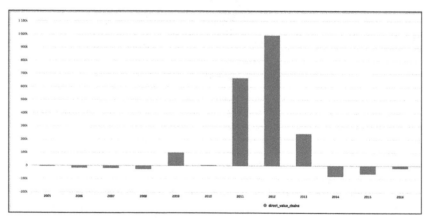

When do we use Histogram Visualization?

Use a histogram for the following reason:

- To make comparisons in data sets over an interval or time.

- To show a distribution of data.

Don't use a histogram for the following reason:

- To compare 3+ variables in data sets.

Best Practices for a Histogram Visualization

If you use a histogram, here are the key design best practices:

- Avoid bars that are too wide that can hide important details or too narrow that can cause a lot of noise.

- Use equal round numbers to create bar sizes.

- Use consistent colors and labeling throughout so that you can identify relationships more easily.

Box Plot

A box plot, or box and whisker diagram is a visual representation of displaying a distribution of data, usually across groups, based on a five number summary: the minimum, first quartile, the median (second quartile), third quartile, and the maximum.

The simplest of box plots display the full range of variation from minimum to maximum, the likely range of variation, and a typical value. A box plot will also show the outliers.

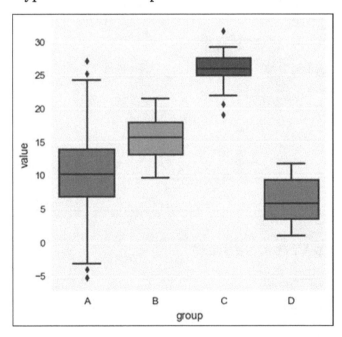

When do we use Box Plot Visualization?

Use a box plot for the following reasons:

- To display or compare a distribution of data.

- To identify the minimum, maximum and median of data.

Don't use a box plot for the following reason:

- To visualize individual, unconnected data sets.

Best Practices for a Box Plot Visualization

If you use a box plot, here are the key design best practices:

- Ensure font sizes for labels and legends are big enough and line widths are thick enough to understand the findings easily.

- If plotting multiple datasets, use different symbols, line styles or color to differentiate each.

- Always remove unnecessary clutter from the plots.

Maps

Maps are an amazing visualization to add to your dashboard if organizing data geographically tells an important story for your business. For example, if your dashboard is looking at monthly sales, it could be extremely useful to see the geographic locations of your customers.

You'll find a map visualization that integrates with Sales force to measure accounts by country. Keep in mind that if your dashboard is looking at daily sales, this visualization may provide less value to your day-to-day discussions.

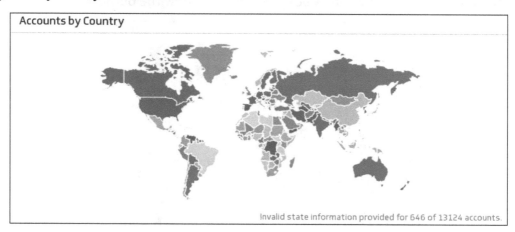

Accounts by Country

Invalid state information provided for 646 of 13124 accounts.

When do we use Map Visualization?

Use a map for the following reason:

- Geography is an important part of your data story.

Don't use a map for the following reasons:

- You want to show precise data points.

- Geography is not an important element of the dashboard's overarching story.

Best Practices for a Map Visualization

If you use map visualization, here are the key design best practices:

- Avoid using multiple colors and patterns on your map. Use varying shades of the same color instead.

- Make sure to include a legend with your map, so that everyone understands what the data means.

Tables

If you're someone who wants a little bit of everything in front of you in order to make thorough decisions, then tables are the visualization to go with. Tables are great because you can display both data points and graphics, such as bullet charts, icons, and sparklines. This visualization type also organizes your data into columns and rows, which is great for reporting.

Above is an example of how to bring in your Google Analytics data into a table, so that you can see all the information you need in one place.

One thing to keep in mind is that tables can sometimes be overwhelming if you have a dashboard with many metrics that you want to display. It's important to find a happy medium between large amounts of data (confusing) and too little data (waste of dashboard space).

Traffic Channels

Apr 01, 2015 to Apr 30, 2015   Last 30 Days
Mar 02, 2015 to Mar 31, 2015 (prev.)

Channel	Sessions	Previous Perio...	Change	Trend
organic	217,883	217,544	-0.15% ▼	∿∿∿
cpc	172,333	138,230	24.67% ▲	∿∿∿
direct	121,528	122,547	-0.83% ▼	∿∿∿
referral	16,529	17,929	7.80% ▲	∿∿∿
retargetting	12,565	10,564	18.94% ▲	∿∿∿

When do we use Table Visualization?

Use a table for the following reasons:

- You want to display two-dimensional data sets that can be organized categorically.

- You can drill-down to break up large data sets with a natural drill-down path.

Don't use a table for the following reason:

- You want to display large amounts of data.

Best Practices for a Table Visualization

If you use a table, here are the key design best practices:

- Be mindful of the order of the data. Make sure that labels, categories and numbers come first then move on to the graphics.

- Try not to have more than 10 different rows in your table to avoid clutter.

Indicators

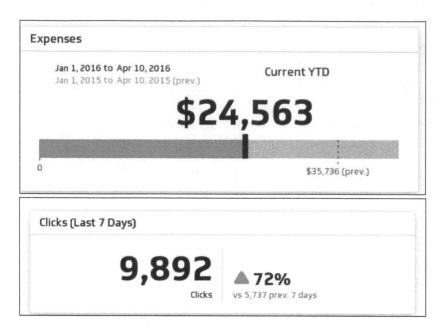

Indicators are useful for an at a glance view of a metric you need to keep track of. An indicator is simply a number showing the current value of whichever performance metric you're tracking. To make it more useful, add a comparison to the previous time period to show whether your metric is tracking up or down. Some people like to get fancy with indicators and use gauges or tickers. They present the same type of information, just in a different visual way.

Area Chart

An area chart is very similar to a line graph but may do a better job at highlighting the relative differences between items. Use an area chart when you want to see how different items stack up or contribute to the whole.

Visualization in Three or More Variables

Pairwise Scatterplots

A scatter plot displays the correlation between a pair of variables. Scatterplot matrices are a great way to roughly determine if you have a linear correlation between multiple variables. This is particularly helpful in pinpointing specific variables that might have similar correlations but can be somewhat ineffective for categorical data.

For a set of data variables (dimensions) X_1, X_2,..., X_k, the scatter plot matrix shows all the pairwise scatter plots of the variables on a single view with multiple scatterplots in a matrix format. For k variables, the scatterplot matrix will contain k rows and k columns. A plot located on the intersection of ith row and j^{th} column is a plot of variables X_i versus X_j. This means that each row and column is one dimension, and each cell plots a scatterplot of two dimensions.

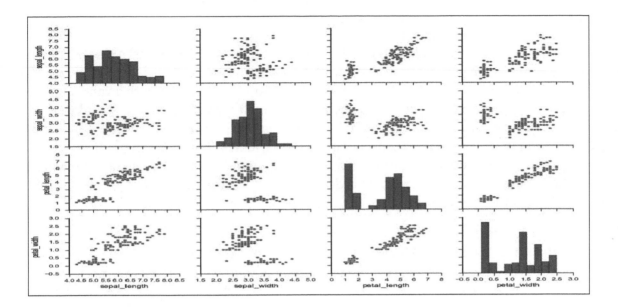

Trellis Graphs or Lattice Plots

Trellis graphs are graphs that display a variable or the relationship between variables, conditioned on one or more other variables. A trellis is a graph whose nodes are ordered into vertical slices (time), and with each node at each time connected to at least one node at an earlier and at least one node at a later time. The earliest and latest times in the trellis have only one node. n coding theory (convolutional codes) the graph called "trellis diagram" is used to visualize something.

Trellis Graphics is a family of techniques for viewing complex, multi-variable data sets. The ideas have been around for a while, but were formalized by researchers at Bell Laboratories during the 1990s. The techniques were given the name Trellis because they usually result in a rectangular array of plots, resembling a garden trellis. A number of statistical software systems provide multi-panel conditioning plots under the name Trellis plots or Cross plots. The trellis graphics system exists in parallel with the normal R graphics system.

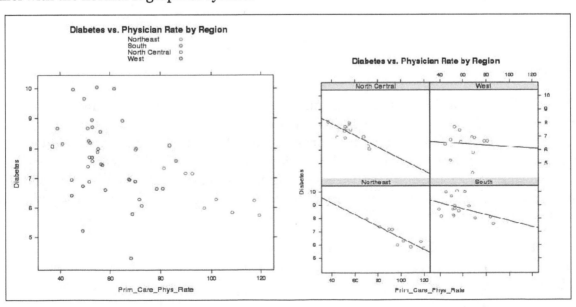

Star Plot

The star plot is a method of displaying multivariate data. Each star represents a single observation. Typically, star plots are generated in a multi-plot format with many stars on each page and each star representing one observation. Star plots are used to examine the relative values for a single data point (e.g., point 3 is large for variables 2 and 4, small for variables 1, 3, 5, and 6) and to locate similar points or dissimilar points. The star plot consists of a sequence of equiangular spokes, called radii, with each spoke representing one of the variables. The data length of a spoke is proportional to the magnitude of the variable for the data point relative to the maximum magnitude of the variable across all data points. A line is drawn connecting the data values for each spoke. This gives the plot a star-like appearance and the origin of the name of this plot.

The star plot consists of a sequence of equiangular spokes, called radii, with each spoke representing one of the variables. The data length of a spoke is proportional to the magnitude of the variable for the data point relative to the maximum magnitude of the variable across all data points. A line is drawn connecting the data values for each spoke. This gives the plot a star-like appearance and the origin of the name of this plot.

Star plots are helpful for small-to-moderate-sized multivariate data sets. Their primary weakness is that their effectiveness is limited to data sets with less than a few hundred points. After that, they tend to be overwhelming.

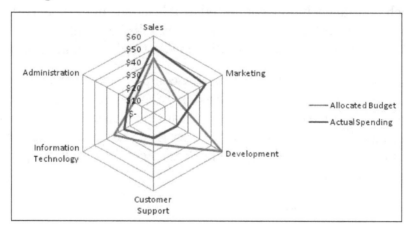

Parallel Coordinates

Parallel coordinates is a visualization technique used to plot individual data elements across many dimensions. Each of the dimensions corresponds to a vertical axis and each data element is displayed as a series of connected points along the dimensions/axes. Parallel coordinates are a common way of visualizing high dimensional geometry and analyzing multivariate data. To show a set of points in an n-dimensional space, a backdrop is drawn consisting of n parallel lines, typically vertical and equally spaced. A point in n-dimensional space is represented as a polyline with vertices on the parallel axes; the position of the vertex on the ith axis corresponds to the ith coordinate of the point.

This visualization is closely related to time series visualization, except that it is applied to data where the axes do not correspond to points in time, and therefore do not have a natural order. Therefore, different axis arrangements may be of interest. This type of visualization also is used for plotting multivariate, numerical data. Parallel Coordinates Plots are ideal for comparing many variables together and seeing the relationships between them. Here the famous iris data is taken to visualize the parallel coordinates.

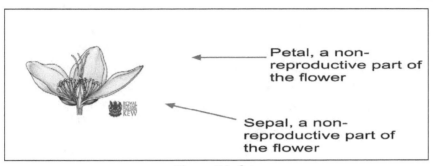

Figure: Iris data

Table: Sepal and petal data.

Sepal Length	Sepal Width	Petal Length	Petal Width
5.1	3.5	1.4	0.2

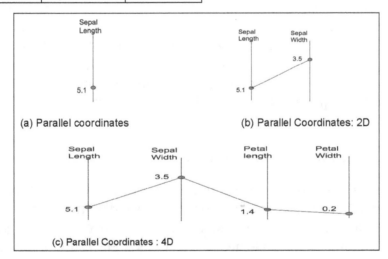

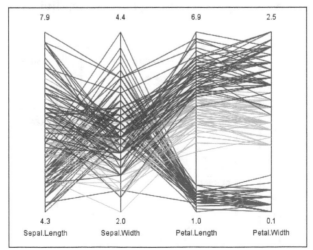

Figure: Parallel Visualization of Iris data.

Higher Dimensions

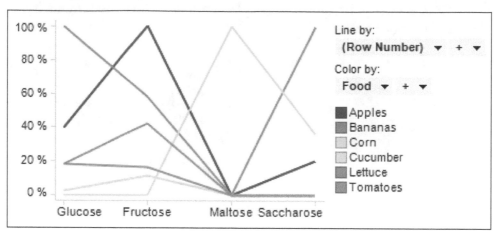

Figure: Parallel coordinate plot.

Adding more dimensions in parallel coordinates (involves adding more axes). The value of parallel coordinates is that certain geometrical properties in high dimensions transform into easily seen 2D patterns. For example, a set of points on a line in n-space transforms to a set of polylines (or curves) in parallel coordinates all intersecting at n − 1 points. For n = 2 this yields a point-line duality pointing out why the mathematical foundations of parallel coordinates are developed in the Projective rather than Euclidean space. Also known are the patterns corresponding to (hyper) planes, curves, several smooth (hyper) surfaces, proximities, convexity and recently non-orientability. Since the process maps a k-dimensional data onto a lower 2D space, some loss of information is expected.

Cleveland Models on Human Perception

Elements of the theory are tested by experimentation in which subjects record their judgments of the quantitative information on graphs. The experiments validate these elements but also suggest that the set of elementary tasks should be expanded. The theory provides a guideline for graph construction: Graphs should employ elementary tasks as high in the ordering as possible. This principle is applied to a variety of graphs, including bar charts, divided bar charts, pie charts, and statistical maps with shading.

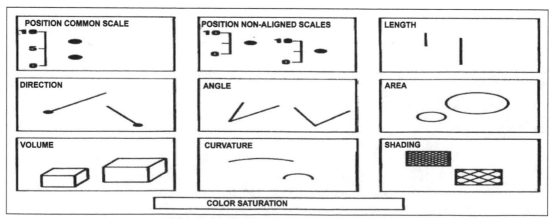

Figure: Position along a Common Scale.

Some other Techniques

Pie Charts and 3D Plot/Graphs

A pie graph (or pie chart) is a specialized graph used in statistics. The independent variable is plotted around a circle in either a clockwise direction or a counterclockwise direction. The dependent variable (usually a percentage) is rendered as an arc whose measure is proportional to the magnitude of the quantity. Each arc is depicted by constructing radial lines from its ends to the center of the circle, creating a wedge-shaped "slice. "The independent variable can attain a finite number of discrete values (for example, five).The dependent variable can attain any value from zero to 100 percent.

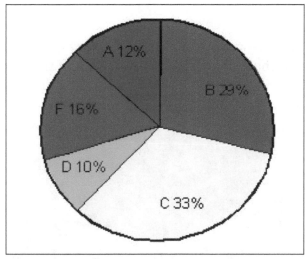

Figure: Pie chart

The illustration is a pie graph depicting the results of a final exam given to a hypothetical class of students. Each grade is denoted by a "slice." The total of the percentages is equal to 100 (this is important; if it were not, the accuracy of the graph would be suspect).The total of the arc measures is equal to 360 degrees.

Highcharts 3D is a Highcharts module providing limited 3D support to charts. It currently allows creating 3D Column charts, 3D Pie charts and 3D Scatter charts.

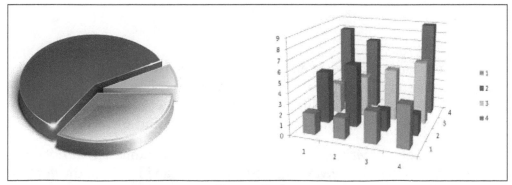

Figure: 3D plots

Color Shading

Shading alters the colors of faces in a 3D model based on the angle of the surface to a light source or light sources. Shading is also dependent on the lighting used. Usually, upon rendering a scene a number of different lighting techniques will be used to make the rendering look more realistic.

- Any graphics primitive (pixel, line, glyph, polygon) can be assigned a color.

- Adding color shading to represent a variable is a useful method of illustration. It is equivalent to adding an extra dimension to the visualization.

- Requires appropriate choice of color map.

False Color

False color (or false color) refers to a group of color rendering methods used to display images in color which were recorded in the visible or non-visible parts of the electromagnetic spectrum. A false-color image is an image that depicts an object in colors that differ from those a photograph (a true-color image) would show.

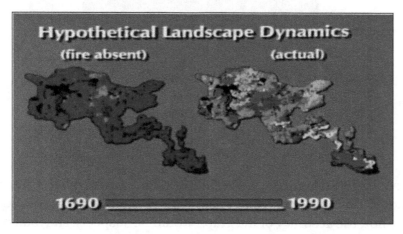

In addition, variants of false color such as pseudo color, density slicing, and choropleths are used for information visualization of either data gathered by a single gray scale channel or data not depicting parts of the electromagnetic spectrum (e.g. elevation in relief maps or tissue types in magnetic resonance imaging).

Glyphs

In typography, a glyph is an elemental symbol within an agreed set of symbols, intended to represent a readable character for the purposes of writing. As such, glyphs are considered to be unique marks that collectively add up to the spelling of a word, or otherwise contribute to a specific meaning of what is written, with that meaning dependent on cultural and social usage.

For example, in most languages written in any variety of the Latin alphabet the dot on a lower-case i is not a glyph because it does not convey any distinction, and an i in which the dot has been accidentally omitted is still likely to be recognized correctly. In Turkish, however, it is a glyph because that language has two distinct versions of the letter i, with and without a dot. Following are some examples of glyphs:

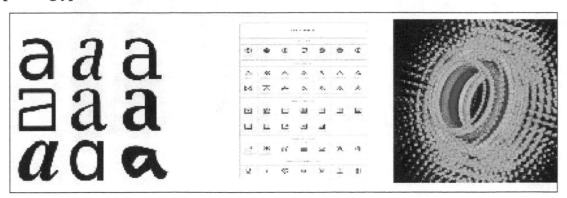

Vector Fields

A region of space under the influence of some vector quantity, such as magnetic field strength, in which each point can be described by a vector, is called vector field. The need to visualize vector fields in two or three dimensions is common in many scientific disciplines, as well as it is necessary in some industrial branches. Examples of vector fields include velocities of wind and ocean currents, results of fluid dynamics solutions, magnetic fields, blood flow or components of stress and strain in materials. Existing techniques for vector field visualization differ in how well they represent such attributes of the vector field as magnitude, direction and critical points.

- Arrows: Vector arrows are used to indicate both direction and magnitude at points in a vector field (e.g., velocity, magnetic fields).Velocity Field for Flow over a Blunt Fin example. When used with a color map, up to three pieces of information can be represented by a vector arrow.

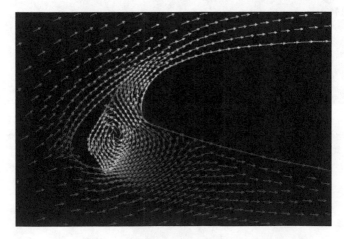

- Streamlines: Streamlines are normally associated with velocity fields.It shows time-history of a massless particle, sometimes depicted as a twisted ribbon to show effect of rotation about streamline axis. It can also show movement of a glyph along the computed streamline. More work, computational resources required to compute motion in a time-varying velocity field.

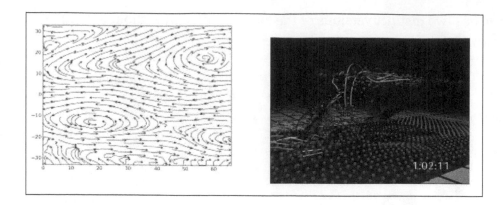

Textures

The surface of any visible object is textured at certain scale. In a general sense, the word texture refers to surface characteristics and appearance of an object given by the size, shape, density, arrangement, proportion of its elementary parts. A texture is usually described as smooth or rough, soft or hard, coarse of fine, matt or glossy, and etc.

Textures might be divided into two categories, namely, tactile and visual textures. Tactile textures refer to the immediate tangible feel of a surface. Visual textures refer to the visual impression that textures produce to human observer, which are related to local spatial variations of simple stimuli like color, orientation and intensity in an image. This thesis focuses only on visual textures, so the term `texture' thereafter is exclusively referred to `visual texture' unless mentioned otherwise.

Figure: Example of natural textures.

Figure: Example of artificial textures.

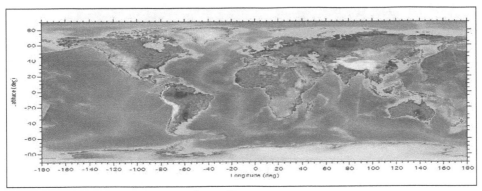

Figure: Texture map.

Animation

Animation is the process of making the illusion of motion and the illusion of change by means of the rapid display of a sequence of images that minimally differ from each other.

Animation creation methods include the traditional animation creation method and that involving stop motion animation of two and three-dimensional objects, paper cut outs, puppets and clay figures. Images are displayed in a rapid succession, usually 24, 25, 30, or 60 frames per second. Computer animation processes generating animated images with the general term computer-generated imagery (CGI). 3D animation uses computer graphics, while 2D animation is used for stylistic, low bandwidth and faster real-time renderings.

Figure: Animation images.

Virtual Reality

Virtual reality (VR) typically refers to computer technologies that use software to generate the realistic images, sounds and other sensations that replicate a real environment (or create an imaginary setting), and simulate a user's physical presence in this environment. VR is a mediated environment which creates the sensation in a user of being present in a (physical) surrounding.

Virtual reality is an artificial environment that is created with software and presented to the user in such a way that the user suspends belief and accepts it as a real environment. VR has so many applications in every field like healthcare, education, and entertainment, military and so on. But irrespective of the use, virtual reality produces a set of data which is then used to develop new models, training methods, communication and interaction. In many ways the possibilities are endless.

Figure: Virtual reality image.

Data Sonification

Sonification is the use of non-speech audio to convey information or perceptualize data. Auditory perception has advantages in temporal, spatial, amplitude, and frequency resolution that open possibilities as an alternative or complement to visualization techniques.

Data sonification is a mapping from data generated by a model, captured in an experiment, or otherwise gathered through observation to one or more parameters of an audio signal or sound synthesis model for the purpose of better understanding, communicating or reasoning about the original model, experiment or system. Although data sonification shares techniques and materials with data-driven music, it is in the interests of the practitioners of both sound art and data sonification to maintain a distinction between the two fields.

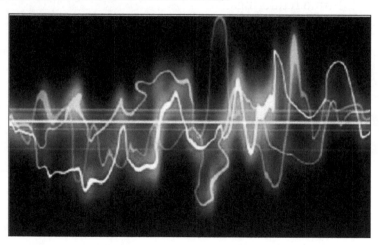

Big Data Visualization

The Big data visualization explains about the description of data by providing the user with effective visualization techniques. The real time data changes, complex data processing results can be easily shown by using the big data visualization. It can displayed in the form of charts, graphs etc. The business people are forced to know about the every piece of information about their data. Some of the important features of data visualization and the role of data visualizations in big data environment are as follows.

Real-Time Data Analysis

The most important feature of data visualization is they play a vital role on real time data by providing deep insights to the user about every piece of information about the data. So that the business people can make a better decision by seeing the result displayed by the dashboards.

Dynamic Nature

The massive data collected from variety of sources can be dynamic by changing the view in different types such as graph (bar, line) charts (pie, bar) scatter plots etc.

Interactive Presentations

The usage of the data visualization tools by the company provides them an interactive presentation of data with reports. It displays all details about the data to the user, so that the user can makes some effective changes according to the result.

In-Memory

The data can be visualized by multiple users, so that each user will produce different opinion in order to improve their business strategies. Many types of data visualizations result are stored in memory for easy access.

Secured

Most of the data displayed in big data environment will be secured by putting some right access to the user. Some data can be viewed by certain users to have security and the data can be compressed to have low memory space.

Errors to Avoid in Data Visualizations

The data visualization in big data environment helps the user to know about the value of data. But they also face some complex problems while handling large volume of data in bigdata environment. Some of the error carried by the business people while displaying the data and makes the user or data analyst in trouble.

- Exposing All Data: It is one of the errors occurred while carrying the data visualization. The importance of data visualization is to give a visual treat for the users and business people. It will give the Knowledge about insights of the data. The dashboard is used to give clear cut information, but some companies will give a clumsy view of data. This kind of approach makes the user in a confused state, where they can't get a proper conclusion on the data.

- Displaying Errors: It is another factor to be noted while visualizing data. The company should know about the wrong side of their business strategies. These methods help the company to know the unnecessary data for making decision. The problem facing while displaying the wrong data is they makes the user to take incorrect decision.

- Lack of Planning: Before displaying the data, the organization should select the proper dashboard for displaying the data. This is because, certain data can be displayed in the form of graphs and it will look worse if the user use some kind of inappropriate dashboards. So they need a proper planning by selecting effective and proper dashboards for displaying the data.

Data Visualization Tools in Big Data

- Data Wrapper: It is used to create data visualization and make it very easy for the end user to grasp the knowledge from the raw data. By using the data wrapper tool the user can easily generate graph and it can be done by simple steps with good web based GUI (Graphics User Interface).The user can save time for creating visualizations. The user should upload the data and they should choose which kind of visualization they need for analyzing.

- Dygraphs: It is one of the main data visualization tool used for representing large volume of data. They use java script based charting library. Even though they use some scripting language they are user friendly with an effective output interface. The user can able to get knowledge due to its flexibility interface. The user should have prior knowledge about web programming to get started with a chart.

- Chart JS: From the name we can understand that it data visualize is carried in the form of chart. The user should include the library in your frontend code. Once the process is completed the user can use the API from the library to work with charts and assign values. D. Charted It is simple to use and the user can upload their data file as input data in.csv file format. If the user needs to customize the chart, they should have simple coding knowledge for fetching the data.

- D3: The term D3 refers to the data driven documents. It contains JavaScript library to help user bind random data to the DOM (document object model). They have the ability to apply data-driven transformations to the document. As you know, DOM is a programming API that allows programmers to access documents as objects. These objects indicate the structure of document they need to model. The user should know about programming knowledge for creating graphs.

  The result can be generated in the form of HTML, CSS documents and SVG.

- Raw: It is a web-based tool that allows user to simply paste the data. It has very simple steps for creating graphs. The Raw is completely based on the D3.js library, which makes the user to easily accessible, so that the user can have all components in packed form of D3 into a format that is ready to be used by non-programmers.

- Timeline: Sometimes the user needs to analyze the data and display events as sequential timelines. In this scenario timeline data visualization tool, helps user to complete the task. The user should need to do before going to timeline visualization, where they should change the format of data to timeline template, in order to have quick and effective result.

- Leaflet: It is a lightweight mobile friendly data visualization tool used to study the data generated by high traffic and good conversion rates. It has JavaScript library to help user for developing interactive maps. It is simple to use and works on both desktop and mobile with good performance.

- Tableau: It is one of the important and most usable data visualization tool in big data environment. The user can gain knowledge with their data, by creating charts, graphs, maps and many other graphics. It helps non-programmers and business types to have deep insights and perfect data ingestion; they can also have fast exploration with interactivity, animation etc.

- Infogram: It is used to access large data sets and it has three simple step processes. The user can customize their visualization by selecting the perfect template and enhance them by having their own idea like charts, map, images and even videos, and you are ready to share your visualization.

- ChartBlocks: It is an online tool that doesn't require any sort of programming skills. The input data can be in databases, live feeds and spreadsheets. The backend process is done in HTML5 by using the powerful JavaScript library D3.js. The visualizations will be responsive and compatible with any screen size and device.

- Plotly: It is very simple to use, where the user can create chart in quick time. The input data can be given from the spreadsheet. The interface is very user-friendly and the user can know the insights of data with short span of time.

- Ember Charts: The name indicates that this tool is completely based on the Ember.js framework and uses D3.js under the hood. They are mostly used for visualize the data in the form time series, bar, pie and scatter charts. The user can provide more amounts of data and the availability is high, where they won't crash when they have bad data on it.

- NVD3: The NVD3 runs top of D3.js, where they have re-usable charts and components. The main of using NVD3 is to provide the user an easily understandable chart which can be reusable and customize according to the need of the user.

- FusionCharts: The java Script chart library is used for creating chart. The user can build own chart in a simple way. It has 90 charts and 900 maps and the Fusion Charts integrates easily with libraries like jQuery. It also frameworks such as Angular JS and React, and they can also support languages like ASP.NET and PHP. JSON and XML data also used in Fusion Charts, the result can be derived in formats like PNG, JPEG, SVG and PDF.

- Highcharts: It is one of the main data visualization tool used by most companies and it has JavaScript API that integrates easily with jQuery. It also contains Highmaps and highstock for carrying data visualization.

- Polymaps: The geographical related data which is generated from country wide level can be visualize by using polymaps. It has JavaScript library that uses SVG to represent geographical data. The user can create a map with integrative data.

Techniques in Big Data Visualization

The existing visualization methods for analyzing data can be categorized based on several factors. According to user task or their requirements the visualization techniques are decided. The visualization techniques include 1D, 2D, 3D, multidimensional, temporal, tree, and network. The user tasks comprises of history, detailed representation of data, general overview of data. Sometimes interaction/distortion techniques are also used for visualize massive volume of data. Some of the important data visualization techniques used by the big data environment to get deep insights about the large volume of data are discussed. Most of the companies are using these techniques for analyzing the data.

- One Dimensional (1-D): The data set which comes under the 1 d consists of one variable and it has only a value per each data item. The histograms are used for carrying data visualizations for one dimensional data

- Two Dimensional (2-D): Mostly two dimensional is used for visualize the data set, which contains two variables. It can be done easily by knowing the relationship between two variables. The 2D visualizations can be represented in the form of line graphs, by comparing the relationship between two variables ad plotting can be done according to it. The 2d can also be represented in form of bar charts, area charts, pie charts, maps, scatter plots and stream line and arrow visualizations.

- Three Dimensional (3-D): The 3 d representation of data will give more knowledge to the user, where they can easily find the merits and demerits of their business flow, study etc. It contains values in three dimensional spaces. it gives information in the form of slicing techniques, 3D bar charts, Iso-surface and realistic renderings.

- Multi-Dimensional: The multi-dimensional visualization gives the user a clear idea in different perspective. The different techniques used such as parallel coordinates, maps, scatterplot matrices, auto-glyphs.

- Temporal Technique: It is a technique, where most of the data can be easily displayed and the temporal technique has the ability to display the data in many views such as timeline, time series and scatter plot.

- Tree Map: It is also known as hierarchical model, where the data is nested in form of rectangle and it represents each branch of the tree. The sub branch is represented as in form of smaller rectangles and leaf node is used for describing the specified dimension on the data. Sometimes the colored leaf nodes are used to display a separate dimension of data. It also provides the user a proper display of data in a hierarchical manner.

- Network Technique: It is mostly used for analyzing all kinds of data extracted from variety of data fields. It has the ability to collect the data in social media, website and blog and present in the form of network. The end user can know which area has to be improved and where the company gains more profit etc. By gaining knowledge from these results the company will have some global idea about their products and place themselves in a better position in the market.

Applications and Challenges of Big Data

6

There are many applications of big data which are used in companies, offices and various organizations. This chapter gives an insight on the different open source tools which are used for data analysis, such as HADOOP and SPARK. This chapter has been carefully written to provide an easy understanding of the these applications of big data.

Open Source Tools for Data Analysis

Hadoop

Big data technologies are important in providing more accurate analysis, which may lead to more concrete decision-making resulting in greater operational efficiencies, cost reductions, and reduced risks for the business.

To harness the power of big data, you would require an infrastructure that can manage and process huge volumes of structured and unstructured data in real-time and can protect data privacy and security.

There are various technologies in the market from different vendors including Amazon, IBM, Microsoft, etc., to handle big data. While looking into the technologies that handle big data, we examine the following two classes of technology.

Operational Big Data

This includes systems like MongoDB that provide operational capabilities for real-time, interactive workloads where data is primarily captured and stored. NoSQL Big Data systems are designed to take advantage of new cloud computing architectures that have emerged over the past decade to allow massive computations to be run inexpensively and efficiently. This makes operational big data workloads much easier to manage, cheaper, and faster to implement.

Some NoSQL systems can provide insights into patterns and trends based on real-time data with minimal coding and without the need for data scientists and additional infrastructure.

Analytical Big Data

These includes systems like Massively Parallel Processing (MPP) database systems and MapReduce that provide analytical capabilities for retrospective and complex analysis that may touch most or all of the data.

MapReduce provides a new method of analyzing data that is complementary to the capabilities provided by SQL, and a system based on MapReduce that can be scaled up from single servers to thousands of high and low end machines. These two classes of technology are complementary and frequently deployed together.

Table: Operational vs. Analytical Systems.

	Operational	Analytical
Latency	1 ms - 100 ms	1 min - 100 min
Concurrency	1000 - 100,000	1 - 10
Access Pattern	Writes and Reads	Reads
Queries	Selective	Unselective
Data Scope	Operational	Retrospective
End User	Customer	Data Scientist
Technology	NoSQL	MapReduce, MPP Database

Big Data Challenges

The major challenges associated with big data are as follows:

- Capturing data
- Curation
- Storage
- Searching
- Sharing
- Transfer
- Analysis
- Presentation

To fulfill the above challenges, organizations normally take the help of enterprise servers.

Hadoop - Big Data Solutions

Traditional Approach

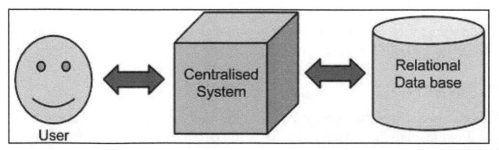

In this approach, an enterprise will have a computer to store and process big data. For storage purpose, the programmers will take the help of their choice of database vendors such as Oracle,

IBM, etc. In this approach, the user interacts with the application, which in turn handles the part of data storage and analysis.

Limitation

This approach works fine with those applications that process less voluminous data that can be accommodated by standard database servers, or up to the limit of the processor that is processing the data. But when it comes to dealing with huge amounts of scalable data, it is a hectic task to process such data through a single database bottleneck.

Google's Solution

Google solved this problem using an algorithm called MapReduce. This algorithm divides the task into small parts and assigns them to many computers, and collects the results from them which when integrated, form the result dataset.

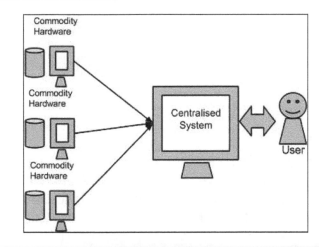

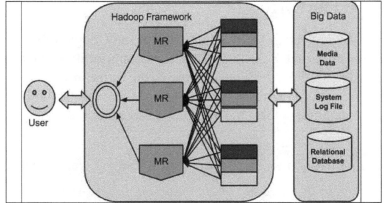

Using the solution provided by Google, Doug Cutting and his team developed an Open Source Project called Hadoop. It runs applications using the MapReduce algorithm, where the data is processed in parallel with others. In short, Hadoop is used to develop applications that could perform complete statistical analysis on huge amounts of data.

Hadoop is an Apache open source framework written in java that allows distributed processing of large datasets across clusters of computers using simple programming models. The Hadoop framework application works in an environment that provides distributed storage and computation across clusters of computers. Hadoop is designed to scale up from single server to thousands of machines, each offering local computation and storage.

Hadoop Architecture

At its core, Hadoop has two major layers namely:

- Processing/Computation layer (MapReduce).

- Storage layer (Hadoop Distributed File System).

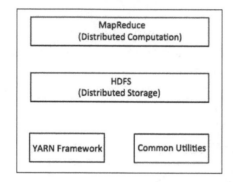

MapReduce

MapReduce is a parallel programming model for writing distributed applications devised at Google for efficient processing of large amounts of data (multi-terabyte data-sets), on large clusters (thousands of nodes) of commodity hardware in a reliable, fault-tolerant manner. The MapReduce program runs on Hadoop which is an Apache open-source framework.

Hadoop Distributed File System

The Hadoop Distributed File System (HDFS) is based on the Google File System (GFS) and provides a distributed file system that is designed to run on commodity hardware. It has many similarities with existing distributed file systems. However, the differences from other distributed file systems are significant. It is highly fault-tolerant and is designed to be deployed on low-cost hardware. It provides high throughput access to application data and is suitable for applications having large datasets.

Apart from the above-mentioned two core components, Hadoop framework also includes the following two modules:

- Hadoop Common: These are Java libraries and utilities required by other Hadoop modules.

- Hadoop YARN: This is a framework for job scheduling and cluster resource management.

How does Hadoop Work?

It is quite expensive to build bigger servers with heavy configurations that handle large scale processing, but as an alternative, you can tie together many commodity computers with single-CPU, as a single functional distributed system and practically, the clustered machines can read the dataset in parallel and provide a much higher throughput. Moreover, it is cheaper than one high-end server. So this is the first motivational factor behind using Hadoop that it runs across clustered and low-cost machines.

Hadoop runs code across a cluster of computers. This process includes the following core tasks that Hadoop performs:

- Data is initially divided into directories and files. Files are divided into uniform sized blocks of 128M and 64M (preferably 128M).

- These files are then distributed across various cluster nodes for further processing.

- HDFS, being on top of the local file system, supervises the processing.

- Blocks are replicated for handling hardware failure.

- Checking that the code was executed successfully.

- Performing the sort that takes place between the map and reduce stages.

- Sending the sorted data to a certain computer.

- Writing the debugging logs for each job.

Advantages of Hadoop

- Hadoop framework allows the user to quickly write and test distributed systems. It is efficient, and it automatic distributes the data and work across the machines and in turn, utilizes the underlying parallelism of the CPU cores.

- Hadoop does not rely on hardware to provide fault-tolerance and high availability (FTHA), rather Hadoop library itself has been designed to detect and handle failures at the application layer.

- Servers can be added or removed from the cluster dynamically and Hadoop continues to operate without interruption.

- Another big advantage of Hadoop is that apart from being open source, it is compatible on all the platforms since it is Java based.

Challenges of Hadoop

Though Hadoop has widely been seen as a key enabler of big data, there are still some challenges to consider. These challenges stem from the nature of its complex ecosystem and the need for advanced technical knowledge to perform Hadoop functions. However, with the right integration platform and tools, the complexity is reduced significantly and hence, makes working with it easier as well.

Steep Learning Curve

To query the Hadoop file system, programmers have to write MapReduce functions in Java. This is not straightforward, and involves a steep learning curve. Also, there are too many components that make up the ecosystem, and it takes time to get familiar with them.

Different Datasets Require Different Approaches

There is no 'one size fits all' solution in Hadoop. Most of the supplementary components discussed above have been built in response to a gap that needed to be addressed.

For example, Hive and Pig provide a simpler way to query the data sets. Additionally, data ingestion tools such as Flume and Sqoop help gather data from multiple sources. There are numerous other components as well and it takes experience to make the right choice.

Limitations of MapReduce

MapReduce is an excellent programming model to batch process big data sets. However, it has its limitations.

Its file-intensive approach, with multiple reads and writes, isn't well-suited for real-time, interactive data analytics or iterative tasks. For such operations, MapReduce isn't efficient enough, and leads to high latencies. (There are workarounds to this problem. Apache is an alternative that is filling the gap of MapReduce.)

Data Security

As big data gets moved to the cloud, sensitive data is dumped into Hadoop servers, creating the need to ensure data security. The vast ecosystem has so many tools that it's important to ensure that each tool has the correct access rights to the data. There needs to be appropriate authentication, provisioning, data encryption, and frequent auditing. Hadoop has the capability to address this challenge, but it's a matter of having the expertise and being meticulous in execution.

Although many tech giants have been using the components of Hadoop discussed here, it is still relatively new in the industry. Most challenges stem from this nascence, but a robust big data integration platform can solve or ease all of them.

Spark

Industries are using Hadoop extensively to analyze their data sets. The reason is that Hadoop framework is based on a simple programming model (MapReduce) and it enables a computing solution that is scalable, flexible, fault-tolerant and cost effective. Here, the main concern is to maintain speed in processing large datasets in terms of waiting time between queries and waiting time to run the program.

Spark was introduced by Apache Software Foundation for speeding up the Hadoop computational computing software process. As against a common belief, Spark is not a modified version of Hadoop and is not, really, dependent on Hadoop because it has its own cluster management. Hadoop is just one of the ways to implement Spark.

Spark uses Hadoop in two ways – one is storage and second is processing. Since Spark has its own cluster management computation, it uses Hadoop for storage purpose only.

Apache Spark

Apache Spark is a lightning-fast cluster computing technology, designed for fast computation. It is based on Hadoop MapReduce and it extends the MapReduce model to efficiently use it for more types of computations, which includes interactive queries and stream processing. The main feature of Spark is its in-memory cluster computing that increases the processing speed of an application.

Spark is designed to cover a wide range of workloads such as batch applications, iterative algorithms, interactive queries and streaming. Apart from supporting all these workload in a respective system, it reduces the management burden of maintaining separate tools.

Evolution of Apache Spark

Spark is one of Hadoop's sub project developed in 2009 in UC Berkeley's AMPLab by Matei Zaharia. It was Open Sourced in 2010 under a BSD license. It was donated to Apache software foundation in 2013, and now Apache Spark has become a top level Apache project from Feb-2014.

Features of Apache Spark

Apache Spark has following features:

- Speed: Spark helps to run an application in Hadoop cluster, up to 100 times faster in memory, and 10 times faster when running on disk. This is possible by reducing number of read/write operations to disk. It stores the intermediate processing data in memory.

- Supports multiple languages: Spark provides built-in APIs in Java, Scala, or Python. Therefore, you can write applications in different languages. Spark comes up with 80 high-level operators for interactive querying.

- Advanced Analytics: Spark not only supports 'Map' and 'reduce'. It also supports SQL queries, Streaming data, Machine learning (ML), and Graph algorithms.

Spark Built on Hadoop

The following diagram shows three ways of how Spark can be built with Hadoop components:

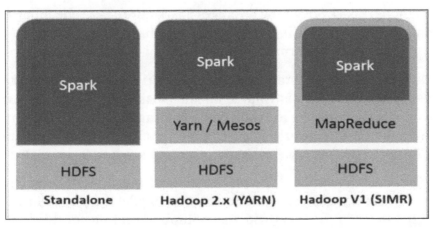

There are three ways of Spark deployment as explained below:

- Standalone: Spark Standalone deployment means Spark occupies the place on top of HDFS (Hadoop Distributed File System) and space is allocated for HDFS, explicitly. Here, Spark and MapReduce will run side by side to cover all spark jobs on cluster.

- Hadoop Yarn: Hadoop Yarn deployment means, simply, spark runs on Yarn without any pre-installation or root access required. It helps to integrate Spark into Hadoop ecosystem or Hadoop stack. It allows other components to run on top of stack.

- Spark in MapReduce (SIMR): Spark in MapReduce is used to launch spark job in addition to standalone deployment. With SIMR, user can start Spark and uses its shell without any administrative access.

Components of Spark

The following illustration depicts the different components of Spark:

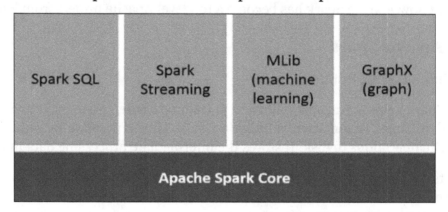

- Apache Spark Core: Spark Core is the underlying general execution engine for spark platform that all other functionality is built upon. It provides In-Memory computing and referencing datasets in external storage systems.

- Spark SQL: Spark SQL is a component on top of Spark Core that introduces a new data abstraction called SchemaRDD, which provides support for structured and semi-structured data.

- Spark Streaming: Spark Streaming leverages Spark Core's fast scheduling capability to perform streaming analytics. It ingests data in mini-batches and performs RDD (Resilient Distributed Datasets) transformations on those mini-batches of data.

- MLlib (Machine Learning Library): MLlib is a distributed machine learning framework above Spark because of the distributed memory-based Spark architecture. It is, according to benchmarks, done by the MLlib developers against the Alternating Least Squares (ALS) implementations. Spark MLlib is nine times as fast as the Hadoop disk-based version of Apache Mahout (before Mahout gained a Spark interface).

- GraphX: GraphX is a distributed graph-processing framework on top of Spark. It provides an API for expressing graph computation that can model the user-defined graphs by using Pregel abstraction API. It also provides an optimized runtime for this abstraction.

Resilient Distributed Datasets

Resilient Distributed Datasets (RDD) is a fundamental data structure of Spark. It is an immutable distributed collection of objects. Each dataset in RDD is divided into logical partitions, which may be computed on different nodes of the cluster. RDDs can contain any type of Python, Java, or Scala objects, including user-defined classes.

Formally, an RDD is a read-only, partitioned collection of records. RDDs can be created through deterministic operations on either data on stable storage or other RDDs. RDD is a fault-tolerant collection of elements that can be operated on in parallel.

There are two ways to create RDDs – parallelizing an existing collection in your driver program, or referencing a dataset in an external storage system, such as a shared file system, HDFS, HBase, or any data source offering a Hadoop Input Format. Spark makes use of the concept of RDD to achieve faster and efficient MapReduce operations. Let us first discuss how MapReduce operations take place and why they are not so efficient.

Data Sharing is Slow in MapReduce

MapReduce is widely adopted for processing and generating large datasets with a parallel, distributed algorithm on a cluster. It allows users to write parallel computations, using a set of high-level operators, without having to worry about work distribution and fault tolerance.

Unfortunately, in most current frameworks, the only way to reuse data between computations (Ex – between two MapReduce jobs) is to write it to an external stable storage system (Ex – HDFS). Although this framework provides numerous abstractions for accessing a cluster's computational resources, users still want more.

Both Iterative and Interactive applications require faster data sharing across parallel jobs. Data sharing is slow in MapReduce due to replication, serialization, and disk IO. Regarding storage system, most of the Hadoop applications, they spend more than 90% of the time doing HDFS read-write operations.

Iterative Operations on MapReduce

Reuse intermediate results across multiple computations in multi-stage applications. The following illustration explains how the current framework works, while doing the iterative operations on MapReduce. This incurs substantial overheads due to data replication, disk I/O, and serialization, which makes the system slow.

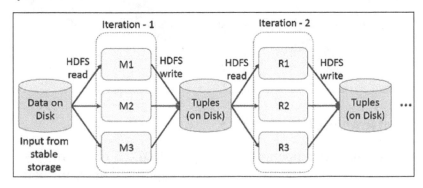

Interactive Operations on MapReduce

User runs ad-hoc queries on the same subset of data. Each query will do the disk I/O on the stable storage, which can dominate application execution time. The following illustration explains how the current framework works while doing the interactive queries on MapReduce:

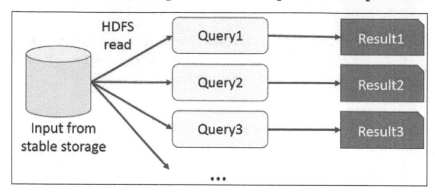

Data Sharing using Spark RDD

Data sharing is slow in MapReduce due to replication, serialization, and disk IO. Most of the Hadoop applications, they spend more than 90% of the time doing HDFS read-write operations.

Recognizing this problem, researchers developed a specialized framework called Apache Spark. The key idea of spark is Resilient Distributed Datasets (RDD); it supports in-memory processing computation. This means, it stores the state of memory as an object across the jobs and the object is sharable between those jobs. Data sharing in memory is 10 to 100 times faster than network and Disk. Let us now try to find out how iterative and interactive operations take place in Spark RDD.

Iterative Operations on Spark RDD

The illustration given below shows the iterative operations on Spark RDD. It will store intermediate results in a distributed memory instead of Stable storage (Disk) and make the system faster. If the Distributed memory (RAM) is not sufficient to store intermediate results (State of the JOB), then it will store those results on the disk.

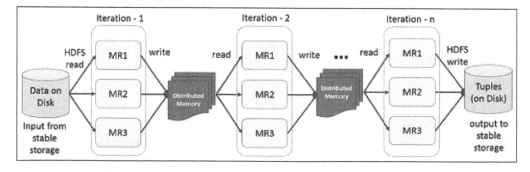

Interactive Operations on Spark RDD

This illustration shows interactive operations on Spark RDD. If different queries are run on the same set of data repeatedly, this particular data can be kept in memory for better execution times.

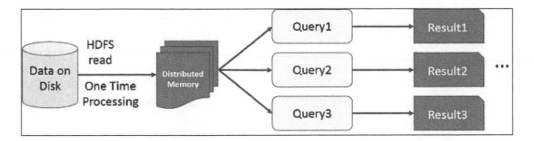

By default, each transformed RDD may be recomputed each time you run an action on it. However, you may also persist an RDD in memory, in which case Spark will keep the elements around on the cluster for much faster access, the next time you query it. There is also support for persisting RDDs on disk, or replicated across multiple nodes.

R Tool

R is a programming language and software environment for statistical analysis, graphics representation and reporting. R was created by Ross Ihaka and Robert Gentleman at the University of Auckland, New Zealand, and is currently developed by the R Development Core Team.

R is freely available under the GNU General Public License, and pre-compiled binary versions are provided for various operating systems like Linux, Windows and Mac. This programming language was named R, based on the first letter of first name of the two R authors (Robert Gentleman and Ross Ihaka), and partly a play on the name of the Bell Labs Language S.

The current R is the result of a collaborative effort with contributions from all over the world. It is highly extensible and flexible. R is an interpreted language; users typically access it through a command-line interpreter.

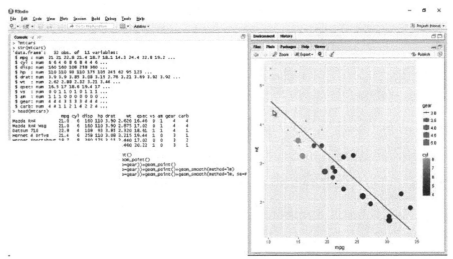

Figure: R graphics.

WEKA

The original non-Java version of WEKA primarily was developed for analyzing data from the agricultural domain. With the Java-based version, the tool is very sophisticated and used in many different applications including visualization and algorithms for data analysis and predictive modeling. Its free under the GNU General Public License, the users can customize it however they please.

WEKA supports several standard data mining tasks, including data preprocessing, clustering, classification, regression, visualization and feature selection. WEKA would be more powerful with the addition of sequence modeling, which currently is not included.

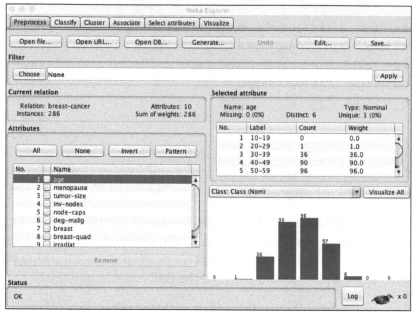

Figure: WEKA tool.

WEKA uses the Attribute Relation File Format for data analysis, by default. But listed below are some formats that Weka supports, from where data can be imported:

- CSV

- ARFF

- Database using ODBC

Attribute Relation File Format (ARFF): This has two parts:

- The header section defines the relation (data set) name, attribute name and the type.

- The data section lists the data instances.

WEKA supports the following data types for attributes:

- Numeric

- <nominal-specification>

- String

- Date

- @data – Defined in the Data section followed by the list of all data segments

Pandas

Pandas is a Python package providing fast, flexible, and expressive data structures designed to make working with "relational" or "labeled" data both easy and intuitive. It aims to be the fundamental high-level building block for doing practical, real world data analysis in Python. Additionally, it has the broader goal of becoming the most powerful and flexible open source data analysis/ manipulation tool available in any language. It is already well on its way toward this goal. Pandas is well suited for many different kinds of data:

- Tabular data with heterogeneously-typed columns, as in an SQL table or Excel spreadsheet.

- Ordered and unordered (not necessarily fixed-frequency) time series data.

- Arbitrary matrix data (homogeneously typed or heterogeneous) with row and column labels.

- Any other form of observational/statistical data sets. The data actually need not be labeled at all to be placed into a pandas data structure.

The two primary data structures of pandas, Series (1-dimensional) and DataFrame (2-dimensional), handle the vast majority of typical use cases in finance, statistics, social science, and many areas of engineering. For R users, Data Frame provides everything that R's dataframe provides and much more. pandas is built on top of NumPy and is intended to integrate well within a scientific computing environment with many other 3rd party libraries.

TANAGRA

TANAGRA is free Data mining software for academic and research purposes. It proposes several data mining methods from exploratory data analysis, statistical learning, machine learning and databases area.

This project is the successor of SIPINA which implements various supervised learning algorithms, especially an interactive and visual construction of decision trees. TANAGRA is more powerful, it contains some supervised learning but also other paradigms such as clustering, factorial analysis, parametric and nonparametric statistics, association rule, feature selection and construction algorithms.

TANAGRA is an "open source project" as every researcher can access to the source code, and add his own algorithms, as far as he agrees and conforms to the software distribution license. The main purpose of Tanagra project is to give researchers and students an easy-to-use data mining software, conforming to the present norms of the software development in this domain (especially in the design of its GUI and the way to use it), and allowing to analyze either real or synthetic data.

The second purpose of TANAGRA is to propose to researchers an architecture allowing them to easily add their own data mining methods, to compare their performances. TANAGRA acts more as an experimental platform in order to let them go to the essential of their work, dispensing them to deal with the unpleasant part in the programmation of this kind of tools: the data management.

The third and last purpose, in direction of novice developers, consists in diffusing a possible methodology for building this kind of software. They should take advantage of free access to source code, to look how this sort of software is built, the problems to avoid, the main steps of the project, and which tools and code libraries to use for. In this way, Tanagra can be considered as a pedagogical tool for learning programming techniques.

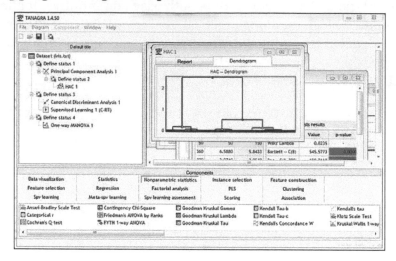

Gephi

Gephi is an open-source network analysis and visualization software package written in Java on the NetBeans platform. Gephi is an open source tool designed for the interactive exploration and visualization of networks. It is designed to facilitate the user's exploratory process through real-time analysis and visualization. Visualization module uses a 3D render engine. It uses the computer's graphic card, while leaving CPU free for computing. Highly scalable (can handle over 20,000 nodes). Built on multi-task model to take advantage of multi-core processors. It runs on Windows, Mac OS X and Linux.

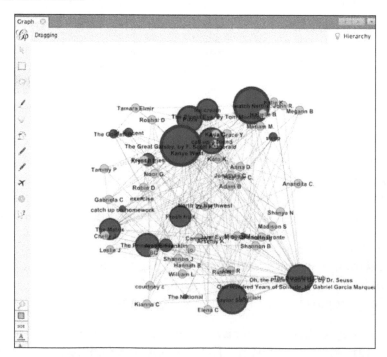

MOA

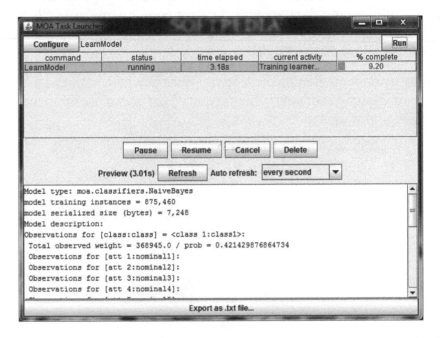

Massive Online Analysis (MOA) is a free open-source software project specific for data stream mining with concept drift. It is written in Java and developed at the University of Waikato, New Zealand. MOA is open-source framework software that allows building and running experiments of machine learning or data mining on evolving data streams. It includes a set of learners and stream generators that can be used from the Graphical User Interface (GUI), the command-line, and the Java API. MOA contains several collections of machine learning algorithms: MOA supports bi-directional interaction with Weka (machine learning).

MOA is free software released under the GNU GPL. MOA is a framework for data stream mining. It includes tools for evaluation and a collection of machine learning algorithms. Related to the WEKA project, it is also written in Java, while scaling to more demanding problems. The goal of MOA is a benchmark framework for running experiments in the data stream mining context by proving:

- Storable settings for data streams (real and synthetic) for repeatable experiments.

- A set of existing algorithms and measures form the literature for comparison.

- An easily extendable framework for new streams, algorithms and evaluation methods.

MOA currently supports stream classification, stream clustering, outlier detection, change detection and concept drift and recommender systems.

Orange

Orange is an open source data mining tool with very strong data visualization capabilities. It allows you to use a GUI (Orange Canvas) to drag and drop modules and connect them to evaluate and test various machine learning algorithms on your data. This hands-on tutorial will go through setting up Orange and getting familiar with its GUI components. We do this by exploring a sample data set with some visualization widgets included with Orange.

Orange is a component-based visual programming software package for data visualization, machine learning, data mining and data analysis. Orange components are called widgets and they range from simple data visualization, subset selection and preprocessing, to empirical evaluation of learning algorithms and predictive modeling.

Visual programming is implemented through an interface in which workflows are created by linking predefined or user-designed widgets, while advanced users can use Orange as a Python library for data manipulation and widget alteration.

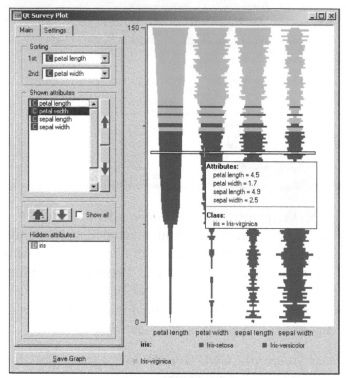

Figure: Orange tool.

RapidMiner

Written in the Java Programming language, this tool offers advanced analytics through template-based frameworks. A bonus: Users hardly have to write any code. Offered as a service, rather than a piece of local software, this tool holds top position on the list of data mining tools.

In addition to data mining, RapidMiner also provides functionality like data preprocessing and visualization, predictive analytics and statistical modeling, evaluation, and deployment. What makes it even more powerful is that it provides learning schemes, models and algorithms from WEKA and R scripts.

RapidMiner, formerly known as YALE (Yet Another Learning Environment), was developed starting in 2001 by Ralf Klinkenberg, Ingo Mierswa, and Simon Fischer at the Artificial Intelligence Unit of the Technical University of Dortmund. Starting in 2006, its development was driven by Rapid-I, a company founded by Ingo Mierswa and Ralf Klinkenberg in the same year. In 2007, the name of the software was changed from YALE to RapidMiner. In 2013, the company rebranded from Rapid-I to RapidMiner.

RapidMiner uses a client/server model with the server offered as either on-premise, or in public or private cloud infrastructures. According to Bloor Research, RapidMiner provides 99% of an advanced analytical solution through template-based frameworks that speed delivery and reduce errors by nearly eliminating the need to write code.

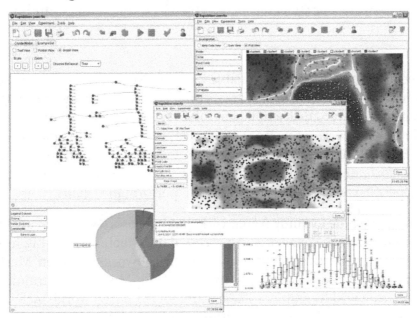

ROOT

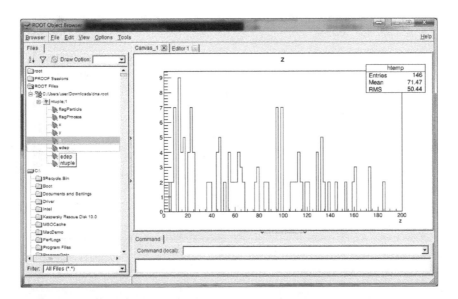

ROOT is an object oriented framework. It has a C/C++ interpreter (CINT) and C/C++ compiler (ACLIC).ROOT is used extensively in High Energy Physics for "data analysis". For reading and writing data files and calculations to produce plots, numbers and fits. A modular scientific software framework. It provides all the functionalities needed to deal with big data processing, statistical analysis, visualization and storage. It is mainly written in C++ but integrated with other languages such as Python and R. It can handle large files (in GB) containing Ntuples and Histograms.It is multiplatform software. It is based on widely known programming language C++. It is free.

The ROOT graphical framework provides support for many different functions including basic graphics, high-level visualization techniques, output on files, 3D viewing etc. They use well-known world standards to render graphics on screen, to produce high-quality output files, and to generate images for Web publishing. Many techniques allow visualization of all the basic ROOT data types, but the graphical framework was still a bit weak in the visualization of multiple variables data sets.

Encog

Encog is a machine learning framework available for Java,.Net, and C++. Encog supports different learning algorithms such as Bayesian Networks, Hidden Markov Models and Support Vector Machines. However, its main strength lies in its neural network algorithms. Encog contains classes to create a wide variety of networks, as well as support classes to normalize and process data for these neural networks. Encog trains, using many different techniques. Multithreading is used to allow optimal training performance on multicore machines. The C++ version of Encog can offload some processing to an OpenCL compatible GPU for further performance gains.

Encog is an advanced machine learning framework that supports a variety of advanced algorithms, as well as support classes to normalize and process data. Machine learning algorithms such as Support Vector Machines, Neural Networks, Bayesian Networks, Hidden Markov Models, Genetic Programming and Genetic Algorithms are supported. Most Encog training algorithms are multi-threaded and scale well to multicore hardware. A GUI based workbench is also provided to help model and train machine learning algorithms. Encog has been in active development since 2008.

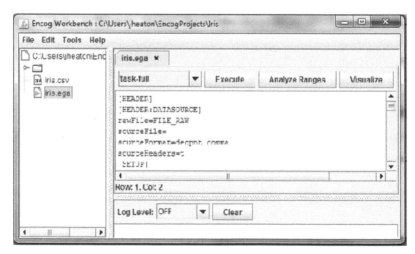

NodeXL

NodeXL Basic is a free and open-source network analysis and visualization software package for Microsoft Excel 2007/2010/2013/2016. NodeXL Pro is a fee based fully featured version of NodeXL that includes access to social media network data importers, advanced network metrics, and automation. It is a popular package similar to other network visualization tools such as Pajek, UCINet, and Gephi. NodeXL is intended for users with little or no programming experience to allow them to collect, analyze, and visualize a variety of networks. NodeXL integrates into Microsoft Excel 2007, 2010, 2013 and 2016 and opens as a workbook with a variety of worksheets containing the elements of a graph structure such as edges and nodes. NodeXL can also import a variety of graph formats such as edgelists, adjacency matrices, GraphML, UCINet.dl, and Pajek.net.

NodeXL workbooks contain four worksheets: Edges, Vertices, Groups, and Overall Metrics. The relevant data about entities in the graph and relationships between them are located in the appropriate worksheet in row format.

NodeXL contains a library of commonly used graph metrics: centrality, clustering coefficient, and diameter. NodeXL differentiates between directed and undirected networks. NodeXL implements a variety of community detection algorithms to allow the user to automatically discover clusters in their social networks.

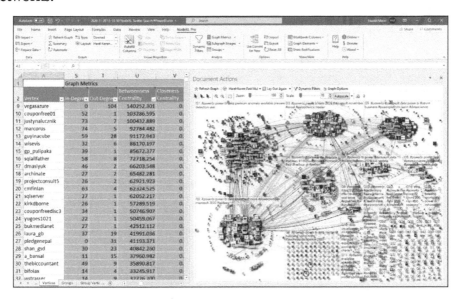

KNIME

KNIME the Konstanz Information Miner is an open source data analytics, reporting and integration platform. KNIME integrates various components for machine learning and data mining through its modular data pipelining concept. A graphical user interface allows assembly of nodes for data preprocessing (ETL: Extraction, Transformation, Loading), for modeling and data analysis and visualization.

The Development of KNIME was started January 2004 by a team of software engineers at University of Konstanz as a proprietary product. The original developer team headed by Michael Berthold came from a company in Silicon Valley providing software for the pharmaceutical industry. The initial goal was to create a modular, highly scalable and open data processing platform which allowed for the easy integration of different data loading, processing, transformation, analysis and visual exploration modules without the focus on any particular application area. The platform was intended to be a collaboration and research platform and should also serve as an integration platform for various other data analysis projects.

KNIME allows users to visually create data flows (or pipelines), selectively execute some or all analysis steps, and later inspect the results, models, and interactive views. KNIME is written in Java and based on Eclipse and makes use of its extension mechanism to add plugins providing additional functionality.

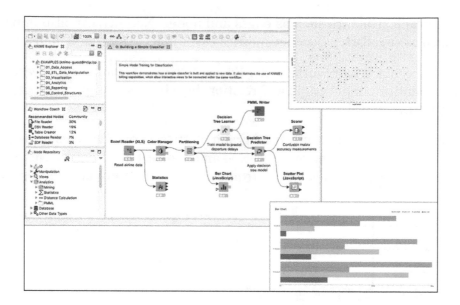

ELKI

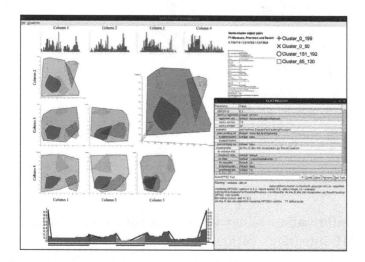

ELKI (for Environment for DeveLoping KDD-Applications Supported by IndexStructures) is a knowledge discovery in databases (KDD, "data mining") software framework developed for use in research and teaching originally at the database systems research unit of Professor Hans-Peter Kriegel at the Ludwig Maximilian University of Munich, Germany. It aims at allowing the development and evaluation of advanced data mining algorithms and their interaction with database index structures.

The ELKI framework is written in Java and built around a modular architecture. Most currently included algorithms belong to clustering, outlier detection and database indexes. A key concept of ELKI is to allow the combination of arbitrary algorithms, data types, distance functions and indexes and evaluate these combinations. When developing new algorithms or index structures, the existing components can be reused and combined.

ELKI is open source (AGPLv3) data mining software written in Java. The focus of ELKI is research in algorithms, with an emphasis on unsupervised methods in cluster analysis and outlier detection. In order to achieve high performance and scalability, ELKI offers data index structures such as the R*-tree that can provide major performance gains. ELKI is designed to be easy to extend for researchers and students in this domain, and welcomes contributions of additional methods. ELKI aims at providing a large collection of highly parameterizable algorithms, in order to allow easy and fair evaluation and benchmarking of algorithms.

Waffles

Waffles are collection of command-line tools for performing machine learning operations developed at Brigham Young University. These tools are written in C++, and are available under the GNU Lesser General Public License.

The Waffles machine learning toolkit contains command-line tools for performing various operations related to machine learning, data mining, and predictive modeling. The primary focus of Waffles is to provide tools that are simple to use in scripted experiments or processes. For example, the supervised learning algorithms included in Waffles are all designed to support multi-dimensional labels, classification and regression, automatically impute missing values, and automatically apply necessary filters to transform the data to a type that the algorithm can support, such that arbitrary learning algorithms can be used with arbitrary data sets. Many other machine learning toolkits provide similar functionality, but require the user to explicitly configure data filters and transformations to make it compatible with a particular learning algorithm. The algorithms provided in Waffles also have the ability to automatically tune their own parameters.

Waffles: Command-line applications:

- waffles_audio: Contains tools for processing audio files.

- waffles_cluster: Contains tools for clustering.

- waffles_dimred: Contains tools for dimensionality reduction, attribute selection, etc.

- waffles_generate: Contains tools to sample distributions, sample manifolds, and generate certain types of data.

- waffles_learn: Contains tools for supervised learning.

- waffles_plot: Contains tools for visualizing data.

- waffles_recommend: Contains tools for collaborative filtering, recommendation systems, imputation, etc.

- waffles_sparse: Contains tools to learning from sparse data, document classification, etc.

- waffles_transform: Contains tools for manipulating data, shuffling rows, swapping columns, matrix operations, etc.

Application of Big Data Analytics

The concept of big data analytics has left no sector untouched. Few sectors like Telecommunication, Retail and Finance have been early adopters of big data analytics, followed by other sectors.

Healthcare

Data analysts obtain and analyze information from multiple sources to gain insights. The multiple sources are electronic patient record; clinical decision support system including medical imaging, physician's written notes and prescription, pharmacy and laboratories; clinical data; and machine generated sensor data. The integration of clinical, public health and behavioral data helps to develop a robust treatment system, which can reduce the cost and at the same time, improve the quality of treatment.

Obtaining information from external sources such as social media helps in early detection of epidemics and precautionary efforts. After the earthquake in Haiti in January 2010, analysis of tweets helped to track the spread of Cholera in the region. The data from the sensors are monitored and analyzed for adverse event prediction and safety monitoring.

Artemis, a system developed by Blount et al., monitors and analyzes the physiological data from sensors in the intensive care units to detect the onset of medical complications, especially, in the case of neo-natal care. The real-time analysis of a huge number of claims requests can minimize fraud.

Telecommunication

Low adoption of mobile services and churn management are few of the most common problems faced by the mobile service providers (MSPs). The cost of acquiring new customer is higher than retaining the existing ones. Customer experience is correlated with customer loyalty and revenue. In order to improve the customer experience, MSPs analyze a number of factors such as demographic data (gender, age, marital status, and language preferences), customer preferences, household structure and usage details (CDR, internet usage, value-added services (VAS)) to model the customer preferences and offer a relevant personalized service to them. This is known as targeted marketing, which improves the adoption of mobile services, reduces churn, thus, increasing the revenue of MSPs.

Telecom companies are working towards combating telecom frauds. Often, traditional fraud management systems are poor at detecting new types of fraud. Even they detect the occurrence of fraud lately, by then fraudsters would have changed their strategy. In order to overcome the limitations of traditional fraud management system, MSPs are analyzing real-time data to minimize the losses due to fraud. Mobileum Inc., one of the leading telecom analytics solution providers, is working towards providing a real-time fraud detection system using predictive analytics and machine learning.

Network Analytics is the next big thing in Telecom, where MSPs can monitor the network speed and manage the entire network. This helps to resolve the network problems within few minutes and helps to improve the quality of service and the customer experience. With the diffusion of Smartphones, based on analysis of real-time location and behavioral data, location-based services/context-based services can be offered to the customers when requested. This would increase the adoption of mobile services.

Financial Firms

Currently, capital firms are using advanced technology to store huge volumes of data. But increasing data sources like Internet and Social media require them to adopt big data storage systems. Capital markets are using big data in preparation for regulations like EMIR, Solvency II, Basel II etc., anti-money laundering, fraud mitigation, pre-trade decision-support analytics including sentiment analysis, predictive analytics and data tagging to identify trades. The timeliness of finding value plays an important role in both investment banking and capital markets; hence, there is a need for real-time processing of data.

Retail

Evolution of e-commerce, online purchasing, social-network conversations and recently location specific smartphone interactions contribute to the volume and the quality of data for data-driven customization in retailing. Major retail stores might place CCTV not only to observe the instances of theft but also to track the flow of customers. It helps to observe the age group, gender and purchasing patterns of the customers during weekdays and weekends. Based on the purchasing patterns of the customers, retailers group their items using a well-known data mining technique called Market Basket Analysis, so that a customer buying bread and milk might purchase jam as well. This helps to decide on the placement of objects and decide on the prices. Nowadays, e-commerce firms use market basket analysis and recommender systems to segment and target the customers. They collect the click stream data, observe behavior and recommend products in the real time.

Analytics help the retail companies to manage their inventory. For example, Stage stores, one of the brand names of Stage Stores Inc. which operates in more 40 American states, used to analytics to forecast the order for different sizes of garments for different geographical regions.

Law Enforcement

Law enforcement officials try to predict the next crime location using past data i.e., type of crime, place and time; social media data; drone and smartphone tracking. Researchers at Rutgers University developed an app called RTM Dx to prevent crime and is being used by police department at Illinois, Texas, Arizona, New Jersey, Missouri and Colorado. With the help the app, the police department could measure the spatial correlation between the location of crime and features of the environment.

A new technology called facial analytics that examines images of people without violating their privacy. Facial analytics is used to check child pornography. This saves the time of manual examination. Child pornography can be identified by integration of various technologies like Artemis and PhotoDNA by comparing files and image hashes with existing files to identify the subject as adult or child. It also identifies the cartoon based pornography.

Marketing

Marketing analytics helps the organizations to evaluate their marketing performance, to analyze the consumer behavior and their purchasing patterns, to analyze the marketing trends which would aid in modifying the marketing strategies like the positioning of advertisements in a webpage, implementation of dynamic pricing and offering personalized products.

New Product Development

There is a huge risk associated with new product development. Enterprises can integrate both external sources, i.e., twitter and Facebook page and internal data sources, i.e., customer relationship management (CRM) systems to understand the customers' requirement for a new product, to gather ideas for new product and to understand the added feature included in a competitor's product. Proper analysis and planning during the development stage can minimize the risk associated with the product, increase the customer lifetime value and promote brand engagement. Ribbon UI in Microsoft 2007 was created by analyzing the customer data from previous releases of the product to identify the commonly used features and making intelligent decisions.

Banking

The investment worthiness of the customers can be analyzed using demographic details, behavioral data, and financial employment. The concept of cross-selling can be used here to target specific customer segments based on past buying behavior, demographic details, sentiment analysis along with CRM data.

Energy and Utilities

Consumption of water, gas and electricity can be measured using smart meters at regular intervals of one hour. During this interval, a huge amount of data is generated and analyzed to change the patterns of power usage. The real-time analysis reveals energy consumption pattern, instances of electricity thefts and price fluctuations.

Insurance

Personalized insurance plan is tailored for each customer using updated profiles of changes in wealth, customer risk, home asset value, and other data inputs. Recently, driving data of customers such as miles driven, routes driven, time of day, and braking abruptness are collected by the insurance companies by using sensors in their cars. Comparing individual driving pattern and driver risk with the statistical information available such as peak hours of drivers on the road develops a personalized insurance plan. This analysis of driver risk and policy gives a competitive advantage to the insurance companies.

Education

With the advent of computerized course modules, it is possible to assess the academic performance real time. This helps to monitor the performance of the students after each module and give immediate feedback on their learning pattern. It also helps the teachers to assess their teaching pedagogy and modify based on the students" performance and needs. Dropout patterns, students requiring special attention and students who can handle challenging assignments can be predicted. Beck and Mostow studied the student reading comprehension using intelligent tutor software and observed that reading mistakes reduced considerably when the students re-read an old story instead of a new story.

Research Areas of Big Data Analytics

Big data analytics is gaining so much attention these days but there are a number of research problems that still need to be addressed:

- Storage and Retrieval of Images, Audios and Videos: Multidimensional data should be integrated with analytics over big data hence array-based in-memory representation models can be explored. Integration of multidimensional data models over big data requires the enhancement of query language HiveQL with multidimensional extensions. With the proliferation of smart phones Images, Audios and Videos are being generated at an unremarkable pace. However, storage, retrieval and processing of these unstructured data require immense research in each dimension.

- Life-cycle of Data: Most application scenarios require real-time performance of the big data analytics. There is a need to define the life cycle of the data; the value it can provide and the computing process to make the analytics process real time, thus, increasing the value of the analysis. Big data is always not always better; hence proper data filtering techniques can be developed to ensure correctness in the data. Another big issue is related to the availability of data that is complete and reliable. In most of the cases, data are sparse and do not show clear distribution, yielding misleading conclusions. A method to overcome these problems needs proper attention and sometimes handling of unbalanced data sets leads to biased conclusion.

- Big Data Computations: Apart from current big data paradigms like Map-Reduce, other paradigms such as YarcData (Big Data Graph Analytics) and High-Performance Computing cluster (HPCC explores Hadoop alternatives), are being explored.

- Visualization of High-Dimensional Data: Visualization aids in decision analysis at each and every step of the data analysis. Visualization issues are still part of data warehousing and OLAP research. There is a scope for visualization tools for high-dimensional data.

- Development of Algorithms for handling domain specific data: Machine learning algorithms are developed to meet general requirements for processing data. However, it cannot replace the domain specific requirements and specific algorithms will be needed to gain insights from the desired discipline.

- Real time processing algorithms: The pace at which data is being generated and the expectations from these algorithms may not be met, if the desired time delay is not met.

- Efficient storage devices: The demand for storing digital information is increasing continuously. Purchasing and using available storage devices cannot meet this demand. Research towards developing efficient storage device that can replace the need for HDFS systems that is fault tolerant can improve the data processing activity and replace the need for software management layer.

- Social perspectives dimensions: It is important to understand that any technology can yield faster results however; it is up to the decision makers to use it wisely. These results may have several social and cultural implications and sometimes leading to cynicism towards online platforms. There are few questions whether large scale search data would help in creating better tools and services or will it usher in privacy incursions and invasive marketing. Whether data analytics would help in understanding the online behavior, communities and political movements or will it be used to track protesters and suppress freedom of speech.

Challenges of Big Data

Business Challenges

- Questions before answers: Big Data holds the potential to offer answers to many business problems. But, depending on how data is queried (i.e. the algorithms used), the same problem can throw up very different answers. It is therefore vital that businesses spend time working out the right questions to ask of the data.

- Know the unknowns: Businesses also need to be able to quantify the latent value within the data. There are many unknowns in Big Data analysis — it often uncovers hidden insights that can generate previously impossible-to-realize value. For example, Big Data can provide more acute market and competitive analyses that might signal the need for fundamental changes to a company's business model.

- Don't trust all sources equally: The increasing use of third-party data sources is creating a requirement for platforms that can guarantee their data can be trusted. This is essential to enable the safe trading of information with appropriate checks and balances (just as with long-established credit reference systems used in the financial services sector). Businesses generally trust their internal data, but when dealing with external sources it is vital to understand the provenance and reputation of those sources. It is useful to consider data sources as sitting at different points on a continuum from 'trusted' (e.g. open government data) to 'untrusted' (e.g. social networks). The level of trustworthiness can also (but not necessarily) equate to whether the source is internal or external, paid or unpaid, the age of the data and the size of the sample.

- Data source dependency: If a business model relies on a particular external data source, it is important to consider what would happen if that source were no longer available, or if a previously free source started to levy access charges. For example, GPS sensor data may provide critical location data, but in the event of a war it might become unavailable in a certain region or its accuracy could be reduced. Another example is the use of (currently free) open data from government sources. A change of policy might lead to the introduction of charges for commercial use of certain sources.

- Avoid analytical paralysis: Access to near real-time analytics can offer incredible advantages. But the sheer quantity of potential analyses that a business can conduct means there's a danger of 'analytical paralysis' — generating such a wealth of information and insight (some of it contradictory) that it's impossible to interpret. Organizations need to ensure they are sufficiently informed to react without becoming overwhelmed.

- Manage the information lifecycle: While some of the concerns around handling information at different stages in its lifecycle are technical, there are also business issues to consider. For example, how should a record containing personal information be processed and what needs to be done when that record expires? Businesses need to decide, for instance, if such records are stored in an anonymised format or removed after a time.

- Overcome employee resistance: In common with many business change projects, senior managers need to ensure Big Data initiatives are not undermined by employee resistance to change. For example, one utility company's Big Data project identified a large number of customers who weren't on the billing system despite the fact they'd received services for months (and, in some cases, years). While this should have been an opportunity to increase revenues, the news was met with a combination of disbelief, messenger-shooting and protective behaviour as some employees believed the discovery of the error had cast them in a poor light. Such resistance might have been avoided had the company paid more attention in advance to pre-empting staff concerns, assuaging their fears and communicating the positive aims of the project. Another potential cause of employee resistance is the fear that advanced predictive analytics undermines the role of skilled teams in areas such as forecasting, marketing and risk profiling. If their fears aren't comprehensively addressed at the outset, such employees may attempt to discredit the Big Data initiative in its early stages — and could potentially derail it.

Technical Challenges

Many of Big Data's technical challenges also apply to data it general. However, Big Data makes some of these more complex, as well as creating several fresh issues.

Data Integration

Since data is a key asset, it is increasingly important to have a clear understanding of how to ingest, understand and share that data in standard formats in order that business leaders can make better-informed decisions. Even seemingly trivial data formatting issues can cause confusion. For example, some countries use a comma to express a decimal place, while others use commas to separate thousands, millions, etc. — a potential cause of error when integrating numerical data from different sources. Similarly, although the format may be the same across different name and address records, the importance of 'first name' and 'family name' may be reversed in certain cultures, leading to the data being incorrectly integrated.

Organizations might also need to decide if textual data is to be handled in its native language or translated. Translation introduces considerable complexity — for example, the need to handle multiple character sets and alphabets.

Further integration challenges arise when a business attempts to transfer external data to its system. Whether this is migrated as a batch or streamed, the infrastructure must be able to keep up with the speed or size of the incoming data. The selected technology therefore has to be adequately scalable, and the IT organization must be able to estimate capacity requirements effectively. Another important consideration is the stability of the system's connectors (the points where it interfaces with and 'talks' to the systems supplying external data). Companies such as Twitter and Facebook regularly make changes to their application programming interfaces (APIs) which may not necessarily be published in advance. This can result in the need to make changes quickly to ensure the data can still be accessed.

Data Transformation

Another challenge is data transformation — the need to define rules for handling data. For example, it may be straightforward to transform data between two systems where one contains the fields 'given name' and 'family name' and the other has an additional field for 'middle initial' — but transformation rules will be more complex when, say, one system records the whole name in a single field.

Organizations also need to consider which data source is primary (i.e. the correct, 'master' source) when records conflict, or whether to maintain multiple records. Handling duplicate records from disparate systems also requires a focus on data quality.

Complex Event Processing

Complex event processing (CEP) effectively means (near) real-time analytics. Matches are triggered from data based on either business or data management rules. For example, a rule might look for people with similar addresses in different types of data. But it is important to consider precisely how similar two records are before accepting a match. For example, is there only a spelling difference in the name or is there a different house number in the address line? There may well be two Tom Joneses living in the same street in Pontypridd — but Tom Jones and Thomas Jones at the same address are probably the same person.

IT professionals are used to storing data and running queries against it, but CEP stores queries that are processed as data passes through the system. This means rules can contain time-based elements, which are more complicated to define. For example, a rule that says 'if more than 2% of all shares drop by 20% in less than 30 seconds, shut down the stock market' may sound reasonable, but the trigger parameters need to be thought through very carefully. What if it takes 31 seconds for the drop to occur? Or if 1% of shares drop by 40%? The impact is similar, but the rule will not be triggered.

Semantic Analysis

Semantic analysis is a way of extracting meaning from unstructured data. Used effectively, it can uncover people's sentiments towards, for example, organizations and products, as well as unearthing trends, untapped customer needs, etc. However, it is important to be aware of its limitations. For example, computers are not yet very good at understanding sarcasm or irony, and human intervention might be required to create an initial schema and validate the data analysis.

Historical Analysis

Historical analysis could be concerned with data from any point in the past. That is not necessarily last week or last month — it could equally be data from 10 seconds ago. While IT professionals may be familiar with such an application its meaning can sometimes be misinterpreted by non-technical personnel encountering it.

Search

Search is not always as simple as typing a word or phrase into a single text input box. Searching unstructured data might return a large number of irrelevant or unrelated results. Sometimes, users need to conduct more complicated searches containing multiple options and fields. IT organizations need to ensure their solution provides the right type and variety of search interfaces to meet the business's differing needs.

Another consideration is how search results are presented. For example, the data required by a particular search could be contained in a single record (e.g. a specific customer), in a ranked listing of records (e.g. articles listed according to their relevance to a particular topic), or in an unranked set of records (e.g. products discontinued in the past 12 months). This means IT professionals need to consider the order and format in which results are returned from particular types of searches. And once the system starts to make inferences from data, there must also be a way to determine the value and accuracy of its choices.

Data Storage

As data volumes increase storage systems are becoming ever more critical. Big Data requires reliable, fast-access storage. This will hasten the demise of older technologies such as magnetic tape, but it also has implications for the management of storage systems. Internal IT may increasingly need to take a similar, commodity-based approach to storage as third-party cloud storage suppliers do today — i.e. removing (rather than replacing) individual failed components until they need to refresh the entire infrastructure. There are also challenges around how to store the data — for example, whether in a structured database or within an unstructured (NoSQL) system — or how to integrate multiple data sources without over-complicating the solution.

Data Integrity

For any analysis to be truly meaningful it is important that the data being analysed is as accurate, complete and up to date as possible. Erroneous data will produce misleading results and potentially incorrect insights. Since data is increasingly used to make business-critical decisions, consumers of data services need to have confidence in the integrity of the information those services are providing.

Data Lifecycle Management

In order to manage the lifecycle of any data, IT organizations need to understand what that data is and its purpose. But the potentially vast number of records involved with Big Data, and the speed at which the data changes, can give rise to the need for a new approach to data management. It may not be possible to capture all of the data. Instead, the system might take samples from a stream of data. If so, IT needs to ensure the sample includes the required data, or that the sampled data is sufficiently representative to provide the required level of insight.

Data Replication

Generally, data is stored in multiple locations in case one copy becomes corrupted or unavailable. This is known as data replication. The volumes involved in a Big Data solution raise questions about the scalability of such an approach. However, Big Data technologies may take alternative approaches. For example, Big Data frameworks such as Hadoop are inherently resilient, which may mean it is not necessary to introduce another layer of replication.

Data Migration

When moving data in and out of a Big Data system, or migrating from one platform to another, organizations should consider the impact that the size of the data may have. Not only does the 'extract, transform and load' process need to be able to deal with data in a variety of formats, but the volumes of data will often mean that it is not possible to operate on the data during a migration — or at the very least there needs to be a system to understand what is currently available or unavailable.

Visualization

While it is important to present data in a visually meaningful form, it is equally important to ensure presentation does not undermine the effectiveness of the system. Organizations need to consider the most appropriate way to display the results of Big Data analytics so that the data does not mislead. For example, a graph might look good rendered in three dimensions, but in some cases a simpler representation may make the meaning of the data stand out more clearly. In addition, IT should take into account the impact of visualizations on the various target devices, on network bandwidth and on data storage systems.

Data Access

The final technical challenge relates to controlling who can access the data, what they can access, and when. Data security and access control is vital in order to ensure data is protected. Access controls should be fine-grained, allowing organizations not only to limit access, but also to limit knowledge of its existence.

One issue raised by advanced analytics is the possibility that the aggregation of different data sources reveals information that would otherwise be deemed a security or privacy risk. Enterprises therefore need to pay attention to the classification of data. This should be designed to ensure that data is not locked away unnecessarily (limiting its potential to provide actionable insights) but equally that it doesn't present a security or privacy risk to any individual or company.

In addition, open-ended queries (searching with wildcards) may have performance implications — or cause concerns from a data extraction perspective. For example, organizations may invest significant resources in consolidating data to give them a 'single view' of customers or other key competitive information which could become a target for hacking, theft or sabotage.

If a business provides an external interface to its data by means of an API, this needs to be maintained, echoing the challenge referred to above (under Data integration), but this time as a provider of data rather than as a consumer. Finally, application developers need to be aware that the move from serial to parallel processing may affect the way that applications are designed and implemented.

Legislative Challenges

From a legal standpoint, many of the challenges relate to data ownership, privacy and intellectual property rights. Over time, we can expect a societal shift in attitudes towards data handling, but currently organizations have to take into account that:

- Depending on where data originates, there may be issues around ownership, intellectual property and licensing — all of which will need to be resolved before data can be used.

- As data is aggregated even anonymised data may contain identifiable information, which may place a business in breach of data protection regulations.

- With data being stored on various systems across the globe, there may be issues of data sovereignty and residency (i.e. questions over which country or countries can claim legal jurisdiction over particular data) depending on the type of data being stored and processed.

References

- Hadoop-quick-guide, hadoop: tutorialspoint.com, Retrieved 05, April 2020

- What-is-hadoop: talend.com, Retrieved 27, May 2020

- Apache-spark-introduction, apache-spark: tutorialspoint.com, Retrieved 05, Feb 2020

- Apache-spark-rdd, apache-spark: tutorialspoint.com, Retrieved 07, July 2020

- White-Book-of-Big-Data: fujitsu.com, Retrieved 17, May 2020

Permissions

Index

Printed in the USA
CPSIA information can be obtained
at www.ICGtesting.com
JSHW051416221024
72173JS00006B/1369

9 781639 891450